TALKING DOUBLE
DUTCH

PAUL HOLLAND
TALKING DOUBLE
DUTCH

breedon **books**
PUBLISHING

First published in Great Britain in 2009 by
The Breedon Books Publishing Company Limited
Breedon House, 3 The Parker Centre,
Derby, DE21 4SZ.

ISBN 978-1-85983-697-2

Printed and bound by TJ International Ltd, Padstow, Cornwall.

Contents

Dedication

Football has been a large part of my life and I have, over the years, earned a good living from doing something that I love with a passion.

Bill Shankly once said 'Football isn't about life and death it's more important than that!' I do not agree. Success and adulation are not bad things but the thing I remember most is the opportunity to have met some extraordinary characters and made some lifelong friendships. That to me is what football is about.

I would like to thank my mum and dad who were there when the journey began, Ivan Hollett who has been a constant friend and mentor throughout my career, and my wife Clare for being there when it came to an end.

Acknowledgements

I would like to thank the following people for many different reasons, but they all know themselves what for: Clare Holland; Chelsea Holland; Jak Holland; Megan Holland; Christopher Holland; Mum and Dad; Enid Dolby; Lisa Tighe; Martin Watkins; Colin Dolby; Oliver, Rachel, Harriet and Matilda Dolby; Jamie, Claire, Isabel and Daniel Holland; Banny Isaac and family; Eleanor, Marco and Lucia Scotece; Vicky and Neil Doherty; Ian and Julie Foster; Clare, Dave and Haydn Roberts; Wendy, Perry, Lewis and Charlotte Palmer; Hiroko, Andy, Alisa and Hannah Clark; Colin and Rhona White; Becky, Mark and Abbie Taylor; George Naufahu; Paul Madin; Ivan and Ann Hollett; Phil and Helen Shields; all my aunties, uncles and cousins and, finally, all at Breedon Books, especially Michelle Harrison for her help and advice.

Foreword

I go back a long way with Paul Holland. I had just returned to Mansfield Town Football Club to coach the Youth Team at the request of the then manager Ian Greaves and his Youth Development Officer, John Jarman. It was a Sunday morning at Nottingham Forest's training ground, Mansfield Under-15s were playing Nottingham Forest's Under-15s, and the management asked me if I would have a look who the next group of youngsters were who would become part of the youth team at Under-18 level.

I was not disappointed. Paul was very impressive playing mid-field and looked a very exciting prospect. A year passed and sure enough he was featuring in the youth team. He was mature beyond his years as one Saturday I asked him to play striker at Stoke City, and without any objections he played as if he had been in that position all his young career! That typified Paul, 'Get on with the job!'

The next move for him was to be his debut at Crewe Alexandra for Mansfield's first team; I was privileged to see him take the field at Crewe and he did himself proud. By now he was developing into a really good player and indeed got selected for the England Youth Team. All of us at Mansfield Town were proud for him.

Paul's career took off and he moved on in the football world, as no doubt you will learn as you read this biography.

Years later we again met up at Mansfield Town. Paul (Dutch as he was now known) had to retire from football because of serious injuries to his knees. He was still quite young to be finished playing and consequently he was offered a position at Mansfield Town to coach the youth team and I would assist him.

He took to the position wonderfully well. He was bubbly, full of fun and a real practical joker, as they say 'never a dull moment'.

As a pair we pushed through quite a few young footballers into the first team.

A few years later, I performed a reading at Paul and Clare's wedding and I was privileged to do so. We annually celebrate the occasion.

Later he was to assist Carlton Palmer, Peter Shirtliff and more recently Billy Dearden. Finally he was made caretaker manager but ran out of matches to save Mansfield's fate of going out of League football.

Overall, I personally feel privileged to be part of his life and career and I believe he will bounce back and achieve managerial positions because he has a good knowledge of the game, a super personality and gets the best out of people.

Good Luck Paul

Ivan Hollett 2008

Chapter One

My First Pair of Boots

I have never understood why some young boys are not interested in football. For me it was always football, football, football. I have had some incredible highs, some incredible lows and have made some great friends. I have also had a lot of laughs and a few tears. For all those of you who have a passion for football, I want to share the highs and lows with you.

I was born in Sleaford on 8 July 1973, the second son to Sue and Jim, and younger brother to Jamie, two years my senior.

My first real footballing memory is from my third birthday when I received my first pair of football boots, bought for me by my late nan, Doris. What I remember about the boots was the bright yellow stripes stitched on to the shiny black plastic. Looking back, they were obviously a cheap pair but they meant the world to me. At the time money was tight, my dad was working two jobs and my mum was a full-time housewife taking care of myself and my brother Jamie. From this moment, it was unlikely that anybody would see me without these boots, my pride and joy, and people commented that they never saw me without a football, either at my feet or in my hands.

Up until the age of eight I was never signed on for a local team so all my football knowledge was taught to me by my dad (a good local goalkeeper, who could have had trials at Football League clubs but did not because his parents could not afford the transport to get him there and back). Just before the age of four we moved from the small village of Leasingham to the then small market town of Sleaford. This was great news for me as a football mad three-year-old. I was not bothered about my brand new bedroom, in my brand new house, because more importantly 30 yards up the road was the place where I would spend most of my spare time over the next few years, a place known as 'the rec'.

My earliest memories of the rec were that it was my Wembley. In those days I was allowed on Saturday afternoons to wander up the street and watch the local teams play their games against other small towns.

At that age, without any fear or trepidation, there was many a time when my dad had to come and drag me away from the local teams' warm up in order for the game to start. Once or twice, I think my dad got in heated discussions with some of the players because it was great amusement for them to kick the ball out of their hands as high as they possibly could and watch me run for the ball and get smacked squarely in the face by it on the way down. This may explain a few things to those of you who know me.

The next few years were much of the same – kickabouts with family and generally watching as much football as possible. (It is only recently that my wife Clare pointed out to me that my mum must have had a 'if you can't beat them join them' philosophy, as she often ended up in goal and had to tolerate endless football on the television. It never crossed my mind at the time that it may not have been her first choice of activity at a weekend, so wrapped up was I in the game.)

The big highlight in Sleaford's footballing season was the infamous Sleaford Festival of Sport. This was a selection of competitions in varying sports where local sportsmen could compete individually or collectively in a team, against other teams put together by local people. It was so frustrating watching the football competitions on the rec, being only a wide-eyed, frustrated seven-year-old dying to get involved in what seemed like the FA Cup and World Cup rolled into one. The only downside to this festival was that the youngest age group were under-11s and I was only seven. However, many an evening was spent walking round asking the various teams whether they were a man short and could they do with an extra member for their team. Monday, Tuesday and Wednesday passed without any luck and the frustration was mounting as all that was left now was the Under-16 age group before the adults started their tournament on the Friday night. That Thursday was probably the start of my football career and probably the end of my dreams of being a goalkeeper! I did my usual circuit of teams, asking for a game, and finally came to a group of young lads not as smartly turned out as the rest, in different kits that comprised of numerous shades of white with multi-coloured shorts and socks. The usual spiel came out from my seven-year-old mouth, asking to play in an Under-16 competition. To my delight and amazement they were a man short and the position they were short of was goalkeeper. I was wearing my plain green cotton goalkeeper's top with my Manchester United badge sewn on and my red cotton gloves with the black grip that I thought were top of the range goalkeeping gloves, but later found out were bicycle gloves from Halfords.

At this point, none of my family had any idea that the youngest son was about to be playing with lads nearly 10 years his senior. The team I played my first competitive game for were called the mighty Ireland's Own comprised of mainly two Irish families called the Harlands and the Dohertys. To me the next four games were the best minutes of my life so far. Me, playing in goal for a 'proper' team, in a 'proper' tournament.

At the tournament you got four points for a goal and one point for a corner. It did not matter to me that Ireland's Own, failed to score a point and conceded 164 points (over 40 goals conceded in four games!) – I absolutely loved it. Goal after goal went past me but people told me in future years they have never seen such a proud youngster, so obviously doing something that he loved, with a huge smile that stretched from ear to ear.

I think it was probably in the third game that my mum and dad came to look for me as they thought I would still be pestering, bending people's ears for a game. Their eyes scanned the various teams sat around the pitches but obviously not looking onto the actual pitches themselves where near 'grown men' were doing their bit. My mum eventually spotted me after somebody said, 'Have you seen your Paul?' and there I was – picking the ball out of the net, yet again.

I think mum and dad wanted me to go home and not cause any more embarrassment to the young lads of Ireland's Own but my new teammates were not bothered about winning, it really was the taking part that counted.

Needless to say we failed to qualify for the next stages of the tournament but I went home having played my first proper matches and felt on top of the world.

I thought that this was my Festival of Sports experience over for the year but a strange night happened in October. After finishing another evening meal (my mum was now back working full-time in a bank but never once was there not a proper dinner prepared for the family), mum and dad announced that we were going to the Carre's Grammar School for the presentation night. We all had to be suitably dressed – hair smart, teeth brushed and shoes cleaned. They said we were going just to watch people receive their winners' trophies.

I can remember arriving to a packed school hall full of people smartly dressed but none smarter than me in my elastic bow tie and beige suit! That night I promised myself that one day I would be on stage receiving an award from the mayor.

The presentation night, while probably dragging on for many people, did not for me. I was loudly clapping people, who I saw as heroes, receiving their trophies. It came to the final award of the night – the Mayor's trophy. I listened to him as he talked about the spirit of sport, and how the winner of this award had not actually won a winners' medal but the way he had enjoyed himself so much and put a smile on so many people's faces by his obvious love of football deserved to be recognised. I was looking round wondering who was going to collect this award – the biggest trophy of the night – when the name was announced. It was my own name, but it still did not sink in that the award was mine. Mum and dad had to push me out of my seat and I made the marathon walk to receive the Mayor's trophy. After numerous photographs there could never have been a more proud recipient. Even now while writing this piece and thinking about all the awards I have received since, this award is still probably the closest to my heart. How mum, dad and Jamie managed to keep it quiet amazes me and this was only the first instance of the help and dedication given to me by my family. At this point I would like to thank my first ever team, Ireland's Own, and my first manager, for giving me the chance and the start of my life in football.

I still use this story when I go to watch my son play football – particularly when he is forced from his favoured position and made to go in goal, looking gloomy, while their team is 4–0 down. I will stand on the edge of the touchline and tell him to keep smiling, as I remember the drubbings received by Ireland's Own in the summer of 1980.

At this time I was at the William Alvey Primary School and though I enjoyed my time there immensely, my mind was always on football and getting home as quickly as possible in order to get my kit on and get over to the rec. Most nights were spent with mates for as long as possible having a 'kick about', pretending I was one of my Manchester United heroes. The players of Sleaford Town were also among my heroes and I can still vividly remember watching them claim the League and Cup double in the 1980–81 season. The team comprising of Messrs Smith, Woodcock, Cox, Brankin, Rowland, Clawson, Ogden, Kelby, Winters, Mason and Bartlett among others have gone down in Sleaford folklore and I owe them a big thank you because I watched them so closely and saw how they did different things. I can honestly say that at this time I would rather have seen my beloved Manchester United lose than watch the Greens lose.

In the following September my first full season in football started. Strangely for a town the size of Sleaford, there was no junior football club so my first team was to be Ruskington Tigers Under-11s. My brother was also in the team, despite being over two years my senior. I think competing against older boys accelerated my football progression and a few years later we were to be playing again in the same team for Swinderby Under-16s under the guidance of Nadge Anderson (quite a colourful character but more of that later). My first manager was to be a great man called Norman Hill, whose lad Philip also played for Tigers. It was to be a very long hard season, with us finishing bottom (this was becoming a habit!), but we steadily progressed and from being beaten out of sight in our games before Christmas we were only being beaten by the odd goal come the end of the season. In fact, we improved so much that we beat the League winners Navenby in the Final of the Digby six-a-side tournament. We only won one league game all season but I had got the bug and the new season could not come quick enough.

A new season brought a new team for the two Holland brothers. We, along with a few others, went to play for a small village team called Navenby. This meant a few more miles for my parents but again they did not complain and many more miles were to be chalked up over the next few years all over the country because of my love for football. Jamie went to play for the Under-12s while I stayed with the younger age group. We had a great season, finishing second, and I was lucky enough to be selected for the trials to play for the league representative team. Three of us from Navenby were fortunate enough to be selected to represent the league. They were Stephen Maplethorpe, Stephen Horswood and myself, still a year younger. Soon we found out that we were going to travel to Germany in June for a week to pit ourselves against foreign opposition. I was so excited but also a little bit worried because I had never been away from my family before, apart from the odd night at my grandparents' who were both very local. Mum thought it would be a good idea for me to stay away for a night before the trip, so the weekend before I stayed at Stephen's house in Metheringham. That passed fairly smoothly, and I can still remember having my photograph taken in the back garden at my home with a big suitcase next to me containing all my changes of clothes and football stuff. I was dropped off in Lincoln late on Sunday afternoon, and I can remember a tearful goodbye. I do not know who was the more upset – me or my mum. The journey was awful and seemed to take forever. The ferry was bad enough but worse was to come – the Black Forest. I can recall the majority of the boys being sick as we ascended the forest in red-hot conditions. There was no air conditioning on the bus and that is still the worst journey I have ever been on. We finally got the football underway and for me that was the only enjoyable part of the trip. I hated being away from home and my mum still has a postcard that I wrote with tear drops smudging the writing on it. I think the team did okay in the tournament and I was lucky enough to receive Player of the Tournament. This was a small bonus for me but I could not wait to get back to Sleaford. The week finally passed and I can remember arriving back in Lincoln a week later, really looking forward to seeing mum, dad and Jamie. Much to their amusement, when I climbed down the stairs of the coach I still had the same clothes on that I had left in a week earlier, and none of the outfits that my mum had packed and ironed so methodically had been worn. Worse still I had chewed a hole in the front of my white Adidas t-shirt. I was not bothered in the slightest, I was home! Let the new season begin.

Before that was the six-week school holiday and that meant my other love – cricket. Again the rec was the venue and from eight in the morning until five in the evening for the whole six weeks there we all were (the same crew as the football) in shorts and cricket gear. In the six-week holiday you could always guarantee the weather and apart from family holidays there would always be at least eight of us there religiously. I am sure that many people must have been walking across the rec on their way to work and smiling to themselves because most mornings Jamie and I would be there at half past seven preparing the wicket. Remember: this was not a cricket pitch and it had a season's worth of football with probably over 100 games played on it. There was not much grass left on it and it was very bumpy, but that did not matter. The rec had changed from our Wembley to our Lords. Mum and dad's old reliable Qualcast push mower would be out in the morning cutting the 'wicket'. Many a time the groundsman would come over and have a quiet word in our ears about giving the grass time to recover for the football season but to no avail.

From the time I started school, mum was back at work full-time, working as the manager's secretary at Barclays, and dad was still doing his bricklaying but combined it with picking vegetables in the fields during the evenings. Looking back now this was obviously done to earn that extra bit of money which was needed for all the miles mum and dad were doing running their two sons about. We never wanted for anything. Money was obviously tight but we never had a clue. I can remember in the last couple of weeks at junior school having a chance to go to Lincoln for some kind of education workshop. The only problem was that we would have to make our own way there so for all of us this was a major problem. All my friends' parents worked full-time as well so have a guess who volunteered his dad to take five of us. Dad asked the obvious question about what the other kids' parents were doing and I promptly said 'Of course they can't take us dad, they are at work!' Dad reminded me in a very subtle way (not!) that, in case I had forgotten, he also worked more than full-time but again he was there for me and did not let us down. As my mum and dad worked during the day my nan used to come round and look after us, which was not very difficult because we were out all day. In fact nan became the drinks lady and the sandwich maker. We would all trudge to our house at about 10.30am where orange squash would be ready and then again at about 1.30pm where plates of sandwiches would be waiting. Perhaps another visit would be made about 3.30pm for the last drinks session of the day and I dread to think how much drink we used to consume over the holidays. By the time the six-week holiday ended we were all totally exhausted but boy did we have a good tan.

Up until this point we had always gone to Butlins in Skegness for a much-needed holiday (for my parents) for a week in August and this again would see Jamie and I spend most of the day on football courses, but this summer we went off to Devon for the first time. It was to be a custom for the next seven or eight years.

I have always been one for practical jokes, something that I must have got from my dad. I can remember how dad used to put my nan's Russian-style hat on the lamp shade to wind her up; one day when we were on our family holiday in Brixham (Devon), before we went for a little walk up to the local pub, I put her hat on the lamp shade next to her bed. My parents and grandparents had a few drinks while Jamie and I had a few games of pool. We all had a bag of chips while we walked back to the guest house and when we went to our rooms I heard my nan shriek. I told my parents that I had put the hat on the lamp next to her bed and I saw the horror on their faces. They rushed towards nan's room and you could see the black smoke and smell the burning down the corridors. I had left the lamp on! The heat from the lamp had burnt a hole right through the hat, nan's pride and joy. How it had not caught fire and burnt the guest house down, I do not know. I apologised profusely and promised that I would buy her a new hat but they realised it was an accident and was only meant to be a joke. Not the way to repay her for all the drinks and sandwiches she had made us!

By this time I was in my last year at the William Alvey School and my teacher was to be Pete Douglas, who also ran the school's football and cricket teams. Lincolnshire is one of the few counties left to have grammar schools, so we had to sit our eleven-plus to determine whether we would go to the all boy's Carre's Grammar School if we passed, or the mixed St Georges School if we failed. Jamie, much more academic than me, had passed two years earlier, so it was a great delight when I passed and so did the majority of my mates. We had had another good year at Navenby, competing yet again with Lowlands for all the awards. In the Lowlands team was Stephen Froggatt, who went on to play for Wolves and Aston Villa before injury forced him to retire early, and Jonathan Kerrigan, who has gone on to be a success in television, appearing in such programmes as *Casualty*, *Merseybeat* and more recently *Heartbeat*. The rivalry was fierce but they were to become very good friends. A new chapter in my life was now starting…

Chapter Two
Carre's

I had just turned 11 years of age in the July and was eagerly awaiting the start of senior school. Jamie had been there now for two years and the stories he came home with meant September could not come quick enough. I knew a lot of Jamie's friends so it was not as if I would not know anybody there and making new friends has never been something I worried about.

One thing that was concerning me a little was that I had started getting problems with my left knee (by the end of this book you will be sick of reading about my knees but remember when it all started!) Whether it was all the sport I was playing, the fact that I was growing, or just the hard ground with all the pounding from cricket and tennis, something was not quite right. My knee had started locking and there was no way it would go straight. The usual treatment consisted of a hot bath and I would basically force it to go straight. This would work for a couple of days but again and again it would happen. My dad took me to see a very experienced physiotherapist in Lincoln called Bert Loxley. He thought it might be a combination of growing and the hard ground and thought it would be a good idea to rest completely from sport for a month, dad agreed and I thought my world had fallen apart. No sport!

The next month consisted of telling mum and dad that I would still go over to Lords (the rec) but only to umpire. Whether they believed me or not they agreed and every day from 8am until my mum used to pass on her way to work there I was umpiring, doing as I was told. As soon as she had gone out of sight I would be straight back playing. I would carry on until I saw my dad's work van pull up in the distant lay-by at about 4.30pm. My umpiring role would then resume and dad would walk up and usually send a couple of bowls down to see if he could catch one of the lads on an unprotected part of their sunburnt legs. To his delight he did sometimes get a couple of 'stingers' as we called them. Then he would normally ruffle my hair up and say how hot and sweaty I had got when all I had done was umpire all day. He would have known it was too big a temptation for his son to resist joining in.

My new uniform had been bought consisting of a blazer that had to be worn at all times at Carre's. The now customary new school photo by mum was taken and I think this was the smartest I was ever to look in it. Over the next seven years many pairs of shoes were scuffed and ruined, and numerous holes in knees of trousers due to playing football in the playground appeared. Even now my wife,

Clare, teases me about how spoilt Jamie and I were when we were kids. Every morning my mum would be up an hour before us making sure our uniforms were as smart as possible, and she would squeeze about half a dozen oranges to make us orange juice every morning to get our vitamin C intake. To this day we take the mickey out of my mum but never once did we go out to school without breakfast (the most important meal of the day, as it was drilled into us), and when she got home after working a full day at work a hot meal was always on the table.

I met up with my friends and made the mile-long walk up to Carre's for our first day at senior school. We felt so grown up walking through the gates. We were escorted to our new form room where we met our form teacher for the first time. I was pleased to find out it was to be a man called Mr White, who was head of PE and a well-known face around Sleaford due to his connections with the cricket club. He was very sharp and very strict on that first morning and laid the law down quickly. Over the next seven years Colin White would become a huge influence in my development in all sports. His knowledge was second to none and he was to become, and still is, a very close friend who I have so much respect for.

Obviously the main difference when you first start senior school is the sheer size of it and the wide range of subjects you do. From the normal maths and english at primary school, we were now going to be doing religious education, science, history, geography and latin among others. I could not wait to get started. However, I had a rude awakening around the corner in my first lunchtime at Carre's. A group of my mates and I were exploring our new school, minding our business, when I saw Jamie and his mates coming towards us. They gave us a bit of stick about how smart we looked in our brand new uniforms (I am sure all mums have the same idea about their sons growing into an oversized blazer) and I think I can remember saying something back a bit cocky. I knew all of my brother's mates and they gave chase. They soon caught up with me and it was all good natured but I did not count on the stink bombs. They were broken in my blazer pockets and had the desired effect for the rest of the day. To great hilarity I was given a wide berth for the afternoon and when I got home I was given a grilling by mum about what had happened. I played dumb and did not 'grass' on Jamie and his mates. His mates responsible for the stink bombs, Andy Wilkinson, Danny White and John Sabin, were to become teammates and firm friends over my school life.

My life was now getting a bit more complicated. Obviously school was now becoming a lot more important and with homework deadlines and my sport still to fit in round these, I was struggling to get it all in. Again my parents told me in no uncertain terms that school was the priority and football would have to come second for the first time in my life. At this time the next big problem came to light. This may be hard to believe to those of you who know me now, but I was the smallest one in the year and very lightweight! This had never been a problem before but over the next couple of years it was to become a major issue.

I loved my new school life, and I even loved the homework. I had made loads of new friends already and the sport side of the school was brilliant. Colin White, the PE teacher, had organised football practices at lunchtimes and soon I had come through these and, in fact, in my first month at Carre's I had been made captain of my year and had even played for the year above. My first game saw us beat Ruskington Secondary School by double figures but even that did not please Mr White. He said that he would not accept that standard and emphasised the need to improve. Looking back and knowing Colin as I do now, this was obviously pre-empted and a way of knocking these new students into line. We were never allowed to rest upon our laurels, but I was used to this as dad was always a big believer in this and would never let us become too big for our boots.

At this point I was starting to get noticed by a few other people. Unbeknown to me, football scouts had started coming to my games to see this talented but very small individual from Sleaford. The first club to show any real interest was not the nearby Lincoln City, but Notts County. A man called Mel Hackett spoke to my dad and invited us to attend training sessions every Monday night in Nottingham. Nottingham is about an hour away from Sleaford but at that time of day (training started at 6pm) it probably was nearer one and a half hours. Having only finished school at 3.45pm it was a mad rush on Mondays for the next couple of years, getting home as quickly as possible, having something to eat and then leaving the house at 4.30pm. Dad had to finish work early as well but this was yet another sign of his loyalty to his youngest son's ambitions. The first time we went to Meadow Lane (Notts County's ground) the whole family went. Mum and dad were there with me, but the pleasing thing for me was that my elder brother Jamie was there. We have never fallen out, to this day, and not once when we were younger did he show any signs of jealousy about the attention I was attracting, and he has always been a great support.

Amazingly the training sessions I had at Notts were held by the actual first-team manager, a man called Jimmy Sirrel – an absolute legend not only in Nottingham and the East Midlands, but all over the country. I was so nervous (as I was all through my career) and also the smallest. However, Jimmy seemed to take a shine to me and after the first few weeks he and his assistant, Mick Walker, came to speak to my dad. They had been delighted by what they had seen and wanted to see me in some games. These games were to be played on a Sunday morning and because you were not allowed at that time to play under the name of a professional club, I was soon to make my debut for the 'intermediates' in the Under-12 Derby league. Our home games were to be played in Derby. I say home, this was now one and a half hours away from Sleaford, and all away games were to be played in venues all around Derby. This meant more travelling, more petrol and, therefore, more expense.

School games had started on Saturday mornings and probably the occasional mid-week game, so my footballing week was now getting fuller and fuller.

Saturday morning	School Fixture
Saturday afternoon	Occasional game for Navenby
Sunday morning	Notts County game
Sunday afternoon	Occasional game for Navenby or league team
Monday night	Training for Notts County
Wednesday night	Occasional school game
Friday night	Training for Navenby

This did not bother me at all, the more football the better. I was somehow still fitting all my school work in as well, but for the first time I had to sacrifice other things that my friends were doing. They understood this and yet again I had their support. Mr White was pleased that I was getting noticed outside of school, but he told me and my family that if my school work started slipping something would have to give and under no circumstances would it be my work or my participation in school fixtures. He said that this was to be the priority and not Notts County, but I had no qualms about this. There was no way I was going to jeopardise my ambitions by letting anything slip.

After a few weeks of going to Derby and playing for the intermediates, we were yet again called in front of Mick Walker. He was delighted by my progress but was concerned about my size. This had never worried me because I had no fear on a football field, (probably my undoing in later years). Nothing fazed me and I loved the challenges with the much bigger opposition, coming out of the challenge with the ball and the opponent floundering on the floor. However, it did concern Mick and he said I desperately needed to grow. Looking back I think this was harsh because I was only 11/12 years of age and my years of growing were ahead of me. There was always the sense of him doubting my ability. This was the first time I felt somebody had doubted me in anything I had done but, typical of my character, I wanted to prove him wrong. My family talked about the issue of my size with many people, including Colin White, and we all came to the conclusion that I would be fine. In fact I think this hurt Colin more than he let on, that somebody doubted one of his students, and subconsciously I think this was the point where everybody focused on my goal of becoming a professional footballer.

My hero at this point was Bryan Robson, who played for Manchester United. Many of you may say by supporting United I was a glory hunter, but they had not won the League title for many years and were well known as a Cup team. Five or six times a season my family would get up early on a Saturday morning and head off to Manchester. It would take us about two and a half hours to get there and we would park up in the other Old Trafford (the cricket ground). We would have a quick sandwich from the pack-up mum had made and at about 10.45am would make the 10-minute walk up to the 'Theatre of Dreams', otherwise known as Old Trafford. For the next hour Jamie and I would run around like nutters, trying to get the autographs of the United players as they arrived at the ground for a pre-match meal. My main drive would be to get the signature of my hero Bryan Robson, and to have a photograph with him. I still have the autograph book and must have got his autograph over 10 times. For Christmas, one of my main presents was Bryan Robson's autobiography. I could not put it down, it was frighteningly relevant to my issue. My hero was very small up to the age of 16 and when he was in digs at his first club, West Bromwich Albion, he had been put on various diets to try and get him to grow. A bottle of stout would be had after each evening meal which consisted of a mound of potatoes, along with vegetables and a steak. Three or four times a day he would crack a couple of raw eggs into a glass, beat them up, add a bit of sugar and swallow the lot. For the next year, I would have Bryan's diet. Whether it was because I was always on the go and I was burning all the calories off I am not sure, but the diet was not really having the desired effect. Not straight away, anyway.

That first season with Notts in the Derby league, we competed with JCS Garages FC and Littleover Dazzlers FC. You may think this was unfair as we were a professional team playing under a different name, but these teams were in fact representing Nottingham Forest and Derby County. We won the league and many of us in that team went on to play professional football in later years. Mel Hackett had crossed the river and gone to Nottingham Forest as a coach, and I was upset because he had been very supportive to me. The new coach, however, was a man called John Gaunt, whose son was the captain of the intermediates. He made it very enjoyable and was adamant that my size would not matter when the decision to be made about my future at Notts County was made. In the 1980s you could still play for your local team as well as representing a professional league club. I loved going back to play for Navenby and never once did I show off that I was at Notts. I was very level-headed and enjoyed being with my mates. I think this is a major problem nowadays, once you sign or go on trial at a professional club they now insist you leave your local club and even miss some school fixtures. That would not have been allowed to happen at Carre's with Mr White.

I had not signed anything with Notts by this point; the first forms you could sign at a professional club were schoolboy forms, which you could not sign until you were 14 years of age. Therefore, other professional clubs were starting to show a bit of interest. Mel Hackett rang my dad up and asked me to go to trial at Forest, and there were phone calls for Leicester, Watford, Mansfield Town and a Manchester United scout called Ray Medwell. However, I was loyal to Notts County and waited for the word from them.

The phone call came from John Gaunt, who had now got a great team together at Notts, and he said he could not believe what he had to tell my dad. He had given his list to Mick Walker saying who he had wanted to keep and who he thought should be released. My name had been towards the top of the list of people he wanted to keep, because John loved the way I played. I may have been one of the smallest, if not the smallest, but he admired my aggressive style of play. However, the men who made the final decision were Mick Walker and his assistant Russell Slade, the now Yeovil manager. They, especially Mick, were concerned about my lack of inches and disagreed with John about my chances of becoming a professional footballer. Therefore, it was left to John to make the phone call, a phone call he obviously did not want to make. My dad told me the news and it was met with tears – lots of them. Another family chat, another chat with Mr White and it was decided that this was to be the springboard for a career in football with a resolve to prove people wrong – especially the people at Notts. The phone started ringing from clubs now hearing about my release at Notts and this was the next chapter in my footballing life – trials, and lots of them.

Chapter Three
A Long Stretch

S o the Notts County dream had gone – all for being too small. My first year had gone really well at Carre's and I had even won a couple of school prizes for academic work, but the County thing had really got me down. I was even more determined to prove them wrong and my ambition to be a professional footballer had grown even stronger. The six-week holiday was to be full of cricket at the rec again and my cricketing ability had really improved due to Colin White. He was a key member of the Sleaford Cricket Club First XI and got me involved at the weekends down at their London Road ground. My first role at the cricket club was to be scorer for the First XI. This involved both home and away fixtures and so my weekends, those when I was not playing football, were now filled with my next love, cricket. The pay was not exactly good! 10 pence from each player and a free tea, but I loved it. It was the next best thing to playing football and I loved the banter among the cricketers. However, my knee was to start playing up again and, after numerous visits to physios and never really getting to the bottom of the problem, it was decided that rest was the only option. I was a bit better as a patient this time but I think people were starting to get a bit concerned by the problem.

The six-week holiday soon came to an end and school started again, overshadowed by my dodgy knee. Mr White was careful about my participation over the summer months as hard ground was a probable cause of my injury. I was willing for the rain in order to soften up the ground and when it came the knee improved greatly. Fitness at this stage was something that I never had to work at. I can remember representing the school in cross country at the district championships at Burghley Park in Stamford and when I got there, much to my surprise, I found out that I was actually running in the age group above myself. I still started with the same mentality I did in all my running events. I went off as fast as I could for as long as I could. To my amazement, it worked. I fancied myself against my age group but to get a start against older lads was a surprise. The run was about three miles and by the time the last half a mile came up, I was about 100 yards clear. I dug in against the ever-closing pack and crossed the finishing line in first place by about 10 yards. I was ecstatic until I realised that I had now qualified for the county championships to be held at the South Park Common in Lincoln.

The knee was now fine and the phone started ringing about going for football trials. My next step was Nottingham Forest. I went there in the half-term holiday and probably not in the right frame of mind. The Notts County episode had hit my confidence a bit but by the time the week ended I was flying again. We had a trial game on the last day where decisions were to be made about coming again for another week late in the year around Christmas time. I played the game of my life, scoring two goals in a 3–1 victory for my side. It could not have gone any better. Alan Hill, Forest's chief scout, came up to me after the game and asked a bit about my background. He said the club would be in touch about me going over Christmas. I was elated!

The only down side to all this is that my school work was slipping a little. I can remember dreading Christmas coming because that meant my school report. I knew myself that I had let my standards slip and I was ready for an almighty telling-off. I was not disappointed. I got the telling off of my life! I was told until my school work improved football would stop. My dad spoke to Forest on the phone (or I thought he did!) telling them that I would be unable to go and train after Christmas because I was not working hard enough at school. I was absolutely mortified! The day before I was supposed to be going to Forest mum and dad sat me down and told me they wanted to see a drastic change in my school work and that they had not really spoken to Forest. It was a shock tactic, and god did it work. I cried with relief.

After another good trial Forest said they were pleased with my progress and would see me again at Easter. Mansfield Town started showing an interest around now, and I went down there a few times. It was a good friendly club and I think my dad even got a bit of petrol money for going over every Thursday night. However, misfortune was around the corner.

Around Easter time, and having played a lot of football, the athletics, tennis and cricket seasons were about to start. This meant the grounds were becoming harder and harder and my knee was getting stiffer and stiffer. Yet again it locked!

This was getting too common now and we decided that whatever it took, it had to get sorted. After many telephone calls we decided to go and see a knee specialist in Boston. He told us that the reason my knee was locking was not because of a fault mechanically within it, but because of a trapped nerve in my back. He thought that the problem could be sorted out, but it would involve a stay in hospital on traction. I was not really listening to him, as I was working out the time I would be out of sport. He said to my dad that the traction would not be available until the end of June and that I required three weeks of it. My dad asked how often I would need the traction over the three weeks, and to our amazement he said that I would be in a hospital bed for the entire time.

It was the end of June, and I can remember arriving at the Pilgrim Hospital with my suitcase packed with the usual hospital attire. A couple of pairs of pyjamas, some puzzle books and the customary bag of grapes. I was still confused about what traction was all about, but if it meant the end of my knee problems I was prepared to do anything. I saw the specialist again on that first morning and he explained what traction was and the idea of how it was going to help me. They were going to put a girdle around my pelvis, and have bands run from it down the side of my legs to a contraption at the end of the bed which had weights attached to it. Basically they were going to stretch me in order to try and release the trapped nerve in my back. I was not allowed to get out of my bed for the whole three weeks, not even to the toilet. Bed pans and bed baths were the order of the day, a bit embarrassing for a young boy who was going to become a teenager in 10 days.

On that first morning I was strapped to the bed and it was the start of the most boring three weeks of my life. The only consolation to being in hospital was that I was going to miss three weeks of school, no homework, no teachers. How wrong I was! All of the nurses introduced themselves and sat on the end of the bed trying to lighten my mood. That first morning dragged but then to my horror I was wheeled off down the corridor in my bed to a room containing a person I did not think I would be seeing – Mrs Hillyer, my form teacher from Carre's was sitting there in the hospital classroom. She had come over with all my schoolwork for the next three weeks and beyond, so not only would I not be behind any of my mates at Carre's, I would actually be ahead of them. To be fair to Mrs Hillyer, she probably did me a great favour on that first morning but I did not realise it at the time.

The first week was horrible. I was alone in a ward for six with no one to talk to. I felt so low. I had visitors every afternoon, uncles, aunts, teachers, mates and grandparents, and then at night my mum and dad would come over. Boston was about half an hour away from Sleaford so a lot of people put themselves out to try and keep my spirits up. I had my birthday to look forward to in a few days, and in the second week two other boys came into the ward to liven things up. Firstly there was a young ginger-haired boy called Ryan who was probably no more than seven. He was a real character who was afraid of nobody and I can recall him telling the senior staff nurse that he had seen the spitting image of her earlier. She asked him to show her if he saw her again and he said, 'There she is now lady! In the middle of that field scaring the birds off. You look like that scarecrow!' He was a cheeky little so-and-so but he did lighten the mood over the next two weeks. Secondly, there was the lad opposite me, a boy called Matthew Gross. He was not somebody I would have normally hit it off with but for the next two weeks we did. I think we probably realised that we could make the rest of our stays at the Pilgrim easier by getting on and having a laugh and we certainly did that. I think the nurses turned a blind eye to a lot of things, but I think they were pleased just to see a smile on two faces. Never once did we ask each other what the other one was in for and along with young Ryan, Matthew made the last two weeks go a lot quicker.

Not one visiting session was missed and every night when mum, dad and usually Jamie came over mum would have plated a dinner up, because the hospital food was not that great. My birthday came and went – not many people can say they have become a teenager while wearing a girdle and being stretched.

As the three weeks came to an end my thoughts were wandering to what lay ahead in the the next few weeks. The last week at school, two weeks in Devon with my family, and straight after that a week at Forest. I could not wait to leave hospital. My mum and dad arrived to pick me up at about three in the afternoon and after a final chat with the specialist all they had to do now was weigh me, measure me and take that infamous girdle off. I had not put a foot on the floor for three weeks so I was desperate once the girdle had been removed along with the weights to get going. To my disgust, the nurses brought me a wheelchair down to take me to get measured and weighed. They advised me to use it as my balance would have gone with being laid in bed for the last three weeks. Instead, I chose to jump out of bed and promptly fell flat on the floor. My balance, co-ordination and senses had completely gone (some football supporters would say never to come back!) All I could think of was that I had a trial at Forest in less than a month and that I had a lot of hard work to do before then. My dad asked the specialist about the trial, and he said I would probably have to miss it. He said the chances were about 20:80. Being as stubborn as ever, I refused the wheelchair and used the arms of mum and dad to get down to the car.

The last week at school involved no sport, I missed sports day and generally felt a bit out of place. I did my bit encouraging my mates, but I was worried. My balance and co-ordination were coming back slowly but in three weeks time I was going to Forest to try and impress. I kept trying to test myself. I would have a little jog on the way home but it felt foreign to me, as if I had never run before. How on earth was I going to be fit for a football trial?

We set off for Torquay for our two-week family holiday: mum, dad and Jamie in one car, me in the back of my grandparents' car. I loved the holidays in Torquay but on the long drive down to the south-west at 4 o'clock on a Saturday morning I promised myself that even if I had to test myself for the whole fortnight I would, if it meant I could go on that damn football trial. Mum and dad kept telling me that there would be many more chances and that I should just relax and enjoy my holiday like the specialist had advised me to do. No way; every chance I had, I would be on the move. Every morning I was up before everybody else and volunteered myself to go and get the daily papers. I worked out that it would probably take me about half an hour to walk there and back to the paper shop, so once I was out of sight of the guest house I would set off jogging. I knew dad was looking of the window but he knew what I was up to. I would run as fast as I could to the shop and then go for about a four-mile run with two papers in my hand. Dad told me many years later that he used to wait until I had gone and then walk up to the Downs where he guessed I would be. I put myself through it. I would be throwing myself on to the floor and getting up as quick as possible and then sprinting various distances trying to recreate football situations. Day after day, I was getting stronger and fitter and, remarkably, taller. The traction in hospital had stretched me so well that not only had the trapped nerve been released and my knee better, but I had grown three inches. Every afternoon I would walk up the steep hill from Anstey's Cove (a little beach opposite the guest house), until again I was out of view, and set off on another long run. Looking back I probably ran over 100 miles in those two weeks, not bad for somebody who was supposed to be resting. On the penultimate day of our holidays we got the bus in to the centre of Torquay and looked around the shops. As the morning was coming to an end, I persuaded everybody to go into GT Sports and have a look. There I found what were to be my best ever pair of football boots. A pair of Puma Step Stars, a plain boot compared to some of those of today, but instead of the usual white stripe found on most Puma boots it was orange. They were made from kangaroo leather and they were the softest pair of boots I had ever felt. The only stumbling block, and a massive one at that, was the price. They were £80 – a lot of money in 1986, especially for a pair of boots that would not even see me through a season. I had set my heart on them, I tried them on (they were perfect) but realised they were way too much money so reluctantly I put them back and left the shop. We were having our evening meal that night when dad told me to fetch his wallet that was on his bed. When I got upstairs I could not believe it. There on my bed were my dream boots, along with a bright orange football that the shop had thrown in as part of the deal. I ran back downstairs and hugged everybody. Apparently my mum and dad and my nan and granddad had clubbed together and bought them. I could not believe it and I can remember my grandparents telling me to go to Forest and 'knock them dead'. I looked at my mum and dad and they nodded their heads – I was going to Forest. Straightaway I did what I always did with new boots, I put them on and then sat in the bath for a couple of hours to get the boots to mould perfectly. I vowed that night to make everybody proud of me.

The next morning, the last full day of the holiday, we went, as we had done every day, down the steep hill to the beach. After a couple of hours of playing in the sea with my brother I asked my parents if I could go back to the guest house and get my boots and ball and play on a grass area halfway down the hill. My dad said it would be all right but told me that under no circumstances was I to wear my boots on the concrete or bounce or kick my ball down the hill. 'No problem', I said. I sprinted all the way back up the hill and got my boots and ball. I obeyed half of my dad's instructions. I carried the boots, but was messing about with the ball as I walked down. As I got about 200 yards from the grass I lost control of the ball and it rolled down the hill, bouncing against the kerb as it picked up speed. I was not too concerned: it would end up on the grass area. How wrong I was. I did not realise that about 100 yards ahead there was a pipe in the kerb, obviously to allow water to pass through and flow down the cliff face rather than go all the way down to the beach. Where did the ball end up? Not down on the grass area but on a ledge about 50 feet down the slope. Not a real cliff face, but far too steep to walk or climb down. My heart sank. What on earth was I going to tell my dad? I walked down to the beach trying to get the story straight in my head, when I finally got my words out I could tell he was fuming. He told me to go back up to his car and get the rope out of the boot. Yet again I sprinted back up the hill and got the rope, still not sure what dad was planning. When I got back to my dad I showed him exactly where the ball was. He tied the rope around my waist and told me to start making my way down the slope while he held the other end. I thought he was joking. To the amazement of the few people now watching, I was lowered towards my ball. Looking back it could not have been that dangerous otherwise my dad would not have let me do it. When I finally got the ball and made it back up the slope, he told me not to tell mum what I had just done. I promised not to, and for the next hour or so we had a kick about. I was feeling ready for Forest.

Chapter Four
Decision Time

F ootball was now getting more and more serious. My trial had gone well at Forest, mainly due to the fact that they knew how hard I had worked to get fit. The interest was starting to come from different Football League clubs but for me it was between two: Nottingham Forest, a First Division club, and Mansfield Town, a Third Division club. Many would say it was not a hard decision to make, Forest were a top-League club who, a few years earlier, had twice been champions of Europe. I was not sure. I spoke to a few people and had lengthy discussions with my parents and Colin White. They were concerned about my long-term prospects at Forest and the possibilty that I might be better at a smaller club like Mansfield where I could start at the bottom and work my way up. However, at this point it did not really matter as neither club had offered me anything yet. Christmas came and went and then the phone started ringing every night. One night it would be Forest, the next it would be Mansfield. Mansfield was a much friendlier club, but Forest was a lot more professionally run. Forest was the first to offer schoolboy forms. These could not be signed until my 14th birthday in July, and upon hearing this Mansfield bettered this by offering schoolboy forms and a guaranteed two-year youth team apprenticeship place when I finished my GCSEs. When I told Forest this, or should I say when my dad told Forest, they said they thought I had a very good future in the game but they were not going to be held to ransom by a 13-year-old. I could understand this so the decision was Forest or the Stags.

Then came a phone call out of the blue. The local Football League club in my area, Lincoln City, wanted me to go down and play in a trial game. It had always confused me why clubs over an hour away had shown an interest in me, but Lincoln, only 20 minutes away, had never once rang. I agreed to go and play for Lincoln City in that trial game and had an absolute blinder. The game was played on Sincil Bank, Lincoln's main ground, and I scored a hat-trick. As soon as the game ended I was pulled to one side by the chap who had organised the trial game. He told me that the first-team manager, Peter Daniel, wanted to see me in his office as soon as I had showered and changed. I was shown down the corridor to his office where I tentatively knocked and waited for the shout to come in. For the first time my dad had not come to watch me, and here I was going in to see the first-team manager at a football club. I entered the room and was told to sit down on the other side of his desk. He said he was very impressed by what he had seen, and that despite having only seen me play once he was prepared to offer me something. He asked me what other clubs I had been to and I told him that

Forest had offered me schoolboy forms, and Mansfield had offered me schoolboy forms plus a guaranteed two-year youth team deal. He said there was no way he could offer the same as those two clubs, and my heart sank. Not rejection again. Amazingly he offered me schoolboy forms, a two-year youth team scheme and a one-year professional contract on the basis of one game. So now it was Forest, Mansfield and Lincoln.

My parents and Colin were surprised that Lincoln could offer that much after one game. It appeared as if they were letting Forest and Mansfield do all the hard work in coaching me and then they would come in at the last minute with the best deal. I was flattered by the deal Lincoln had put on the table but at the same time a little bit confused. Another chat with my parents and we decided to ring Peter Daniel back. We thanked him for his kind offer but declined to accept it. Again it was down to two.

One night in March the decision was made a little bit easier. It is not commonplace for a first-team manager to take an interest in a young 13-year-old, but that is what happened. Ian Greaves, manager at Mansfield Town, came over to Sleaford with chief scout Bob Shaw, the man who got me to Mansfield a few years earlier. They sat there for over two hours, taking time out from more important issues, to try and convince me to sign for them. The thing that impressed my parents and Colin White the most was the issue of education. Ian Greaves told us that my education was more important than football and that basically he thought I should stay on at school at 16 and do my A-levels. He said I could still play for the youth team and if I did well enough the reserve team, while I was still at school studying. This sounded brilliant to my parents and Colin but confused me a little. How could they want me to join their club but still want me to stay at school? Looking back now it was the right decision and I have found myself telling numerous young players to stay on at school and concentrate on their studies even when I was manager of Mansfield Town. Football, as I found out much later, can be a very short career and as the years have gone by there is less and less loyalty in the industry as well.

Towards the end of the season the cricket had restarted and so had my scoring for the First XI. It was FA Cup Final day between Spurs and Coventry, and the cricket club were playing Burghley Park away at Stamford. A very good left-arm spinner who played for Sleaford, called Dick Johnson, was going to be about 90 minutes late for the game due to a wedding he was photographer at. Sleaford asked the opposition captain if I could stand in for an hour if we had to field. They agreed, we lost the toss and they put us in the field. I was ecstatic. The captain, a great chap called Chris Travers, tried to keep me out of the way but with not much luck. After a couple of overs Burghley Park's opening batsman (and also a minor county cricketer) absolutely cracked the ball in the air towards me. Instinctively I put my hand out to stop it and it stuck. I had caught their danger man out! The Sleaford players rushed over to congratulate me and a real character called Chris Perkins gave me a high five. Delighted, I smacked his hand and the pain hit me. When taking the catch I had dislocated my little finger on my right hand. Even in those days I was injury prone!

The end of the football season was coming fast and so was decision time. The day that finally convinced me that Mansfield Town was the club for me was Sunday 24 May 1987. That date will be a significant one for any true Mansfield fan and will not need any explaining. We had been given two complimentary tickets by Nicky Anderson, Nadge's eldest son and a young professional at Mansfield, to go and watch the Stags play at Wembley in the Freight Rover Final against Bristol City. It is strange that many years later I went on to play for both clubs and also that one of the Bristol City penalty takers that day was going to be manager of Mansfield Town in future years.

I was enthralled by the game which Mansfield won on penalties after finishing 1–1 after extra-time. The big crowd, the venue and the fact that I knew so many of the Stags players was amazing to me and I promised myself that one day I would play at the Twin Towers in front of a big crowd. That Sunday afternoon was the one that convinced me that Mansfield Town was my club.

I did not feel as if I was improving enough at Lowlands FC, not because I failed to enjoy it but because it was too easy. We were winning comfortably every week and it was not a test. Therefore, for that season I was to join forces with my brother yet again, playing for Swinderby Under-16s. I would now be playing against boys two years older than me, and they were much stronger physically. All my managers up until now had been really nice characters and did not really raise their voices. My new manager was Nadge Anderson, still a real nice character but boy could he give you a rollicking. I now had to do it week in week out else I would know about it. Not only was the pressure on to perform well in school football, it was also there in my local football. We had a great season winning the League and Cup double but all the games were competitive and I felt an improvement not only in my football but also in my confidence.

I finally signed for Mansfield Town at the start of the 1987–88 season. This was a massive year for me, both in my academic work and in my football career. I was now in the fourth year at Carre's and because I was in the top set at both Maths and English, I would sit my Maths and English Language GCSE a year earlier.

Football wise, this season would see me playing for numerous teams: the fourth-year school team, the fifth-year school team, South Kesteven District team and, hopefully, the Lincolnshire Under-15 team. I was now travelling to Mansfield every Thursday night for training and Sunday morning for games so, as you can imagine, the legs were tired but the knees were holding up. My confidence was high, and I was now to meet a man who was to become my best friend in football.

Ivan Hollett, a legend in both Mansfield and Chesterfield, had started up the Centre of Excellence at Mansfield alongside Dennis Petitt. The training I was receiving was greatly beneficial and I can never thank Ivan enough. You will see his name many times over the course of this book, but I make no apologies for it. I see this man as a legend and a true friend.

There was to be a bit of a knock to my confidence, not in school football or at Mansfield but at the county trials. Everybody had expected me to breeze into the county Under-15 team playing in my favourite central-midfield role. I only just scraped in! I had been in this situation many times and after the trial game I thought I had easily done enough to get through, so imagine my surprise when they called out the names of 16 definites and four more to have decisions made in the future and I was one of the four. Nobody could believe it. I think there may have been a bit of history between Alec Brader (the county Under-15 manager) and Colin White, but I do not know for certain. Other teachers who I had got to know from other schools could not get their heads round it. I was not a show-off – far from it. I was not one to kick up a fuss so I just let it go. I was about to get into Colin's car to go back to Sleaford when I got the shout to go back and see Mr Brader. I think other teachers had felt so strongly about my omission from the squad they had told him he had made a wrong decision. Not Colin, he was too proud to lower himself. I was told to report to the county squad training sessions over the next few weeks. I thanked him but was not looking forward to the trip home with Colin, who had a face like thunder. Not one word was uttered over the half-hour trip back to Sleaford. I knew Colin well by this time and realised he was fuming. He felt that there was a hidden agenda over the decision and there definitely was. I would have been the first to admit it if I had failed to do enough in the game to be selected but that was not the case. I never fell out with Mr Brader, he was a nice chap, but for the first time in my footballing career I did not enjoy those county games that season. I did get picked eventually, starting in all of their games that season, but I played at right-back, not my usual position of midfield. Again I do not know whether it was done to get a reaction but I kept my head down and just got on with it.

At that time that was my way. Later on in my career if I did not agree with something I would say. I always would do it in the right way and would always show managers and teammates respect, but if I felt something could be done to improve the tactics or results I would put my point of view across. Perhaps that is why I captained most of the teams I played for. I always was, and still am, a firm believer that a captain should change things on the field if he sees something the manager has not. I did this many times when I played for Chesterfield under John Duncan, and we had plenty of disagreements but we both had the utmost respect for each other as we both wanted, and mostly got, the same things.

I could not wait for the county games to end. That was the only time in my entire footballing career that I did not enjoy games. Colin White, ever the perfectionist, got me out of a couple of lunch times a week, practicing delivering passes from the right-back position and learning the positional play of a full-back – the position he had played as a schoolboy at Tottenham Hotspur many years earlier. I can not believe that nowadays any professional footballer worth his salt cannot play any position on a football field if asked and play it to an adequate standard. They should not only understand the responsibilities and positional sense of their preferred position but also that of all their teammates. In my professional career I started a League game in every outfield position but never appeared as a goalkeeper, something I would have loved to have done. Many times when teams I played in went without a goalkeeper on the bench I would have been the stand-in 'keeper if he was injured or sent off. It was never to happen; perhaps somebody had seen me many years earlier playing for my first team, 'Ireland's Own'!

I was really enjoying playing for Mansfield Town and learning the professional side of football. Mansfield were very keen for me to spend as much time as possible training with them, so in the February half-term they put myself and Jonathan Kerrigan up in a hotel near Mansfield called Redbrick House. For two 14-year-olds with no transport, it was in the wrong location. We used to get picked up there in the morning and dropped off at the ground to prepare for a day in the life of a youth-team footballer. It was a real eye-opener. The home team dressing room was used by about 12 senior professionals, while the away dressing room 10 or so. The 15 to 20 youth team players changed in the prison cell (with about room for 12 people maximum); the second-year youth team on the police side of the bars while the younger ones actually changed behind the bars (some of them getting practise for later on in life). The banter between them all was brilliant and that was really the first insight into what being a footballer was all about. The camaraderie was amazing to see for the first time, but also the discipline that Ian Greaves instilled was unbelievable. His presence was everywhere.

This was the week that I really met and got to know two very different people at Mansfield: Billy Dearden and John Jarman. Although they were so different they both had the same resolve to make Mansfield Town a success. Their way of doing it was as diverse as it could have been, but they were both characters and I still have massive respect for both.

Around this time I made my debut for the Mansfield Town Under-18s against Derby County at Derby's old training ground, Ramarena. I was on the bench and could not believe the pace and power of the game. As the two teams went in at half-time Derby were leading 2–0, and with Derby having a few Youth internationals in their line up I did not think we had done badly. John Jarman did not agree. He went absolutely berserk, immediately targeting the likeable Glen Wathall and tearing him to shreds. With tears welling in his eyes, Glenn started taking his boots off and John told him that if he took them off, he would never play for the Stags again. He waited for Glen to put his boots back on and when he had done so told him to take them off again as he was being made substitute. What an insight into a dressing room at half-time! John told me I was going on and just to go out and enjoy myself. I have never walked off a pitch feeling as tired after a full 90 minutes as I did that day at Derby after playing only 45 minutes. I think the game finished 4–2 in their favour, but I had done okay. My dad and I then did what we were to do many times over the next three years, get back to Mansfield and go to the Old Talbot Inn on Nottingham Road for a bite to eat before going to watch Mansfield in the afternoon. I can recall them playing Gillingham that afternoon and Mark Place, the captain of the youth team, was making his home debut. I may be wrong but I am sure Mark needed stitches before the game for a head wound he had suffered warming up in the dressing room. I apologise, Mark, if that was not true but I am sure if it was you will not mind me telling all the Stags fans.

The football season was coming to an end so now I focused my mind on the upcoming cricket season, or so I thought. Mansfield wanted me to go in to train in the last week of the Easter holidays, and they had found me new digs. I spent the week on a street named Mackworth Court in the town with an elderly family called the Martins. They were lovely people and made me very welcome. Mr Martin used to take me to the ground every morning and pick me up after training in his old reliable Austin Maxi. I had my own room, the cooking was good and I could really see this becoming my digs when I joined Mansfield, if I was to take the youth team option that the club still held open. I actually joined in some sessions with the professionals that week, an even quicker pace, and I could not believe how helpful they were and how quick they were to offer advice to a young schoolboy. It was very much appreciated, as I was very nervous and lacking in confidence before those sessions.

The football season ended and now my efforts centred on the two GCSEs I was taking. My mum would virtually lock me in my room to do my revising and if I was lucky I could go downstairs and do a bit of work around the dining room table while listening to some music. One night everybody was out. My parents had recently re-covered the dining room chairs and had had the ceiling artexed in the lounge and dining room about two weeks earlier, as was the fashion at the time. My mum was so proud of it. The tape had stopped and I decided to change the music. For some unknown reason I decided to flick my pen about in the air while I was doing it. It was not a pen that you would expect to flick any ink, but to my horror when I looked at the ceiling there were dots forming in a line, not wide but about a metre in length. 'Oh my God! Mum is going to kill me!' I thought. 'What is going to get permanent black ink off of the ceiling?' The only thing I could think of was the ever-trustworthy Jif. Things were going to get even worse very quickly! I got one of my mum's newly covered dining room chairs, got a cloth and administered Jif to the stain. Disaster! The thin line of ink had just turned into a one metre grey-coloured smudge, with grey Jif dripping off the cloth onto the dining room chair. Panicking, I rubbed and rubbed but to no avail. The chair was ruined and the ceiling was not much better. Admitting defeat, I cycled round to my nan's house not far enough away to think of a reasonable excuse. When I knocked on the door, I told my mum she had better come home. She knew me well enough to know something was wrong and we cycled back home. She went into the living room, looked up at the ceiling, looked at the chair, turned to me and quite calmly told me to go to my room and get as far away from her sight as possible. I remember being awake in bed when dad got home and heard him march upstairs. I pretended to be asleep as I did in the morning until I heard dad go to work. The atmosphere in the morning was still very frosty and on the way home from school I went to get mum a 'sorry' present. You can not get a lot for a pound but I managed to get a bell from Wise Owl (I did try). I gave it to mum when she got home and it did a bit to lighten the mood, but only for a couple of weeks.

Things had calmed down a little since the pen episode and I was playing on the rec with a good friend, Wayne Louth, when I suddenly remembered that I needed to go to nan's for something. Not having a bike, I borrowed Wayne's brand new one. I set off and was just going round the corner when I decided to test the bike out. As I changed gear, there was a strange noise from the chain. I looked down and bang, straight into a parked car. Even worse, it was outside PC Shakespeare's house. I was sat on the bonnet of the car, looking round madly to check if anybody had seen. My shoulder was killing but could I get away before anyone knew it was me? No such luck! The door on the car opened, PC Shakespeare was only sat in the car! He asked me my name and address and told me that he would be round later to see my father. I surveyed the damage and I did not think it was as bad as it might have been. The bike was still rideable. Should I tell my dad or take a risk? After the pen episode a couple of weeks earlier, I took the latter choice. We had our tea and I was praying for nobody to knock at the door. Tea passed and I told mum and dad that I was going down to the cricket club to watch some mates play. I sat on the bench, and after about an hour I saw my dad's car pull into the car park. I immediately knew it was bad news. I made the walk round the boundary edge to my dad's car, opened the door and the telling-off began. My dad is a fairly laid back guy but when he loses it, he really loses it. I was sent to my room and told there was over a hundred pounds worth of damage to the car. Much to my horror, just as I was about to fall asleep, the phone rang. I listened mortified when I heard the conversation. It was from 'Tango' Louth (Wayne's father). I had caused damage to Wayne's bike to the cost of about 30 pounds. I may not have been a really naughty kid, but I was a clumsy one who may have had brains but no common sense. I got back into the good books when the results of my GCSEs came through though; two Bs in Maths and English Language.

Chapter Five
National Finals

After doing well in my previous year's GCSEs, I would be taking eight more at the end of the school year. My parents kept stressing to me how important this next year at school was and that my sport, especially football, might have to take a bit of a back seat, particularly after Christmas. I reluctantly agreed but how wrong we all were. It was to be my busiest and most enjoyable football year to date.

It all started early on in my fifth year, potentially my last at Carre's. The decision was still to be made – would I stay on and do my A-levels or would I go on and do my apprenticeship at Mansfield Town. There was plenty of time to make the decision and the club said they would leave it totally up to me as to when I made it. This year was to be a very important football year for the school First XI, the team my brother played for. They had been the most successful school team in the history of Carre's and they had not been beaten throughout the six years they had been there. They would enter the Lincolnshire Schools County Cup and hopefully win that, then enter the English Schools Football Association Cup representing Lincolnshire. After a couple of weeks Colin asked me to go out and train with them to get a bit of experience and what I thought was to make the numbers up.

By this time I was playing for my own school team and also Mansfield Town Under-16s on a Sunday morning. Ivan was the coach and I just loved playing for him. I found him so approachable and my game was coming on fast working with him. We were to play all the East Midlands clubs in what were competitive friendlies. They wanted me to get involved as much as possible with the youth team playing in the Midland Purity League on a Saturday morning. This was a really strong League and you would find yourself competing against future international players at Leicester, Villa etc. I did this whenever there was not a school fixture on a Saturday morning but Mansfield were really keen for me to get more involved, they believed that youth-team football would be a lot more beneficial than playing for the Under-16s on a Sunday morning. School football on a Saturday morning usually involved playing for my own year school team. This was not really testing me and apparently, after a few drinks at the cricket club one weekend, my dad and Colin had a heated discussion about my football. My dad thought it would be better for me to play for the youth team while Colin was absolutely adamant that if there was a school fixture I would represent the school. They did not fall out, they had far too much respect for each other, but Colin said it was a massive year for school football and that I would be playing for the school First XI in the County Cup and hopefully later in the Nationals. This appeased my dad a little and they agreed that for this year I would be a bit more selective in my games. This meant cutting down a bit on other sports as well, but I could still do my cricket. By this time we had spoken to Mansfield about the situation and they were happy with me not playing for the Under-16s on a Sunday morning but still representing the youth team whenever possible. However, they wanted me in all of the school holidays.

The school XI progressed easily through the opening rounds of the County Cup and I had cemented my place in midfield. Again I was playing with lads much older than me but this was so much more beneficial to my game. Much to my surprise, the whole of our First XI had been selected to go for the county trials for the chance to represent the county Under-19 team. The usual process, but this time I did not expect to get in. I thought I might scrape into the B squad which was announced first: I did not. 'Never mind' I thought, but I nearly fell through the floor when my name got called out for the A squad along with six others from Carre's while the other four had all been chosen for the B. I thought one of the lads who had been chosen for the B squad deserved to be in the A squad on merit but he went on to captain the B squad – my brother Jamie. I felt awful that he had not been selected but he once again was big enough to show no signs of jealousy. (He has since told me that he was really pissed off!)

Around about November time Mansfield youth team had drawn Manchester City in the FA Youth Cup. Manchester City had about four or five Irish Youth internationals, of which I am sure Neil Lennon was one, in their line up and they played their full strength side with six 18-year-olds and five 17-year-olds. However, we were decimated by injuries. I think some of the youth team knew what was coming but we lined up with one second year youth-team player (Tony Clarke), goalkeeper and first year youth-team player (Jason Pearcey) and nine Under-16 players. I can remember the team talk vividly, even now. Kevin Randall, the youth team manager, told us it was damage limitation and that we were to waste as much time as possible whatever the stage of the game. It meant that even if we were trailing by a couple of goals we were to take our time and frustrate them. The plan worked brilliantly. We battled and had a lot of luck. We eventually lost 1–0 but that was a great score for such a young team against a club who went on to reach the semi-finals. Later on when I joined Chesterfield, I had many laughs with assistant manager Kevin Randall about how he had masterminded the greatest 1–0 defeat in the history of football! Kevin was a tremendous person to work with and I thoroughly enjoyed playing in his teams.

Throughout the 1988–89 season for every school holiday I would go to Mansfield and stay in digs. Not at the Martin's as I expected (Mr Martin was ill), but at a new digs on Rutland Street with the Ferry family. This was to be my Mansfield home for the next six or seven years. Colin was a miner and was broad Irish and Brenda was a lady with a heart of gold. They had four grown-up children and a younger son called David who would have been about nine at that time. It was ideal. We would get up and walk down to the ground in the morning and get ready for a day with Kevin Randall. Every morning had the same ritual. You would get down to the ground for about 8.45am, do any jobs that needed doing straight away and then report to the old gym behind Quarry Lane goal to do three circuits. After completing these, you would go on the track around the main pitch and do eight timed 'fast laps'. This was bloody hard work and by the time the professionals rolled in around 10am, we looked and felt like we had done a day's work already.

Kevin really saw me as a utility player and he used me in various positions, not just centre midfield but also centre-half and centre-forward. I especially felt comfortable playing at centre-half. One time I can remember playing against Stoke City youth team at their training ground, which was right next to the A500. Playing up front for Stoke that day was a really tall, gangly striker who later went on to play for the Stags. Mark Sale thought this was going to be his morning, playing against a much smaller and younger opponent, and I think he thought there were plenty of goals to be had. I can remember going up for the first header with him and landing with a bloody nose and watering eyes. Rather than being fazed by this, I loved it (I always did like the physical side of football). We kicked and elbowed each other for about 85 minutes, not one of us moaning to the referee, picking each other up off the floor with a smile and a wink. Most of my teachers at school always said how could someone so polite and gentle in a classroom turn into a raving lunatic as soon as he went onto a football field. I can remember going for a header towards the end of the game and Mark ended up on the floor while I was still in the air. As I looked down to see where I was landing, all I could see was a hand with two fingers strapped together protecting an injury. As I landed straight bang with my studs on his fingers he let out an almighty cry. I apologised and gave him a wink, but he knew it was part and parcel of the game. The final whistle went and we gave each other a firm handshake and a smile. We had both given our all and enjoyed the game. That is what sport is all about to me, competing to win but also showing your opponent the respect they deserve.

The county team had started well also and it looked like we were going to represent the East Midlands region in the Nationals. So as Christmas was approaching football was going well. The school team had gone on to qualify, along with Lincoln College, to represent the county in the national competition, while the county team had to win one more game to qualify through from their Midland group. We promptly did that so after Christmas there would be some really important football coming up. I did well in my mock GCSEs and I had been predicted A to C grades. My brother was studying as well for his A-levels, so Christmas was a welcome respite.

First in the National school competitions was a trip to take on a college side in Norfolk (it may have been Wymondham College). We beat them comfortably 4–0 with my brother scoring a couple of goals. This meant we were through to the last 16 schools in the country. We really felt we could go on and win it, and I know Colin did as well. The football was coming thick and fast and next up was the final Midland Group game. We won that, therefore progressing to the next round of the National competition.

Around this time my dad had a phone call from Kevin Randall asking if I could play for Mansfield Town Reserves at Hillsborough against Sheffield Wednesday. At that time Hillsborough was known for its infamous Kop and even though I had played at a few League grounds by this time, nothing in the realm of this. Even though the ground was practically empty the feeling I had when I ran out there as a 15-year-old to face Wednesday was incredible. I played centre-half (this was becoming a regular thing with Mansfield) and found myself marking a legend at the club, Imre Varadi. I loved pitting myself against the players I had seen on the television, and even though I probably struggled I did okay for my age. Between then and the end of the season I found myself playing a few times for the reserves, always at centre-half, and I loved the challenge. The Stags were really fast-tracking me and I enjoyed learning the game from their senior players.

Next up for me was the game in the last 16 of the school Nationals. We had been drawn against The Josiah Mason College from Birmingham and I can honestly say I have never felt so intimidated playing in a football match. I have played at some notorious grounds like Millwall, Leeds and Bradford but you still feel a bit protected, but not on that Saturday afternoon in Birmingham. While the game was going on we were spat at, punched and verbally abused, something that we were not used to coming from a small town in Lincolnshire. We were winning the game comfortably with about 20 minutes to go and I genuinely believe we were worried what might happen to us when the game ended. Their players looked a lot older than us, especially me, and some even had full-grown beards. They had a very good striker who netted a hat-trick in the last 10 minutes to draw the game 5–5. A great match but one I was so relieved had finished. The striker who scored a hat-trick was to become a teammate of mine at Mansfield a few years later, a man by the name of O'Neill Donaldson. The game ended and we could not wait to get back to the relative safety of our coach. We had a replay against them coming up, but that surely could not be as bad?

The replay was at Carre's on a midweek afternoon. The entire school had come out to watch and the atmosphere was like nothing the school had ever seen before. Josiah Mason had brought a couple of buses with them and their supporters were making a lot of noise and our school mates sang back. It must have been a bit worrying for the teachers at Carre's because it felt at any minute like they would have a full-blown riot on their hands. We raced into an early lead with Andy Wilkinson reacting first to the rebound off the crossbar after I had missed a penalty (why on earth did I try to take penalties – I never scored them!) Half-time came and went and we were winning comfortably. Then it happened again. Was lightning going to strike twice? 5–2 became 5–3 which became 5–4. I remember our 'keeper Dan White pulling off a great save from the last kick of the game to win us the game. We had got to the National quarter-finals.

We progressed through a couple of rounds in the Nationals for Lincolnshire Under-19s and were to meet Devon in the semi-finals. We had been drawn at home and were to play at Boston United's York Street ground. It was another great game and with a minute remaining the scores were tied at 2–2. Their centre-half made a reckless tackle on Andy Wilkinson and we had a penalty. If we scored we were through, if we missed the Lincolnshire County Schools committee would have to fork out for a few days in Devon for the replay. I think they were more nervous than the penalty taker, who happened to be yours truly. I can remember placing the ball on the spot and looking up behind the goal to see my brother and a few school mates. I could picture being the hero; I ran up and hit it perfectly, straight over the bar into my brother's hands! The referee's whistle went and the game ended 2–2. Mr Dunn, the team manager, tried his best to put on a brave face, but had I just wrecked his dream of being the manager of the National County Champions?

We went down to Torquay for a few days for the replay at the expense of the County Schools Association. I was telling everybody that they should thank me for missing that penalty and getting everybody a short break. We actually drew that game as well which was played at Exeter City's ground. This was the only game that I ever got cramp in and I was actually pleased when the final whistle went. It was decided that the next replay would be played somewhere between the two counties, Redditch United being the venue (a small non-League club in Worcestershire). However, before that was the quarter-final for the school against Dr Challoner's Grammar School in Buckinghamshire. It was to be played at Bisham Abbey, a place where England used to, and still does, occasionally train. We absolutely battered them from the first minute to the last, but we ended up losing the game 2–1. They were actually the weakest team we had played so far in the Nationals but lady luck was not on our side. We must have hit the woodwork four or five times and their 'keeper had the game of his life. They actually went on to win their semi-final but lose in the national Final. Fair play to them, they had won the game and we were good losers but deep down we could not believe it. This was the last school game for most of the team and after having gone through so much as a group of players it was heartbreaking. There were a few tears on the journey back, but really we should have been proud of ourselves. I know Carre's have gone on to represent the county in the Nationals in later years, but Colin will say this was by far his best team. (The Nationals are now split into two sections, schools and colleges, where as before it was all one competition.) We went on to beat Lincoln College in the County Final but this was scant consolation for us – we wanted the big one.

We went on to beat Devon 3–1 at Redditch so we were to face West Midlands in the ESFA Under-19 County Final. The two counties tossed a coin to see who would host the Final; we were desperate for them to win the toss because it was to be played at Villa Park. However, we won the toss and it was to be played at York Street again. There were some very tired legs in the Lincolnshire team that night and we deservedly got beaten. All that was left now football-wise in this season was the County Soccer Festival which was held in Skegness. You played five games in five days, with a showpiece game one night involving the England Schoolboy Under-18s against England Under-18s. The FA team won comfortably with Steve McManaman starring. My dad took me to Skegness while the rest of the Carre's lads got onto the train, the wrong one. They ended up in Peterborough and as my dad always said 'Carre's boys — all brain and no common sense'. The week dragged a little but most nights the lads would go down to the local pub The Dunes for a couple of pints. They were all 18 now and I think I was the nominated 'look out' when they missed their curfew. Getting back into the place where we were staying involved scaling a wall about six feet high. Not difficult you may think, but quite a bit more so with tar painted on top of it to deter unwanted guests. Being the youngest, I was the one to go up first so I got the worst of the tar!

All there was to do now was sit my remaining GCSEs. I had done some revision but, as you can imagine, with all the football, it was a case of doing it whenever I had a spare minute. By this time I had sat down with Mansfield and told them I would not be accepting their offer of an apprenticeship. The new manager at Mansfield, George Foster, told me he was desperate to hold onto me. He offered me a one-year professional contract to start two years later, when I had finished my A-levels. The only thing they asked was that I continued to play for the youth and reserve teams and come down every holiday to train. This was all done and agreed by a handshake and that was it. I had got the best of both worlds; I was still continuing my education which delighted my mum, and I had the guarantee of a football contract which my dad was ecstatic with.

One thing at the back of my mind, however, was how my fellow Under-16s at Mansfield felt. They were about to start a two-year apprenticeship scheme, if they had been lucky enough to have been offered one, to try and earn a professional contract and there I was being offered a professional contract. It did not seem fair.

I now had 10 GCSEs to my name, all A–C grades, but what was really exciting me was the next two years. Could I break into Mansfield Town first team and could I get in to the England Under-18 Schoolboy squad?

Chapter Six
Schoolboy Pranks

S chool football was to be a bit strange over the next couple of years. I obviously still enjoyed playing with my mates from my own year, but it felt a bit of an anticlimax after the previous season with the incredible highs and an exceptional low. My brother had got four A-levels and it seemed strange that he, along with all his mates, had now left Carre's and gone off to pastures new. It was decided between my family and the school that it would be most beneficial if I only studied for two A-levels plus my general studies. This gave me more time for my football commitments, which I was thankful for because the next two years were going to be so hectic. Looking back the school were very lenient with me about work deadlines and basically let me do my work at my own pace. I decided to do geography and English literature at A-level. Why I chose to do English I will never know, but geography I enjoyed and my brother had done it over the last two years and I had his work!

For my geography coursework we visited North Yorkshire. Eight of us got dropped off, and we had to make our way through various little villages with our questionnaires and look at different geographical formations. We walked for about eight miles with the map and directions given to us by our A-level geography teachers, Mrs Hillyer and Mr Mouncer. We finally reached our youth hostel – our base for the next few days. After our evening meal we would normally walk down the road to the local pub and have a few games of pool. We might have had a couple of shandies as well but it was all good fun and we had some great laughs. We got back to our dorms one night and the six lads decided to have a bit of fun. We were daring each other to do stuff, and they were getting a bit worse and a bit more daring when it came to my turn. My friend Robert Stahel dared me to go across the corridor into Mr Mouncer's room, bring his pyjamas into our dorm and then get them back into his room without him knowing. So off I went. It was about 10.30pm and when I knocked on his door there was no reply. He must have been downstairs having a drink. I tried the door handle and it opened. I tiptoed across the room and there it was laid neatly on his bed. Not pyjamas but a nightgown! I opened it up and saw Wee Willie Winkie on the front. This was getting better. I decided to go one better and put it on. I opened the door, looking to see if the coast was clear, and burst into our bedroom. My mates could not stop laughing as I pranced about in a nightgown. Then their faces dropped and I froze. I turned round and there was Mr Mouncer, he went out of the room and I followed him into his bedroom. I was getting ready for the blast (he had one of the loudest voices I have ever heard), but when he turned round he burst out laughing. 'Very funny Holland! That's a good one. Now if you would like to kindly take off my nightgown and go back to your room, I would appreciate it!' I had got away with it and my mates could not believe it. This would happen a few more times over the next couple of years.

When we arrived back at Carre's, we had to complete some coursework talking about what we had done over the week. Remembering that my brother had been on exactly the same trip a couple of years earlier, this did not hold many fears for me as I would use my notes and Jamie's assignment to create my own work. Upon reading Jamie's it was obvious that his essay was going to be a lot better than mine so I decided to copy his work, changing a few words to make it look like my own. I used my own photographs and the essay was really flowing when I came across a photo and a few lines about the 'striations at Elterwater'. Looking back through my photos I realised that I had not got a photograph of Elterwater so I promptly took Jamie's and stuck it into my essay, with a few lines about the striations from Jamie's work. I was delighted with my essay when I handed it in to Mrs Hillyer to get marked. When I got my book back I opened it quickly expecting a good grade. The mark B+ was good but the comment not so. It went something like this: 'Great piece of work Paul. Particularly like the piece on Elterwater – pity we didn't even go there!'

As I was doing only the two A-levels I had lots of spare time and many a time I would be in the common rooms playing football with anybody I could find. A couple of broken windows later, all of the sixth form were called into a meeting with Mr Cattermole, the deputy headmaster. I got on really well with him, probably due to his love of football. He was a mad Newcastle United fan and we used to give each other a bit of stick about our respective clubs. In the meeting he went mad about the windows and he said whoever was responsible for them was to go to his room in 10 minutes. He left the room and all eyes turned to me. I held my hands up and 10 minutes later I was knocking on his office door. 'Enter', I heard, and without even looking up from his desk he said 'I bet it's Holland'. 'Yes sir, I am sorry, I am responsible for those windows and it won't happen again'. 'It better not, now go back and keep your shots down. You are getting more like Manchester United players everyday!' We laughed and I left the room and yet again my mates could not believe how lightly I had been punished, embarrassed, I told them I had a litter pick at lunch time.

A couple of days later we were playing in the 'headmaster's garden' at school, which was a big area where you could have a kick about, but on this particular day we were playing dodgeball. I had the tennis ball in my hand, chasing one of my mates, and I aimed an almighty throw for his back. My mate ducked, and it went crashing through a window. Not just any window but the window of Mr Cattermole's office. All my mates scarpered and Mr Cattermole came out with bits of broken glass in his hair. He had been sat at his desk with his back to the window when it had smashed, showering him with glass. This time he did go mad and I may have had a couple of detentions, but we did have a few laughs about it over the next year.

In the final year at school you had the chance to be a prefect. A decision would be made by Mr Freeman, the head of Carre's, and Mr Cattermole on who would be prefects, who would be deputy head boy and who would be head boy. Somehow I got picked for deputy head boy. It must have been for my sporting abilities rather than my academic skills. I was not thick but I was not the cleverest, not by a long way. The head boy, Jon Paul Fahy, was brilliant at the job. He organised rotas and meetings and I probably should have helped more, but I was too busy with my football and was not at school for long periods of the year. Every other Tuesday afternoon we would have a prefects meeting with Mr Cattermole. It usually only lasted about five minutes but on one particular day Mr Cattermole was late. We were getting a bit bored and restless waiting so we had a little competition – who could get round the whole perimeter of the common room without touching the floor. Game for a laugh I volunteered first. The first half was no problem. Walking on window frames and backs of settees was easy, now came the hard part. There was about a six-foot gap between a settee and a wall desk that ran all the way down two walls of the common room. If I could jump and land on the desk I would be home and dry. Up I went, landed and then disaster struck. The whole of the wall desk came crashing down to the floor throwing out a massive cloud of dust. Mr Cattermole had sent a message across that he would be there in 10 minutes. Ten minutes to try and get the room looking like nothing had happened. We propped the wall desk up as best as we could but there was no way it would now take anybody's weight. Mr Cattermole entered the room and must have been surprised to see all the prefects crowded into one side of the room. However, he did not say a word and started the meeting. There was a knock on the door a couple of minutes later and in flew my mate William Meredith. He came in like a whirlwind, apologised for being late and headed towards the wall desk. We tried to warn him but it was too late. He flung his bag onto the desk and jumped up to sit on it. The noise and dust it created as it hit the floor was unbelievable. The whole room erupted in laughter, but Mr Cattermole did not see the funny side and he went berserk. Yet again he said whoever was responsible was to go to his office. I waited outside the room as I could hear him on the phone. He was in hysterics while he recounted the story. After he finished I went into his office and he started laughing. I sat down and we chatted for half an hour about things.

Only a few months later Mr Cattermole tragically died; I would like to dedicate this chapter to him and if he is reading this somewhere I would like to apologise for being a pain in the ass over those two years.

Chapter Seven
England Recognition

My target in school football over the next couple of years would be to break into the England Under-18 Schoolboy squad. This was an ambition not only for myself but for all those who helped me at school, and in particular Colin. The teachers had turned a blind eye to a lot of things, not particularly bad things but things they could definitely have pulled me up for. My first aim this year would be to start the season well for both school and county. This was achieved without too much bother, and I found that I had been selected for the England trials. I was a year younger than all the other trialists, and luckily for me another lad had also been selected from the school. Colin took me and Craig Lynch to the trials and on the way there he told us what he thought the selectors would be looking for. He felt the way we conducted ourselves on and off the field would be vitally important, as well as having the confidence to express our ability while striving to be a team player. I had no problem with that at all. I thought I would go and enjoy it and play with a smile on my face like I always tried to do throughout my professional career. We were split into four squads of 15 and each team played the other. Colin had told me to mention I could also play at full-back but I felt midfield was my biggest chance. I thought the games went really well, it was now just a case of waiting to see if I had been successful when they cut it down from 60 to 32. It seemed like ages. Eventually the letter came through saying I had been successful and that the 'last 32' trials would be held in a couple of weeks.

Unfortunately Craig had not made it through but he had said he did not think he had done enough to get through. I was quietly confident but kept my feelings close to my chest, so when the letter came through I was delighted.

As I mentioned previously, school and county games were carrying on as normal but there was not that same buzz as the previous season. Therefore my eyes were firmly set on representing my country this year. As before Colin took me to Nottingham to catch the train to Stafford. We both knew this was the last chance to impress so I think we were both a bit nervous on the journey. Just before I got on the train, Colin shook my hand and said, 'Go on Paul. Go and make everybody proud of you. You can do it. It's just a question of believing in yourself.' I wanted so badly to represent England Under-18 Schoolboys, the highest accolade you can receive in schoolboy football.

I was used to the trial situation as I had encountered it many times already. 'You don't get a second chance to impress', I kept saying to myself. The trial games went well and again it was a case of waiting for a letter to come through. I was not as confident this time, I thought I had done very well in the games but something had happened in the last one that made me unsure. I had gone in for a 50/50 challenge with a lad much bigger than myself, had won the ball but caught the lad at the same time. The referee blew for a foul and he told me to be careful as it was only a trial game. 'Exactly', I said. I have always got stuck in whether it is in training or a game and that is what I always demanded in later years when I was coaching players – youngsters or professionals.

The letter eventually came through and I had failed to get into the squad. I felt low in myself but more importantly I felt I had let so many people down. The reason they eventually came up with was that I was too aggressive. I would run the risk of getting sent off in an international and that would not look good for the ESFA. The following year I was to find out that it was not the choice of Mr Philliskirk, the team manager, or Pete Amos, the assistant manager – they had wanted me in the squad – but that of the ESFA council members. I accepted their decision and this made me even more determined the following year. However, in my own head I was going to go there and play in exactly the same way. Everybody I had played for previously liked the aggressive style of play I used and therefore I was not about to change just to please some council members who were more interested in socialising with their international counterparts. I was now a boy on a mission!

This had to be the year. I had got to the last 32 the year before, now it was time to make the squad. I think people expected me to breeze into the squad this year but I knew that at trials, and especially school football trials, anything can happen. Once again Colin took me to the train station in Nottingham to get the train from Stafford to Lilleshall. I felt very comfortable in the surroundings because of my experiences the previous season, but I felt sorry for some very nervous-looking boys. When we arrived Mr Philliskirk and Pete Amos made a bit of a fuss of me which probably made some of the other boys feel as if my place in the squad was already sorted, if only they knew what had happened the year before. I got through the first trials and it was only a matter of weeks before I found myself back at Lilleshall for the 'last 32' trials. I think deep down I knew I was going to get in the squad but I felt I was on trial at a trial. I knew the manager wanted me in the squad but I felt as if some people were waiting for me to make a mistake.

When I arrived back home after the trials it was just a case of waiting. When the letter eventually arrived, I tore it open. I had been selected and had to attend a squad training session at Lilleshall in a few weeks time. I was over the moon and everybody was really pleased, from my family, to school, to Mansfield Town. Everybody had played their part in getting me there and now it was time to pay them back. I went to Lilleshall for the training days and we received all our kit. From boots to training kit, polo shirts, t-shirts, tracksuits and blazer, all with the three lions on. This was the real McCoy and I loved it. We played two games against British Universities which we won 1–0 and we also beat the British Services 2–1, while I managed to score in both games. We got treated like royalty while we were there. Now all that was left was for the international season to start. Before we left Lilleshall we received our fixtures. It read:

Holland (A) venue TBC
Switzerland (H) at Carrow Road, Norwich City FC
Wales (H) at Gloucester
Republic of Ireland (A) at Tolka Park, Dublin
England FA Under-18s at Morecambe during County Soccer Festival

There was not a fixture at a really big ground but that did not bother me: I was playing for my country.

We set off for Holland and I roomed with a lad from Northumberland called Alistair Hails. We really hit it off and, looking back, I was probably the joker in the squad. We had a laugh but we were all looking forward to the game against the Dutch. My dad and Colin travelled to Holland to watch the game and I have never been as proud as when the national anthems were played. I enjoyed the game but we deservedly got beaten 2–0. They were much better than us on the night and it was a pleasure to play against them. I did okay, although I have played much better, but I really enjoyed the occasion. Back at the hotel we were presented with our caps. That cap, along with my England Under-21 cap which I got a few years later, are my proudest possessions in football.

Before our next game against Wales at Gloucester, the family had some bad news. My mum's dad Reg passed away and with our family being so close it hit everybody hard. He died on the 12 March and I was due to play against Wales on the 16 March and Switzerland on the 19th. Therefore there was a good chance that the funeral would be between the two games. The squad were due to meet together on Thursday 14th and stay together until the 20th.

The funeral was set for the 20 March, the day after the Switzerland game. I spoke to my nan and she said Reg would have wanted me to play in both games and do everything that the squad was doing. She did not want me to come back early for the funeral, instead I was to travel properly with England. Before the kick-off against Wales I was determined to score a goal for my grandad. I felt a lot more comfortable in this game than I did in the game against the Dutch, and we were playing well. The conditions underfoot were bad and it was absolutely pouring down, just as I liked it. I had a good game and with about 15 minutes remaining the goal I wanted so badly was at my mercy. All I needed was to get a good connection and it was in. I failed. My chance had gone. The ball rolled towards the goalkeeper for a routine save. He went down to collect the ball but somehow it slipped through his grasp, the ball trickled towards the line and crossed but did not have the pace to hit the net. It virtually stopped a foot over the line. I had scored the goal I had so desperately wanted for grandad but 'sorry grandad, it wasn't a classic'. The game ended 2–2 with Wales getting a last gasp equaliser. I met my mum and dad after the game briefly and gave mum a big hug. We both had tears in our eyes and I told her I would get back as quickly as possible for the funeral on Wednesday.

About three or four coaches from Carre's were going to the Switzerland game at Norwich. I ran out to see a lot of familiar faces in the crowd as we lined up for the national anthems. I looked out for mum and dad and found them. I also saw Jamie and sat next to him was somebody who had not seen me play football for a few years (probably not since I wore those boots she had bought for me with the yellow stripes when I was two). My nan waved at me and I had tears in my eyes for about the first five minutes of the game. I do not think I played particularly well in that game but it was nice to see so many people who had helped me along the way to winning my cap. The game finished 1–1, a good result against a very good Swiss team. My grandad's funeral was the next day and I arrived for the wake at my uncle John and aunt Steph's house.

Next up in that international season was the game against England FA Under-18s comprising of Redknapp (Liverpool), Pollock (Middlesbrough) and Flitcroft (Manchester City) among others. We were widely tipped to get heavily beaten and rightly so. Jamie Redknapp had just been transferred to Liverpool for a lot of money and I was determined to be up against him to see how I compared. The crowd were very much behind us as the majority of them were lads playing for their respective counties in the Football Festival. I think Redknapp got fed up with me following him all over the park. We scored to lead 1–0 and somehow managed to hang on to that score. It was a great scalp and I am sure (my eyes might have been deceiving me) I saw some of the ESFA council members actually smiling!

The final game in the season was against the Republic of Ireland and we won the game 1–0. It was a fitting farewell to our time together in international football and it was hard saying goodbye to some good friends I had made that year. Over the years ahead, I was to come across a few of them in professional football and only the other day I saw Robert Price, who played a few games for Oldham Athletic, sat behind Rafa Benitez as physiotherapist in the Liverpool dugout.

I promise this is the last time I will do it in this book but I dedicate this chapter to my late grandad (and all my grandparents) and to Colin White – a massive influence. Thank you to all of them.

Chapter Eight
Football League Debut

As you can imagine, Mansfield had to take a little bit of a back seat in these years because of the hectic schedule of school, county and international football. It was decided fairly early on in the 1989–90 season that because of this, I would not play for the youth team a lot in these two years but instead concentrate on playing as much reserve-team football as possible. I had by this time already sat down with George Foster (the new manager) and decided my short-term future. One thing he mentioned in this chat, which did surprise me a little, was that while he thought I had a definite future in the game, if I was to play at a higher level in the game he could see me as a centre-half. George was a real old-fashioned centre-half and was still playing league football. He was a very well-respected figure in the lower leagues and when he said something, you sat up and listened. At this time I had played the majority of my football in my preferred position of centre midfield at Mansfield but he wanted me to have a run at centre-half for the reserves. This worried me a little as I was only abut 5ft 9in, but George said 'You read the game as well as anybody I have seen, you have no fear and you are good in the air.' In the pre-season the first team were playing Stafford Rangers in a friendly. My dad received a phone call from Kevin Randall asking if I could report to Stafford because George wanted me to observe how he played in the centre-half role. I took my boots along with me because they said I might be able to join in the warm up before the game. To digress a little, I had done this once a couple of years earlier. John Jarman was keen to get me involved in the build up to what was the highlight of a youth team player's season, an FA Youth Cup on Field Mill. At this time you were only allowed one substitute, so the ones who had not made the squad had room to sit in the dugout. One of the lads, Johnny Blair, had not made the squad and was sat next to me on the bench dressed in his suit and tie. After about 60 minutes, without taking his eyes of the pitch, John barked at Blair to warm up, forgetting he was not even in his kit. 'But John…' Blair piped up. 'Just do it! And don't argue!' John bellowed. I have never seen anything as funny as Blair doing his stretches and warm-up routine in a suit, tie and shoes! Anyway, back to Stafford. I had been named as a substitute but was not expecting to get on. With about 25 minutes remaining, Billy Dearden gave me the nod. I was coming on in midfield and my instructions were to just go and enjoy it. After running around aimlessly for what seemed like an eternity without actually touching the ball, their centre-half headed a cross clear and the ball looped towards me. I instinctively hit it first time and it flew into the net. My best-ever goal to date and what a time to do it, my first-team debut. Even if it was only in a pre-season friendly. However, over the next few months it was back to the reserves and the start of my run at centre-half. I played with numerous partners in the centre of defence over the next couple of years, my best mate at Mansfield Kevin Gray, Mark Smalley (ex-Forest and Birmingham), and one night even the manager George Foster himself. This was against West Bromwich Albion at the Hawthorns. For the first 10 minutes I was slightly intimidated and worried about making a mistake playing next to 'the gaffer', but over the next 80 minutes I have never learnt as much on a football pitch. He practically talked me through the whole game, telling me where I should position myself in different situations. It was as if the whole game was put on especially for my own individual training session in how to play in the centre-half position. I was one of those footballers who only needed to be told a bit of advice once, and I can remember many times over my career, when playing in centre-half, recalling that lesson I received at the Hawthorns. I was still going to Mansfield every school holiday and staying at Brenda and Colin's. They had a three-storey house with five bedrooms and the house was getting fuller and fuller by the week. At this time I think Suzanne, the youngest daughter, was still at the house, so staying there at this time was Brenda, Colin, David, Suzanne and youth team players Kevin Gray, Justin Elkington, Chris Hodges and an Irish lad called Tony Gorman. With me coming down in the holidays, you can imagine how busy meal times were. Breakfast was laid ready on the table for when you came down in the mornings, Brenda would do us a packed lunch, and when we got back from training there would be a hot evening meal ready for us, usually a roast dinner. I think with the amount of people she was feeding, this was the easiest option but there was always plenty and it was always delicious. Those two seasons flew by with a lot of football being played. It was good publicity for the Stags that I was picked for England Under-18 Schoolboy squad international duty. I think by this time I was getting noticed by a few of the Mansfield fans as somebody who could break into the first-team squad over the next few years. After receiving my Under-18 cap against Holland, I was presented with it by John Pratt, the Mansfield chairman, on the pitch at half-time. There was quite a big crowd there and they gave me a really nice ovation. I could not wait for the 1991–92 season to start as I was now a full-time professional, the only downside being that we had been relegated with a game to go. With only one game to go for the Stags – an away match against Crewe Alexandra – George and his backroom staff were already planning for the next season. We had agreed a one-year contract, no money had been talked about (how times change!), but they rang me and said they wanted me to forget that deal and discuss a new one. The one-year deal had been 'ripped up' and replaced by an offer of a three-year contract. They did not need a decision straight away, but would appreciate an answer before Saturday's game with Crewe – a game that they had made the decision would see me make my professional League debut. I could not believe it. What a way to finish the season, and my time at Carre's. The deal was all agreed and it was decided that George Foster, Billy Dearden and Steve Wilkinson (the Stags centre-forward, and ex-Carre's boy and brother of Andy Wilkinson) would come to school and I would sign my professional contract in front of the whole of Carre's. Numerous photographs were taken but all I could think of was the game the following day against Crewe. I did not sleep particularly well on the night before the game but that was the norm. Whatever game I was to play throughout my career I would be as nervous as hell, worrying about my performance. That morning we set off for Mansfield with a full car to meet the team bus. Dad was driving with Colin White in the front, and squashed in the back with me were Jamie and mum. I can remember that journey as if it was yesterday, and I am sure Jamie can for all the wrong reasons. He had been out the night before to a football presentation evening and he had had a few too many beers. He felt and he definitely looked awful. I kept glancing over at him and he was as pale as I have ever seen anybody. Sweat was literally dripping off him, and he kept heaving. I felt sorry for him as he knew it was a big day for me and we could not really stop for him to be sick as we were following the team bus. We arrived at Gresty Road, and after all the hugs and handshakes I went off to the changing rooms to get ready for the biggest game in my career – my Football League debut. I can remember changing next to Trevor Christie, a really experienced centre-forward who was coming to the end of his career. He did everything to try and make me feel comfortable but none of it really working. It was a really hot day and Crewe were renowned for being a passing team. They certainly passed it that day. I found myself up against Neil Lennon again (from that Manchester City FA Youth Cup tie) and also in the Crewe team that day was Rob Jones who went on to play for Liverpool and England. We were beaten comfortably 3–0 and I can remember after the final whistle some of the Stags players clapping the Stags fans and they went mad. They must have felt a bit let down after a long and hard season had ultimately ended in relegation, so when I clapped them I did not really know what reception I was going to get. Their mood changed quickly and they clapped me back and that was the start of a long mutual respect between myself and the Mansfield public. I had done okay, only average really, but I had been determined to remember that day – you only make one debut. All the way through my playing and coaching career, I have always made a point of congratulating a young player on making their debut. As I said, it only happens once and should always be remembered. I still, and will always, remember May 1991, the month I made my Football League debut, and I bet Jamie does too, but for very different reasons! So that was the end of my time at Carre's. I had passed my A-levels and a week after finishing them I was to start out on the long road of professional football, with many highs and lows ahead of me and the chance to meet some great characters. Next came my first pre-season.

Chapter Nine
A Shock to the System

I thought I was quite a fit lad, but those first few days of pre-season in 1991 were hard, very hard! I think the biggest difference was the now full-time training, that with being at school I was not used to. Brenda and Colin were no longer having players stay at their house. Therefore, I was staying at Kevin Gray's parents' house, about 25 minutes away from the ground at a very small village, more of a hamlet, called Fledborough. It was very, very quiet and after a few hard days of pre-season it was the ideal place just to wind down and prepare for training, which I was finding very tough. There was not a lot to do at Kevin's house, it was literally miles from anywhere and I did not yet have my own car. I had passed my test but could not afford to buy one. Kev was into his steam engines, many centre-forwards would say it was like running into one when colliding with him, and he would spend most of his spare time down the garden, putting together and then taking apart different parts of his engines. They were his pride and joy, but, sorry Kev, not for me. I enjoyed my time at Kev's but missed Brenda and Colin's. Not only for their hospitality but because of their closeness to the ground and the town itself. I think Kevin enjoyed it at Brenda's as well, he had not been the reason why Brenda and Colin had decided not to have any more footballers. After a few weeks of gentle persuasion (on the phone every night!) they agreed to have myself and Kevin back, but nobody else. The rules were laid out early on and just before the start of the actual playing season we moved back.

I felt a lot more at home at Rutland Street, and really started to get stuck into the rest of pre-season. I lost count of the times we were up at Thieves Wood on Nottingham Road to do the infamous 'blue run'. We set off in groups and the run was probably about 20 minutes, but at a very good pace. I say it was 20 minutes, it was for most of us, but about 18 minutes for Steve Charles. Charlie was a fit lad who looked after himself. As soon as he set off on the 'blue run' (about two minutes behind everybody) he would just get his head down and try his hardest. There were a lot of senior professionals at Mansfield at the time but they were a very fit group. I can remember thinking that this was their 12th or 13th pre-season and yet they were still putting their all in. We were given times to get in for (everybody under 21 minutes), and it amazed me how some of the pros, namely Fordy (Gary Ford) and Stanty (Phil Stant), would cross the line just as 20:57, 20:58, 20:59, 21:00 were being shouted. Every time to the second; I suppose that is experience for you. I can remember people having a joke with Fordy about it and he said whatever time he was given he would get within a second of it. He called it 'just doing enough', and he joked it was not the running that was his job it was delivering crosses, and that all the hard graft and slog was to be done by the central midfielders (and there was a lot of them). Steve Spooner, Steve Charles, Wayne Fairclough, Martin Clark, Nick Roddis, Gary Castledine and myself could all play in there, so I knew I would have to bide my time and wait for injuries or suspensions to hit before I would be given my chance to impress.

Pre-season did not go well at all for the team, with the lowlight being a defeat at the hands of non-League Matlock Town. This was our last real run out before the season opener away at League new boys Scarborough. George Foster was not best pleased and did he let the squad know it! We may have been an experienced squad, but he let us have it both barrels blazing. He let us know in no uncertain terms that nobody was guaranteed a starting place in the team and that night at Matlock, looking back, probably did me a favour. I was not outstanding, far from it, but I was consistent.

On the Thursday before the opening game of the season we had a practise game and the teams were read out. It was obvious the first squad he was naming would be the team that would face Scarborough. Beasley, Fleming, Withe, Fee, Gray, Ford, Holland…I did not hear the rest. The rest of the training session was a bit of a blur and I was on cloud nine. As soon as I got back to my digs, I was on the phone to my mum and dad telling them the good news. They were delighted and said they would be making the long trip to Scarborough to watch the first game. (They never missed a game while I played with Mansfield.) I really had settled into the club well, and felt part of things early on. What probably helped was that we had spent a week down in Devon at Exeter University where the players trained exceptionally hard, but we also had quite a bit of spare time on our hands to get to know each other better. There was a real closeness about that squad and it was probably that which would get us through that really long hard season, my first in professional football.

One thing that went on at Mansfield, and I am sure at all other clubs at that time, was the divide between senior professionals and the younger squad. Out on the pitch you were together but when you came in for training the senior pros still changed in the home dressing room while the younger pros, myself included, changed in the away dressing room. When you went up the corridor for a team meeting in the home dressing room, you would have to knock on the door and wait for the shout to come in – it was a respect thing. As a young professional you would have to wait for the invitation to go and change in their room and that would be after you had proved yourself in the game. I think this is massively important, even nowadays, but it is not done in football anymore. As soon as you turn professional you are placed with the senior pros, even if you have yet to make your League debut, and I think that is wrong. I feel that it is a shame that respect for older pros has gone somewhat out of the game. Even after playing 40-odd games that first season I was expected to knock and I think that was right and something I would have brought back to Mansfield this season if I had still been at the club – a respect for not only senior players but a respect for everybody whether it be the groundsman, office staff, whoever.

The season did not start particularly well for the team. We drew at Scarborough 0–0, and then got knocked out of the League Cup convincingly by Blackpool with Dave Bamber being a thorn in our sides. (There is a song in there somewhere).

Sandwiched between those League Cup ties was the visit of Barnet for their first away fixture in the Football League. They beat us 2–1 but that scoreline does not really tell the full story: they absolutely battered us. As bank holiday weekend approached the pressure was mounting on George Foster, and many people believed that if we did not get a result at Saltergate against Chesterfield, our bitter rivals, he would lose his job. The build up to that game was something I was not used to, the press were at every training session and the pressure was firmly on us to keep George in a job, especially after the previous season's relegation.

Saturday 31 August was the day our season changed, and the date of my first professional goal. The game was a typical local derby, with both sides frightened of making a mistake. Just before half-time Gary Ford put us 1–0 ahead and when we went into the Saltergate dressing rooms at the interval, George really gave an emotional team talk. He had brought himself back into the starting XI for that game, something that surprised not only the press but his fellow teammates. It was typical of the man: when the pressure was on him most he stood up to be counted and turned in a masterful performance. He said that if we managed to win this game, it would turn our season around. He said his job was on the line and that he was going out for that second half to save it, and who was willing to join him. That second half was probably the longest half of my life. Chesterfield came at us hard, but we had found a new strength and resolve and there was no way we were going to lose that game. My goal came midway through the half. Andy Beasley took a long goal-kick that got headed down into midfield and I managed to just get in front of my opponent and the ball sat up nicely waiting to be hit. Long-range shooting was not my strong point, but what the hell; it was there to be hit. I struck it perfectly and it arrowed into the corner, probably my best goal. I was engulfed by teammates! I felt like I had been accepted and for the first time was worthy of my place. The rest of the game was back to the wall stuff, with incessant pressure from the Spireites. I managed to clear one off the line with about five minutes remaining and when the final whistle went there was much relief. I have never been in a happier dressing room and after six professional games, I was now savouring my first victory and my first-ever goal. There were a few beers had on the short journey back to Mansfield and I felt on top of the world.

We went unbeaten in our next 10 games, with the run seeing eight victories and two draws. In this run we even won seven away games on the spin and we really did have a settled side. Phil Stant rapidly became a cult hero with the Stags fans, and Steve Wilkinson was scoring for fun. I managed to grab my second goal with a diving header at Rochdale to secure a 2–0 victory. In this run of away victories came a game against Scunthorpe at Glanford Park. This was, and still is to this day, the best away support I have ever seen from Stags fans. It was expected to be a very tough game, and the first half proved this. For the second half we came out kicking towards our fans and absolutely ripped Scunthorpe to shreds. We went on to win the game 4–1 and I am sure that all Mansfield fans can remember Stanty climbing on the railings behind the goal. A fantastic following for a fantastic game. We were now on a roll and were competing for top spot with Burnley in what in those days was known as Barclay's League Division Four. (Forget League Two and all that crap, it is Division Four!)

We went to Turf Moor, home of Burnley, at the start of November. We arrived full of confidence after coming back from 2–0 down with three minutes to go to draw 2–2 (both goals from Stanty) against Doncaster in our previous game. In front of a 12,000 crowd the two teams put on a tremendous advert for Division Four football, with Burnley eventually coming out on top in a titanic battle 3–2. Over the next few months things settled down a bit and from then to the end of the season it was really down to four teams – Blackpool, Burnley, Rotherham and ourselves – to see who would get the three automatic promotion places.

Over the Christmas months our form was really up and down, but we managed to secure the double, winning 2–1 over Chesterfield at Field Mill in front of 6,500 fans. This game saw me score again, this time with a close range header from a well rehearsed corner-kick. Gary Ford floated it perfectly to the near stick where Greg Fee got the slightest of flicks on to it and I was there to bundle it in. This corner was to work again a few weeks later at York City, and by this time I had managed to score five goals (the other one being against Gillingham), not bad for a centre-half now playing in midfield.

One thing that people always look forward to at Christmas is the works 'do', and footballers are no different. I was looking forward to it, having heard so many stories from the players about previous ones they had been on. It was decided that this year's Christmas party would be fancy dress. I arrived at the pub at dinner time in my Mr T outfit, comprising of black boots, old blue jeans, a red sweatshirt, black leather waistcoat with all the studs on it (spelling 'Mr T' on the back), and his legendary collection of chains. To complete the outfit was a full head, not just a mask, with his infamous Mohican. The suit came complete with padding (I would not need that now!) and I looked great. The lads arrived over the next half hour or so and they looked brilliant. The only people missing now were the Nottingham crew of Stant, Fairclough and Pearcey. Stanty's wife dropped them off and Fairclough and Pearcey rushed into the pub in their outfits. They told us that Stanty was not in fancy dress but was in his navy blue Mansfield Town blazer and slacks. The lads could not believe it and got ready to give him some stick. Stanty came in to the pub and got a real earbashing from the lads. He commented on how daft we all looked and said that we were supposed to be representing the club. He was facing us all the time he was in the pub, but when he turned round to go to the toilet the whole place erupted in laughter. He had cut the back out of his blazer, shirt and trousers and was wearing a black basque with stockings and suspenders. We should have known!

Towards the middle of January we travelled to Millmoor to face our promotion rivals Rotherham United. I can remember my brother Jamie, who was by now studying at Hull University, saying that he saw numerous scuffles between the two sets of fans and a lot of blood spattered over people's faces. The game was a highly charged affair and we went into the break leading 1–0 courtesy of a debut goal for Paul McLoughlin, a recent acquisition from Wolves along with defender Nicky Clarke. During the second half the bitter intensity was transferring itself from the terraces to the pitch. I can remember a ball bouncing just in front of the dugouts and as I bent down to head it I got a full boot in the face from Dean Barrick, the Rotherham left-winger. I reacted by throwing my arm back as we both went for the ball and hit him squarely in the chest. He went down, poleaxed, holding his face. The referee, Mr Lupton (I will never forget his name), came running up brandishing the red card. I started the long walk towards the Millmoor dressing rooms with boos ringing from the Rotherham fans. They were vicious in what they had to say and it was pure hatred. It seemed strange listening to the game from the changing rooms, trying to guess by the volume of the cheers what was happening. I heard a massive cheer by the home fans, followed by a massive cheer from what must have been the Stags fans, and then another roar from the Millmoor faithful. I did not have a clue what the score was. I was dreading the final whistle because I felt I had let my teammates down and I was expecting a rollicking from George for not keeping my discipline. The players came in and a few tried to say that I was unlucky and not to be worried. Rotherham had missed a penalty but had equalised with not long left to draw 1–1. To my surprise George came in and did not say a word – I think that was worse – and congratulated the team on their 'back to the wall' second half display. I went home that night and waited and waited. Eventually on Sunday afternoon George rang me at home and said I should learn from it and not let it happen again (although he was not quite as polite as that). I took it on board and apologised to him. He said I had nothing to be sorry about, I had had a tremendous start to my season, and now I had to finish it off well. I really appreciated that little wake-up call.

We then went on a terrible run, not winning for five games. We had trained really hard that season before Christmas, and it may have been starting to take its toll. Every Monday morning without fail, win, lose or draw, we would go up to Thieves Wood for a timed 'blue run' and 40 minutes of 'interval running' with Dennis Pettit, the physio. Dennis would be on his bike, barking out his instructions, and the lads would be giving him some fearful stick, telling him precisely what they were going to do with his bike and where it was going to end up! Interval running is where the squad would jog continuously for a length of time, in our case 40 minutes, and every so often Dennis would whistle and you would have to up the pace to a three-quarter pace (not quite sprinting), until you heard the next whistle. It was a bloody hard session, especially after a 'blue run', but when you saw George there, blowing and with a bright red face, you knew you should not complain too much. We did that win, lose or draw and that first season was a great education for me about how senior players conducted themselves out on the training pitch or a 'forest', as it was so often that season.

With the lads looking a bit tired and in need of a boost, George and his staff decided to ask the chairman and directors whether they would pay for a trip away to recharge the batteries, a sort of training camp they put it. It was a good job the board of directors did not see our training as I do not think we even packed any balls!

After the disappointing 1–1 draw at home to Hereford, we were told to meet the following day at Birmingham Airport. The club were taking us to Fuengirola, mainland Spain, for a little break. George sat us down in the airport and explained what the break was going to be about – basically time together, a few beers and rest. A FEW BEERS! George went to the bar and bought everybody a pint and as a group we had a chat abut the season so far, then John Newman (first-team coach) went to the bar and bought a round and so on, and so on. By the time we boarded the plane we must have had five or six pints, and we had had a real laugh and got things out in the open. Some people had little moans but that was the place to air them, and that is exactly what George wanted to happen. The drinking continued on the plane, continued when we got to Fuengirola and continued all week. The weather was awful, so every morning we would get up and go for an hour long jog/walk as a squad and then it was back to the pub. The togetherness was starting to come back, even though we very nearly came back to Mansfield a player short. After a long afternoon in the pub Greg Fee, a great lad who would always make the squad laugh, decided that he could walk around the thin wall on the inside of the hotel. No problem with that except that it was on the eighth floor of a circular hotel with a massive drop below into the foyer of the hotel. The lads tried to stop him, but he did it. I think the drinking dropped off a little as the week progressed and we were soon back in Mansfield preparing for a Friday night game at Aldershot.

There is an unwritten law in football that you are not allowed in a licensed premise 48 hours before a game whether you are drinking or not. I do not think that this was adhered to in Fuengirola. We somehow managed to scrape a 3–1 victory against Aldershot, but I had never felt as rough as I did during that game (apart from the Exeter away game in the Andy King era). The trip had been brilliant fun but now we were faced with the important part of the season. Results picked up a little, but the performances were not brilliant and I had not scored for a bit. I actually missed a couple of games (the knees were starting to play up again), the home return against Burnley being one of them. The game was played in front of 8,500 supporters at Field Mill and, yet again, Burnley beat us, this time 1–0. A couple more results went against us and really all we could hope for realistically was the third-place promotion spot. We had massive home fixtures against Carlisle and Halifax in April. We were terrible in both games but with Stanty getting a hat-trick against Halifax (a 3–2 victory) and me scoring in a 2–1 victory against Carlisle we somehow managed to win both games. In our penultimate game against Maidstone we drew 0–0, meaning that in order to gain promotion we needed to beat Rochdale at Field Mill and hope that Blackpool, who were on a terrible run, lost at Lincoln in the final game of the season. What a last Saturday of the 1991–92 season it turned out to be.

We stormed into a two-goal lead with Stanty and Ian Stringfellow getting the goals when news came through that Lincoln had taken the lead against Blackpool courtesy of a Jason Lee penalty. Rochdale scored a cracking goal to reduce the arrears but we managed to hold on to our lead to complete our half of the equation. The news coming through from Sincil Bank was confusing; Dave Bamber had equalised, Lincoln were still winning 1–0, we were not sure. The radio was on in the dressing room (the match at Lincoln had been delayed due to crowd trouble), and the score was still 1–0 to Lincoln. Blackpool came close to an equaliser on numerous occasions but, with the last kick of the game, Jason Lee scored again from the spot. Blackpool had lost 2–0, we had won 2–1 and the Stags were promoted. The beer and champagne were soon flowing, and I think I had a good night! My first season in professional football had seen a promotion season full of excitement and tension. It could not have gone better on a club level or for me personally. I had scored six goals (two against the Spireites) and thoroughly enjoyed myself in the process. All that was left to do now was to partake in the end of season trip to Gran Canaria for a celebration. It could not involve more drink than the Fuengirola trip – surely not?

We again met at Birmingham Airport and I think after a long hard season people were ready to relax. A few of the squad, who were not playing regularly in the team and not sure of their future at the club, had been trying to be a bit rebellious towards the end of the season (nothing out of the ordinary at other clubs) because they were not in the team and thought when results dipped they deserved a chance which was not forthcoming. They had set up a little group calling themselves the Crazy Gang. In that squad were Major Malcolm Murray, Corporal Clark (Martin Clark) and Sergeant Stringfellow (Ian Stringfellow), among others. It was all good natured and after a few beers around the pool one day the Crazy Gang went up to one of their rooms, shouted to George who was sunbathing next to the pool with the other members of staff and promptly started up a rendition of the 1960s hit *Please release me, let me go*. It was meant in good spirit, a bit tongue in cheek and it was taken in kind.

Rotherham United were also celebrating in the same hotel as us, and a certain Mr Barrick was playing pool. I asked him how his nose was, and he smiled and said, 'It's all part of football.' After a few heated words we eventually shook hands and it was to be forgotten (which really meant I would bide my time and get revenge if we ever went into a 50/50 challenge).

The trip was brilliant, with the highlights being a Kevin Randall/John Newman duo singing *Unchained Melody* in a karaoke bar and a couple of incidents involving our right-back, the likeable and diminutive Paul Fleming. Paul could not handle his drink very well but he tried his best. After one too many one lunchtime he went to the beach and promptly fell asleep on one of the sunbeds. Paul was a ringer for Bobby Ball (his nickname was Bobby) with all his long dark curls but he was that far gone, he did not feel the lads put mashed up bananas in his hair. In the heat his hair literally baked and you could smell bananas cooking from a good distance. When he woke up you could snap his hair in two. A couple of days later all the squad were in a nightclub having a few drinks when all of a sudden the double doors at the top of the stairs flung open and there was 'Bobby', flying down the stairs on a moped he had 'borrowed' outside.

It had been a long, long season, and it was a great way to wind down and relax. The players and the staff had all played their part in the club's success and we were all determined to enjoy our summer breaks.

Chapter Ten
HMS Raleigh

We were looking forward to the new season with much optimism after our promotion the previous season. The squad remained mostly intact and the season could not start fast enough for us. Before that we had to endure another really tough pre-season, even tougher than the season before. George obviously thought that our fitness had been rewarded so the philosophy at the club was the fitter the better. (I am sure we did not see a ball all that pre-season!)

There was another pre-season training trip, not to the relaxing Exeter University campus of a year earlier but to a navy camp in the South West called HMS Raleigh near Plymouth. I can remember pulling into the car park there and being amazed at the sheer size of the camp. You actually had to catch a ferry from Torpoint across the River Tamar to get to the camp. We were welcomed by senior officers, shown to our dormitories and told to report to the camp gymnasium in an hour's time. We all reported to the gym in our brand new training kit and were on time. While having a chat two lads in navy gym gear (plain white t-shirts, [very short!] shorts, socks and trainers) shouted us over and told us to line up in an orderly fashion. We started to do it at our own pace when one of them bellowed at us to hurry up. I think that shocked a few of us and we knew we were in for a tough week ahead – how tough we did not know! One of the navy lad's arms were covered in tattoos, and with his tight white t-shirt showing off all his muscles he looked remarkably like Popeye. He started to come down the line, making comments about how scruffy and unfit we were, and when he had got halfway down somebody down the end he had just been looking at did an impression of Popeye, 'GeGeGeGeGe'. There were a few stifled laughs and he turned round with a face like thunder (although he must have heard it before, he was such a ringer). I have never heard anybody shout as loud and scare a group of people as much as this navy lad did for the next minute. He said we were on his turf now, not on some poncey training pitch, and whoever had done the immature Popeye gag had better stand a yard ahead of everybody in line. Everybody looked down the line and Paul McLoughlin stood forward with a slight grin on his face. It was soon wiped off. The officer absolutely tore strips off him and made him jog on his own around the gymnasium and when he reached a certain point he would stop and do 10 burpees while saying 'I am being punished. I am a stupid t★★t!' It was so funny and I think even the officer saw the funny side of it, but we knew at this point we were in for a gruelling week. The officer continued down the line and came to me. I had had an operation in the summer to staple all the ligaments in my thumb in order to stop it from dislocating and therefore my right arm was in plaster up to my elbow. 'So you think you are going to have an easy week just because you have a little poorly arm?' he asked, well, shouted, to which I replied 'Of course not'. He screamed, 'Of course not what?' 'Of course not sir' I muttered, a bit embarrassed, feeling like I was back in my first year at Carre's in front of Mr Davies. He told me I was going to work harder than anybody else and I was not to use my arm as an excuse at any time during the week. He then sat us down and had a chat with us while Macca was still running around the gym. He told us that we were not going to be treated like professional footballers, people whom he detested, but for that week we were classed as young cadets. We would report in front of the camp clock at 7 every morning ready for a four to five-mile run, and then shower and report at 8.30 prompt for breakfast in the canteen. We would then be told the day's itinerary. The rest of that first day was ours to do what we wanted, but we had to report to the officer's mess for a welcome drink that evening. We were a bit on edge but after a couple of beers we soon relaxed and chatted away to the navy people. The chap who looked like Popeye was there and he bought Macca a pint to show there were no hard feelings. We probably all had four or five pints and went to bed fairly early knowing we were in for a tough run in the morning.

We were all under the clock, some a bit bleary eyed, at 7 ready for our run, and what a run! It was as if we had not been chatting to the instructors the night before. They were back in PTI mode (Physical Training Instructor) and they absolutely hammered us. It was red hot, even at that time in the morning, and it was bloody hard. After breakfast we did some circuits with them and when dinner came we were all knackered and ready for an afternoon off. However, we were told to report back at 2.30pm under the clock and be ready for a tough afternoon. When we got there, there were three big boxes full of dark blue boiler suits. We were told to find one in our size, go to our room, get changed and be back in 10 minutes. We all reported back in plenty of time, but for one player. Andy Beasley was the one missing and when he came round the corner the whole squad nearly fell over laughing when Gary Ford said 'Watch out, Hannibal Lecter is coming for us'. Beas took it in the spirit it was meant. The assault course lay ahead of us. I have never had such a hard but enjoyable afternoon. It was spent going through pipes, over 8ft walls, going down zip wires, doing press-ups in a foot of mud and going through scramble nets. I had my arm in plaster but was expected to do it all. I loved it and so did the rest of the lads. It was probably the hardest session we had ever done, but you do not notice that as much when you are enjoying it and helping each other get round the course. After our evening meal we again relaxed in the mess, enjoying a game of pool and darts with the navy lads over a couple of beers. We now knew how hard the following day was likely to be so it was another early night.

We did the same run before breakfast and then it was the infamous bleep test. There was a bit of banter flying around between the instructors that their fittest lad could beat our fittest lad, Charlie (Steve Charles). It was decided that we would do our test first and then it would be the race between Charlie and their lad. They started off, and went on and on and on. They easily passed our test results and just wanted to outdo each other. The gymnasium was packed. All the instructors and cadets were shouting for their man, and we were doing the same for Charlie. At first Charlie looked like he was struggling and then their lad did. Neither of them wanted to be beat and they both went on to complete the test and there was immediate respect between the two groups.

After dinner we were to meet in the gymnasium for a gymnastics session. This would involve vaulting among other things. I was a little bit concerned how I was going to do vaulting with my arm in pot, but I had managed to complete the assault course with it and the officer had told me on that first morning in the hall that I was not to use my arm as an excuse once that week. We lined up ready for the instructors and when they appeared one of them said 'how the bloody hell are you going to do vaulting with an arm in pot? Are you thick?' I could not win. I was sent to the camp pool for a swimming session (how the hell was I going to swim with an arm in pot!) with Fordy who had got a slight groin strain (or so you said Gary). You could not have got two more different swimmers than Fordy and I. He swam like the *Man from Atlantis* while I swam like a brick, even without my arm in plaster. When we arrived at the pool the instructor tied a plastic bag around my lower arm and we got in the water. I think we both thought it was going to be a light session, especially Gary with his ability, but it was my hardest training through my whole football career. After each width you had to get out and do an exercise on the side of the pool, either press-ups, burpees, sit ups or squat thrusts. I do not know what was the hardest – the swimming or the exercises. Fordy was moaning that he was doing more press-ups than me because my lengths were taking an eternity, but I was moaning because I was finding the swimming harder and I was not getting a long enough rest because Fordy was so quick at his lengths. We eventually finished and met the rest of the lads. They had had a bit of a 'jolly up' – basically just messing about with the apparatus and that was classed as their rest session. We told them about how hard our session had been but they did not believe us and said we had just gone for a little stretch and warm down in the pool!

On our final full day we did our usual early morning run before completing a different assault course after breakfast. We were to do it in groups, but we had to carry a 16ft wooden pole around with us. If any part of the pole touched the floor you would have to start the course again. The navy lads showed us how it should be done and completed the course in about five minutes, but we were a bit slower – in fact a lot slower. After 20 minutes, yes 20 minutes, there was not a lot between the groups but we were not even halfway round the course. We eventually crossed the line in about 35 minutes. It was a hard but enjoyable session. We were allowed a night out and the navy lads came with us, showing us the better pubs and bars to go to on the infamous Union

Street in Plymouth. We had had a really hard week, and the lads were absolutely knackered but after a few drinks soon got into better spirits. But none more so than Greg Fee. He was on Charlie's shoulders waving his arms in the air holding a pint in his hand. The pint was soon to become half a pint very quickly. He did not spill it; the ceiling fan was just above him and took the top half of his glass completely off, and it did not shatter but literally split in half. I think this sobered Greg up fairly quickly realising that it could easily have been his fingers, but the same could not be said for Charlie. I do not know whether it was because Charlie was so fit, but after a couple of pints he was well on his way. When we arrived back at the camp (the navy lads had gone their own way by now) Charlie got us all to follow him to the swimming pool. He had noticed some canoes down the side of the pool and wanted a go. Not in the normal canoe way, but off the top diving board. We knew we were not supposed to be in there, but every single member of the squad was there so if there was a telling off to be had we were all in the same boat (or canoe). Charlie was pushed off the top board by a few of us, and after a few goes he had mastered the canoe dive. Down he went, hitting the water and basically bouncing his way down the pool.

Somebody not on the top diving board was Kevin Noteman, a non-swimmer. (I am sure it was Kevin disguised as 'Eric the Eel' in the 2000 Olympics.) Parkie (Steve Parkin) told Kevin that he would give him £20 if he went in off the top board. I think the wager eventually went to about £100 and he went up the stairs. He was scared stiff when he looked over the edge but after a couple of pints and with £100 at stake he was determined to jump. Off he went running and jumping, not straight but diagonally. I have never seen anything like it. He landed a foot from the edge of the pool so that when he resurfaced he could immediately grab for the side. He managed it and was £100 better off for it. We got up the next day all in one piece (just) for the long drive to Mansfield ready for the 1992–93 season, after my hardest but most enjoyable pre-season.

Chapter Eleven
Out for the Count

This was always going to be a tough season, not surprising really when you saw the calibre of teams we were going to be coming up against. In Division Three that year we would be competing against West Bromwich Albion, Stoke City, Bolton Wanderers, Hull City, Wigan Athletic and Reading (who in the last two years had all competed in the Barclays Premiership). Some of them are massive clubs with a large fan base, but not Wigan and Hull at this time, who, up to 10 years ago, were playing at the same level as Mansfield. It shows what with a bit of ambition, money spent wisely and people pushing together in the right direction what can be achieved at a small club like Mansfield Town. Our season was to start with a tough home game against Peter Shilton's Plymouth Argyle. George had done a bit of pre-season work but not played any games so I found myself playing at centre-half alongside my roommate Kevin Gray in the season opener. I was a little bit apprehensive about this as it was a long time since I had played there in a competitive game, but the game went really well and we drew 0–0. It was not a bad start for the team but a great start for Kevin and I, aged only 19 and 20. Next up was a slightly harder game, Newcastle United away at St James' Park. Newcastle were to win the League that year, and their messiah Kevin Keegan was back at the club. The place was buzzing and Kevin and I would be up against Gavin Peacock and the legend Mickey Quinn. The game did not start well for us with the Magpies taking a very early lead through Peacock. However, we settled into the game and deservedly drew level. This was how it stayed until very late when Quinn scored to win them the game 2–1. It was a blow with it being so late in the game but it still gave us a chance in the second leg at Field Mill a week later. Sandwiched between the two Newcastle games, we got hammered against a very good Swansea City team 4–0. I think possibly our minds were firmly focused on the upcoming Newcastle game. I hit the crossbar from an early corner and we took the game to our illustrious visitors. Midway through the first half I went up for a header and clashed heads with one of the Newcastle players (I think it was Steve Howey.) The rest is not even a blur, I was knocked out cold. Both sets of players knew it was serious and Dennis Pettit rushed on straight away. When he reached me I had started swallowing my tongue. With quick thinking, Dennis put the 'other end' of a pair of scissors into my mouth and stopped me choking. I was stretchered off still unconscious and came round eventually in the physio room with my mum at my side. Realising it looked very serious for a few minutes she had rushed down the back of the stand to be with her little boy! We went on to draw the game 0–0 but we had given a good performance. Now it was time to start performing in the League.

It did not quite happen straight away. We lost our next couple of games but picked up a good point away at Blackpool. We had a local derby against Bradford City, and the pressure was firmly on George and his team to get a much-needed first victory of the season. Whenever we were under that much pressure we had usually dug out a result and once again we were able to do it, producing our best football of the season to beat the Bantams 5–2. Greg Fee, a fans' favourite, who had only just got back into the team at centre-half scored two, and I notched up my first goal of the season and played my first game back in central midfield. We backed this victory up by beating Chester City away 2–1 and things were starting to look a little bit better for us. We had climbed up to halfway on the board after seven League games, not a bad start.

However, we went on to lose our next three games, and this was typical of us in what was to be a very topsy-turvy season. We failed to get any consistency together and that eventually would lead to our downfall. In this bad run we played Stoke City at home and Stoke cruised to an emphatic 4–0 win. This game sticks in my head for two very different reasons. Firstly, as the game was going on I could hear a noise but could not work out where it was coming from. We continued to play for a few minutes but the noise was getting louder and louder. It was a kind of humming noise and then the Stoke fans broke into song, a rendition of the Tom Jones classic hit *Delilah*. It was deafening, and utterly brilliant.

The other thing that sticks in my head was sitting in the dressing room after the game. We had just been beaten 4–0 at home and we had been crap! We knew it was coming and when George entered the changing room with a bright red face, he started. As he was getting out of his gear all sorts of expletives were coming from his mouth. Nobody dare look up and we sat motionless staring at the floor. George was like a whirlwind. He had got undressed and headed in to the shower area out of our sight where the large team bath was. He must have just jumped in because we could hear the splash – then the scream! Whoever had filled the bath had obviously just filled it with boiling water. We looked at each other and tried not to laugh. George came back through the changing room and he looked like he had bright red football socks on. He had obviously jumped in and the water was just below knee depth. He told us all to 'F★★k off' as he went out of the room shutting the door behind him. We were all in hysterics. We were devastated about the result and the performance but it was impossible not to laugh.

We picked up a couple of wins in our next six or so games, but we needed a break for our League campaign. We had been drawn against Shrewsbury Town away in the first round of the FA Cup. They were riding high in Division Three but it was a game that we knew we should win. I probably should not have played in the tie as I had been whacked on the top of my right foot, but I was desperate to play and had an injection in my foot to get through the game. We were beaten 3–1 and this flattered us. The fans were livid and rightly so. I could not feel myself kicking the ball (my foot was totally numb from the injection) but that could not be used as an excuse. We, and I, had totally let everyone down.

We did not play again for two weeks. Instead we ran and ran that fortnight as punishment for that Shrewsbury game. 'If you can't be bothered to play football in games, I can't be bothered to train you, so just f★★★ing run until I tell you to stop.' Our next game was away at Leyton Orient and we got hammered 5–1. I played at full-back and had another awful game. This continued against Walsall in the Associate Members Cup and George gave me my first real rollicking. He said I looked like a 'little rabbit stuck in headlights' and he was right. It was my first real confidence crisis in professional football. I thought I might be dropped but I stayed in the team. We failed to win a game from 3 November until the New Year and George was under real pressure again. Remembering the Chesterfield game when he was last under pressure the previous season, he did exactly the same again. He had not trained all season, but he picked himself to play against West Brom at the Hawthorns just before Christmas. We lost 2–0 but the performance was much better, personally and on a team level. We drew both of our Christmas fixtures and started the New Year off with a victory against Chester City. We were now unbeaten in three games but yet again could not get any further consistency; we did not win for the next five games. After drawing at home with Blackpool in the middle of February we found ourselves six points away from safety. We had a team meeting and it was decided that the four games would either make or break our season. We won three out of the four, all without conceding a goal. Had things started to turn and were we about to produce that consistency we needed? (No and no).

Yet again the upturn in form proved to be false. We had got ourselves level in points with the teams above the relegation zone, lost the next three games by the odd goal and then won the next two without conceding a goal. We had to be the most inconsistent team ever that season – the team could beat anybody one week and lose to a pub team the week after!

When April arrived we had only nine games to save our season. Level on points with Blackpool (they managed to get promoted through the Play-offs the season before) there were five home games and four away games left. If we played anything like we were capable of we would be safe, if we were to have a run of results like we had had all season we would be down. Simple as. We went without a win for six games, losing four and drawing two. We needed to go to Vale Park and get a result against Port Vale who had been in the top two in the League all season. We went there full of hope but were again very poor on the night and lost comfortably 3–0. We had got what we had deserved over a very long season. Port Vale celebrated as that win all but guaranteed them automatic promotion (they eventually missed out); it was us a year earlier, but we were now on the other side of the coin. The team now had to play away at Preston, who were in trouble themselves, and the final home game of the season at Rotherham.

Preston was a funny place to play at that time, with their artificial pitch, but it was even more bizarre with their eccentric boss, John Beck. There were rumours doing the rounds at the time that he used to get youth team players to urinate in the opposition teapot, flood the away dressing room so it was uncomfortable to change in, leave the heating on full blast and basically do anything to make the opposition feel 'away' from home. Even out on the pitch he would have loads of sand placed in the corners so that when they belted the ball forward (they were very direct as all John Beck teams were) the ball would hold up in the corners and not just run out of play. I am not sure if it was in this game, but I remember playing in a game where he substituted their 'keeper for keeping the ball on the pitch. John used to order his 'keepers to kick the ball out to the wingers to compete for it. He did not like the ball to be infield at all and basically would sooner have the 'keeper kick it out of play than onto the opposition centre-half's head.

As I said Preston were in trouble themselves and the pressure was all on them. We just relaxed and played our football and murdered them 5–1. It yet again showed what we were capable of. I managed to score my third goal of the season in the game but all in all it had been a really disappointing season for us. The team had fought so hard to achieve promotion the previous season. Should we have done things differently? The sale of Phil Stant to Cardiff City had angered the fans but we still should have had enough firepower to stay in the League. Should we have gone on a mid-season trip like we did the previous season to recharge the batteries? We might have done after we had won three games out of four in February but money was getting tighter and tighter in the lower Leagues and the owners were negotiating with a mystery business man about the sale of the club. All 'should haves', but at the end of the day we were not good enough. (I will say this again elsewhere in this book!)

I collected my first Player of the Season trophy before the final game against Rotherham. I also won a couple of awards that were nice on a personal level but I would have swapped them all to have another chance to play in that League the following season. I had enjoyed playing against the bigger opposition and felt as if my game had improved both in midfield and centre-half. We lost the game against Rotherham 3–1, yet again underperforming as a team.

Would the new mystery man reportedly taking over in the summer be the saviour of Mansfield Town?

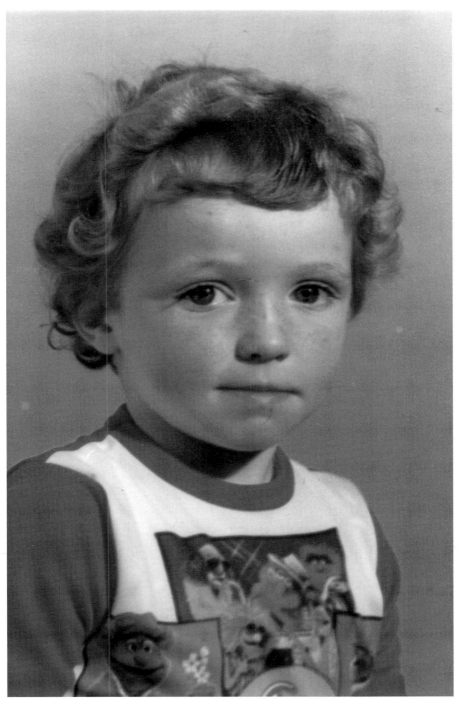

Me aged 5. Mum says I always looked like I was going to cry.

District sports day represtenting The William Alvey School – aged 10.

Going to Germany, first time away from home.

Ruskington Tigers – six-a-side winners 1982.

Festival of Sport – six-a-side winners. From left to right: Jonathan Folland, Richard Cardy, David Stacey, me, Matthew Burchnall, Matthew Pask, Wayne Louth.

My hero Bryan Robson outside Old Trafford.

Receiving the Player of the Year trophy for Navenby from the legendary Jimmy Sirrel.

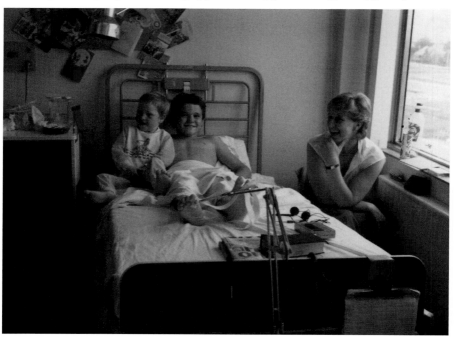

Becoming a teenager in hospital.

Pictured with Jonathan Kerrigan of Heartbeat fame (far left).

My other love, cricket – pictured with David Gower at Sleaford Cricket Club.

National Finalists Lincolnshire Under-19s – May 1989.

England v Wales – Gloucester 1991.

Receiving my England cap 1991.

With my England shirt and cap at my 'second home' Field Mill.

Signing professional forms the day before my debut against Crewe, while still at school – from left to right – Steve Wilkinson, Billy Dearden, Colin White, Peter Freeman (headmaster) and George Foster.

My first professional team photograph – promotion season 1991–92 (I'm behind George Foster and Billy Dearden).

Heading for goal against Newcastle United at Field Mill – August 1992.

From left to right – Colin Ferry, David Ferry and Brenda Ferry – my Mansfield 'family'.

Receiving the Player of the Year trophy from John Lomas (Chad) May 1994.

Kicking my good friend Jamie Hewitt in the local derby – 1993–94.

'The Flying Dutchman' scoring at Rochdale.

Sheffield United July 1995.

Chapter Twelve
Andy King

T he club had been taken over during the summer by Keith Haslam, the son of former Sheffield United Manager Harry. Nobody knew a lot about the new man but he was generally well received by the Mansfield public. I think he bought the club for £1 but took over all the running debts of the club. Keith's reign as chairman at Mansfield was to be a long one and there can not have ever been a more controversial tenure at a lower League football club. The first time I saw Keith he rolled into the car park in a battered, old, beige Mercedes and when he got out I could not believe how young he looked. He was the youngest Football League chairman but he certainly did not lack any confidence. Apparently he had been a professional golfer and from day one, especially in the early days, enjoyed the banter with the footballers. His dad had got Keith interested in football and deep down, even after being so successful in business, he was a frustrated footballer, or manager at the very least. Keith's name will be mentioned many more times in this book, but at this point he was well received by the Stags fans in the summer of 1993.

The feeling in the dressing room was that we had been a massive let-down last season and we were determined to 'bounce' straight back into Division Two. Pre-season was again very tough but there was no trip this year due to the imminent take over at the club. I have always believed that it is vitally important to have a pre-season trip as it breaks the monotony of a very long, hard six weeks of training, and a change of scenery, a change of voice and a different fitness regime can make you actually work harder without realising it because you are enjoying it so much. The pre-season friendlies went okay but the signing of Phil Stant, back on loan from Cardiff City, had given everyone a massive boost, especially the fans who held Stanty in the highest regard. The first game of the season was against Shrewsbury at Field Mill. We had had a team meeting, one of many under George, and it was clear that a good start was vital this season. The squad had a much younger feel abut it, perhaps it was a little too inexperienced, but we went into that first game full of confidence and well prepared for a long season ahead. The first game of any new season is usually a very nervous affair with both teams desperate to make a good start in the new campaign, afraid to make mistakes and therefore playing it very safe. This game was no different and was not a classic by any stretch of the imagination. Stanty was yet again the hero, scoring the goal in a very tense 1–0 victory. We had got the start we so desperately wanted, three points were ours.

Next up was a two-legged League Cup tie against Stoke City, who had been a tough team to play against the previous season and were now plying their trade in League

Division One. I had realised during the summer, when looking back over my first two seasons in professional football, that I had never been on a victorious side for Mansfield in either a League Cup or FA Cup tie, and I was determined to put the record straight this year. Victoria Park, Stoke's old ground, was a great place to play and I have always admired Stoke City as a football club – I personally think it is great to see them playing in the Premiership this season as their fans deserve it more than most. However, we went there with youngsters Steve Foster and Chris Perkins playing and performed admirably to come away with a 2–2 draw. A week later, in a great return game, we eventually conceded two late goals to lose the tie 5–3 on aggregate. I still had not won a Cup tie, but we had done brilliantly over the two legs and had set our standard for the remainder of the season.

The inconsistency was there again when we lost at home to Scunthorpe and there were a few cries for George's head. As it was two years earlier, the game billed as potentially George's last game in charge of Mansfield Town was against our bitterest rivals, Chesterfield, at Saltergate. Could we get the same result for George? We managed to win comfortably, the same result 2–0, but no goal for me this time. I may never have won a Cup tie for the Stags but I had always been on the winning side against the Spireites. I am sure Mansfield fans would have settled for that over a career. But had we saved George's managerial career at Mansfield again? Not this time.

After losing our next home game against Crewe, the chairman relieved George Foster of his duties. George was a legend as a player at Mansfield and it was a sorry way to go. The usual reasons for a manager being sacked were brought out: his 'style of play' was not what we wanted and we needed a 'new face'. Billy Deardon was put in temporary charge and I think the younger players were pleased with this. He was always there to put an arm round your shoulder and preferred the quiet approach rather than the more robust style of George. I had a lot of respect and admiration for the both of them, both having played a massive part in my early days in professional football.

Our first two games under Billy were as tough as you could get. Two local derbies, at home against Lincoln City and away at Doncaster Rovers. We played both games without any fear and won them 1–0. The optimism for the season had returned, we had kept two clean sheets and were climbing the League. However, the Mansfield Town luck, of a problem not far round the corner, would soon come into play. In our next three games, two draws and a victory against Scarborough, we scored eight goals but the worrying thing was that we had also conceded six goals, two in each game. We had got up to eighth in the League but there was always that concern that we would concede in every game. We were right to be worried. The team failed to record a victory in the next five games, which included a couple of hammerings: 1–5 at Northampton and 0–4 at home to Chester City.

Between the Northampton and Chester debacles we got a 1–1 draw away at Carlisle, not a bad result. This was the first game with new physio Barry Statham, a man who was to play a massive part in both my playing and coaching career over the next 10 years.

The game itself was hard fought and with a minute left we were hanging on for what would have been a decent point. I had been booked a bit earlier in the game, deservedly so, for a late tackle, and when the ball dropped to me midway in our own half I toed a touch and played a great 'through ball' for Stringy. He was one on one. I heard the whistle and immediately thought it was for offside. I could not believe what was happening when the referee came up to me holding the yellow card. What the hell for? It got worse! Having realised he had booked me earlier, he then got his red card out. I pleaded with him and asked him what it was for. He said he had given me a second yellow for kicking the ball away! If I was kicking the ball away, I argued, I would not have taken such care as to put my teammate through on goal! I left the field to much bemusement, from both sets of players, staff and fans. It really was that absurd. I did not get fined by the club seeing as it was so unwarranted but I did have to pay for a new away changing room door! I am not proud of the fact but realised that I was going to miss a game, a game that could make a difference to Billy getting the job.

The Chester City game was probably the worst team performance I had ever been involved in. Could it get any worse? It was about to. We were equally as bad the following Saturday away at Wigan where we again conceded four goals in a 4–1 defeat. We knew where the problem lay, and we worked hard on it in training, but the plain truth was that we had conceded 20 goals in our last seven League games. We drew our next game away at Rochdale 1–1, still not finding that elusive clean sheet, and we followed that with a hard-fought victory at home to Gillingham. I think a decision had been made by the hierarchy at Mansfield that the manager's position would be confirmed after the FA Cup tie at home to Preston. We were desperate to win the game to put Billy in a strong position for the vacancy and it must have been the longest caretaker role in the history of football. I was also desperate to get my first win in a Cup tie. Another worrying thing was that I had not yet scored that season. We lost the game 2–1, failing to do the business for Billy, and that week it was announced that Billy had not got the job: a new man was coming in.

At first, a lot of people did not know who this new manager was and asked 'Who the hell is Andy King?' I recognised the name and knew he had played for Everton. What I did not know was just how mad he was and how big an influence he was going to have on me over the next couple of years. Andy King is the most confident person I have ever met in football and he typified this when he first met the lads on the training ground. He told everybody to get a ball and then juggle it, keeping it off the ground with any part of the body apart from the hands. He said whoever got the most, he would double it. Parky came out on top, and Andy King doubled it with ease. He even sat down halfway through it; it was amazing. After he had eventually finished he said in his cockney voice 'Now you know I am still f***ing better than you lot!' It was typical Andy King. He said it in jest, but technically he was still miles ahead of anybody. He would join in every training session and play like it was the last time he would have a football at his feet. He was a centre midfielder by trade and I would learn so much about the position from him, not necessarily the positional side but definitely the things to improve myself technically. Over the next season and a half he was always there with advice and many an afternoon he would have me back on my own, either doing some technical work or playing head tennis (that improves you technically!) He was never beaten in the time I was there but he did bend the rules a little (a lot!) as he did in everything he did, whether it was football, golf, anything.

However, things did not start brilliantly for Andy King and his young team. We lost his first two games in charge, but then won away at York in the Associate Members Cup on penalties. (I did not take one. Penalties and I do not go remember!) Kingy really encouraged me to get forward, chances were coming thick and fast but I still had not scored. He told me to keep getting into the positions and that I would soon be a midfielder who could score double figures in a season. We got our first win under Andy at home to Northampton in our next game and I scored my first goal in a 1–0 victory. We drew our next two fixtures, both away from home, extending our unbeaten run to three games. As always we shot ourselves in the foot by losing our next three League games, got four points out of a possible six in the next two games and then lost the next two. Kingy had had a torrid start to his reign. In his first 12 League games, the team had only won two, drawn three and lost seven. We had slipped down the League and sat in 17th place. Not good enough for a team who only a season earlier had been playing in the League above.

It is strange how one game can change your luck, and usually in the most unforeseen circumstances. Our away fixture at Chester City on 5 February was one such game. We were bloody awful! Yet somehow we drew the game 1–1. The marks awarded in the paper on the Sunday morning were, probably for the first time, right. Darren Ward, our goalkeeper, got a nine, there was one five, and the rest threes and twos. I was one of the players who got a three, and I was lucky to get that. That somehow kick-started our season and we went on to win four out of the next five. We had started to play some really good football and had also started scoring at will. I had scored a few and things were looking rosy. Chesterfield had made a bid for me which was turned down, delighting me. I was really excited about the future with Mansfield and about learning more from Andy King. I was absolutely loving my football. We were 11th in the table; could we get to the Play-offs?

We continued in much the same vein over the next five games with two wins, two draws and one defeat. The team were loving it; we were on a better run than anybody else in the League, scoring more goals, and I have never been in a squad that enjoyed playing together as much. This continued throughout the next season. I was playing as well as I had ever done and the games could not come quick enough for us. We were in a position that we could not have dreamt of only eight weeks earlier. With four games to play in the 1993–94 season, we had given ourselves an outside chance of reaching the Play-offs. Rochdale at home was a make or break game for us: win and we were still there, lose and we would have to wait until next season. We played well but could not quite score. We lost the game 1–0 and that put an end to our season. Losing our next two games but winning the final game of the season at Walsall 2–0, we were disappointed not to have reached the Play-offs after all the optimism of pre-season but after being 17th a couple of months earlier, the future was bright, the future was Andy King!

I was feeling good about my game and had finished the season with seven goals, but a major concern I had was the state of my knees. I was having real trouble again, and there was not a game when I was not in agony with them. They were getting worse and worse and Barry (the physio) and myself were to have many conversations over the weeks to come to try and solve what was becoming a big problem.

One funny episode during this break occurred when I went to spend a week up at Hull University where my brother Jamie was studying. One afternoon Jamie and his housemates went down to the local park and started a football match with some other students who were also in the park. Being very sensible I decided to sit out this game in case I picked up a silly injury. After about half an hour I started to get itchy feet and decided to join in, but only at half pace. Obviously Jamie and his mates knew that football was my job but the other team did not have a clue. One player on the other team, complete with full set of dreadlocks and at about 6ft 4in, fancied himself as a bit of a player and to be fair he was not bad. However, my competitive spirit once again got the better of me and I decided to show him who the proper footballer was. I picked the ball up and dribbled past the majority of their team and nutmegged this guy before slotting the ball into an empty net. I turned round, slightly embarrassed that my ego had got the better of me, to face the guy bearing down on me. He stopped a yard away from me and said, 'Great play, you should consider taking it up professionally'. I did not say a word and went and sat back down behind the goal. That competitive spirit is yet to leave me!

Chapter Thirteen

Scabies

The 1994–95 pre-season was a strange one for me. My knees were now a major concern for the club and myself. I could get through a game or a hard training session but I would be in absolute agony for a couple of days after. I had a meeting with Andy King and Barry Statham and we decided that I had to go and see someone because it was jeopardising my future in the game. We decided that the three of us would keep it to ourselves and from that day it was only us and my parents who knew the severity of the problem. Barry had organised a meeting with one of the top knee specialists in the country, a man called Angus Strover. We travelled to Strovers's Droitwich Knee Clinic not knowing what to expect. He recommended complete rest for at least 18 months.

Barry and I had a real heart-to-heart during the hour-long journey back to Mansfield. I was heartbroken. What should I do? We went straight back into Andy's office and I broke down. Kingy really understood the pain I was in, his knees were not great, and Barry had experienced many people with serious knee injuries. I did not want to rest for that long, that would have been my career over, but how would I be able to perform to my best with my knees in the state they were? I would just have to carry on and see how long they would last, and deal with the consequences later on a personal level. My training throughout that next season was very limited and it was decided that I would have to do a lot of work on my own to keep my fitness levels up. I could not put my knee through too much pounding, so a lot of my physical work was done in the pool, not swimming but with a bright yellow life jacket! Many hours were spent running up and down the pool in deep enough water so that my feet were not on the floor. It was so boring but really beneficial. I was really pushing myself as I knew there was a massive year ahead, both for the club and for me personally.

The best week for me pre-season was the week we spent at Southport, staying at the Pontins Holiday Camp. Kingy had organised a couple of pre-season games up there, and of course he was near his beloved Liverpool. The training schedule was brutal, but because a lot of the physical work was done on Southport beach I was able to do all of the work because it was not putting too much strain on my knees. Anybody who has ever been on the beach at Southport knows how big it is and I feel sorry for Red Rum (three times Grand National winner) who did a lot of his exercise there. Kingy may have been a skilful footballer but he put us through it that pre-season. He had been joined by Colin Harvey who was to help Kingy out in an advisory role. Colin had been involved at Everton in all capacities and Andy had enormous respect for him. After a couple of hours on the training ground with Colin, the whole squad had the same respect. The way he put thing across, his training methods and his opinions on the game were second to none and I learnt so much from him in such a short space of time.

The lads were buzzing. The spirit in the squad was the best I was ever to be involved in. We were a very young squad, and most of them seemed to live at Brenda and Colin's. There were seven of us there now, four professionals and three youth-team players. In my room were Darren Ward, Kevin Lampkin and Stuart Hadley, all first-team players. As you can imagine we had many laughs and the fact we were all so close helped when things were not going well for one of us.

The break at Southport was brilliant, really hard work but enjoyable all the same. Everybody was looking fit and ready for the new season. On the last night we were allowed out to let our hair down and Steve Parkin, our captain, was given strict orders to keep everybody in line. That was not hard for Parky, an absolute beast of a man. He commanded the respect of the squad due to his background in boxing (bare knuckle I think) and when he spoke, you listened. He was a massive believer in the lads staying together, whether it was on a night out or anything we did as a squad. We all had a few drinks, some more so than others, but we all got back to the camp at the same time. We were in good spirits and went straight to the cabaret bar where we found Kingy, Barry and Colin also in very good spirits. We had a few drinks with them and had a laugh, Kingy being the main joker in the pack but not far behind was Adie Boothroyd. They would tear strips off each other, and anybody else in the vicinity. We left the bar, still altogether, and headed for our rooms. The accommodation was typical of a holiday camp, two floors of chalets with all the squad in one block. My room was on the first floor as was Chris Timons, a young centre-half who was on his first real football trip. What Timo did next, only he will ever know why. He decided to do a handstand off the balcony. He looked in perfect shape as he held the handstand for about 10 seconds, but then the nightmare began. He lost his balance and fell onto the ground. It was only about a five metre drop, but as he hit the rock hard ground you could hear the noise. We all rushed to the edge and looked over: Timo was lying there motionless. The next couple of minutes were like a scene out of the Keystone Cops, with bodies rushing in every direction to get down to see the extent of Chris's injuries. Parky was the first there, followed by myself. Timo was not moving but he was making a weird noise. We did not dare touch or move him, we knew that much of first aid procedure, but what was the weird noise? Most of the other lads were gathered round by now, and we were soon to find out what the mysterious noise was. Timo was snoring! The bloody idiot had only fallen asleep! Kingy appeared from around the corner and he went absolutely berserk. We were sent to our rooms and when we woke up in the morning and looked outside, somebody had put an outline of a body in white tape exactly where Timo had landed. Who had done it was a mystery but my money was on the lively roommate pairing of Baraclough and Boothroyd. Again Kingy went mad. We were supposed to be leaving back for Mansfield at 9.30 but we were still on the beach at 11 in the middle of an absolute beast of a running session put on by our illustrious boss. A few of the lads were feeling very fragile and were ill during the session but Kingy was determined to teach us all a lesson. He certainly did that. We came back from Southport united as a squad and looking forward to the new campaign, but unfortunately with an outbreak of scabies. About half of us had caught it from the dirty bedding and towels. It was awful. So all that was left to ponder before the new season got under way was would the knees hold out? Would I win that first elusive Cup tie? Could I get double figures in the goalscoring charts? And would the bloody itching stop!?

Chapter Fourteen
Goals Goals Goals

T he scabies itching finally stopped, thankfully, but I was itching for the season's opener, a Cup game away at Rochdale. The perfect way to 'break my duck' early on in the season. We had a fantastic start to the season, winning the away leg 2–1 and our first League game of the season at home to Colchester, with me getting on the score sheet. Would we finish the job off at home to Rochdale to give me that first Cup tie victory? We did, winning 1–0, and we waited with anticipation to see if we would draw a big club in the next round. It could not have been much bigger at that time. We were drawn to play the Premiership holders Leeds United over two legs with the first game being away at Elland Road. That was a few weeks away yet but we desperately wanted to make it four wins out of four, which would be a fantastic start to the season. The team could not have wished for a better place to try and achieve it, away at Saltergate against our main rivals Chesterfield. We won the game 1–0 but it could have been more. Could we carry on this form through the next few League games before our eagerly anticipated Cup game against Leeds? One thing that you must have realised by now is that you could never put consistent and Mansfield Town in the same sentence. Unless of course you were saying they were the most consistent team in the country at being inconsistent! We lost our next four League games, so we had started the season with four straight victories and backed it up by losing the next four (very consistent!) The Saturday before the Leeds game I managed to get on the score sheet against Northampton in a 1–1 draw, so at least we did not have to travel to Elland Road on the back of five straight League defeats.

Playing against Leeds United at Elland Road was going to be a mighty test of our character and ability as a team. Even though there was not a big crowd on the night, Leeds still played a team packed full of internationals. Kingy had devised a master plan to beat the League Champions, or so he kept telling us, and it was to go there and play with three centre-halves. The usual pairing of Mark Peters and Lee Howarth were to be joined centrally by yours truly. It worked a dream. We did not concede and won the game 1–0, courtesy of a Simon Ireland diving header (something never to be seen again). We had outplayed them on the night and thoroughly deserved our victory. Could this be the start of a promotion push?

The return leg against Leeds was a really tense affair. Everybody expected Leeds to beat us and overturn their one-goal deficit, but we were confident. We had beaten Gillingham away 2–0 and I scored from my favourite midfield position. However, we were to revert back to Kingy's master plan and I was to play as part of a three-man defence again. With a good football brain it is the easiest position on the pitch to play. You never really have to pick up any men, just talk to your fellow centre-halves and cover space. The plan worked perfectly again until we had Colin Hoyle sent off. With a man down, we were under intense pressure and it looked only a matter of time before Leeds went in front. Somehow, with every Stags player outstanding, we managed to hold onto our lead. When the final whistle went the pitch was invaded by jubilant Stags fans and it seemed to take forever to get off the pitch. Gary McAllister, the Leeds captain, waited at the end of the tunnel to shake hands and congratulate every Mansfield player, typical of the man. When we got to the changing room the chairman, Keith Haslam, was there. He had promised us a trip to Magaluf mid-season (before the Elland Road game) if we were successful over the two legs, something he obviously did not expect us to be. We had great pleasure in reminding him of it, and told him to get his wallet out (something I was to ask him many times over the coming seasons, with varying success). As always the squad stuck together and enjoyed a night out before getting on with the important stuff ahead – achieving promotion.

We won our next two League games, the second being away at Northampton at the old County ground. Anyone who has been at this ground will know the crowd stand behind some advertising hoardings down the entire length of one side of the pitch and are literally a couple of yards away from the touchline. About halfway through the first half I went into a sliding tackle only a couple of yards in from the touchline in front of the hoardings. Their lad caught me accidentally on the inside of my left thigh with his studs and I felt a sharp stinging pain. I immediately covered the area with my hand and was subject to the usual abuse from away supporters like 'Get up you fat b★★★ard! There's nowt wrong with you'. I was not in pain, but when I took my hand away it soon shut them up. There was not a lot of blood – just one small trickle running down towards my knee. The problem was that the lad's stud had punctured my thigh and my thigh muscle (or the muscle fibres) were literally hanging out of the puncture wound in my leg. Barry sprinted on and immediately called for the stretcher and the club doctor. There was no way I could carry on in the game and Barry wanted their doctor to stitch my leg as quickly as possible in order to stop any infection getting into the hole. Barry left me in the capable hands of Northampton's club doctor. The only problem being was that I could smell the alcohol coming off his breath. He did not give me any anaesthetic, so the next half an hour was very painful. I had 36 stitches in total, 18 internally and 18 externally. The lads held on for a great 1–0 victory, but on the way home on the coach my wound had opened up. I did not feel it but I was sat playing cards on the bus when I scratched my left leg. When I went to play my next card it was covered in blood. I immediately stood up and from the left pocket near my waist to my left knee of my trousers the blood was soaking through. It was not nice but Barry soon cleaned it up and when I got back to Mansfield it was a trip to A & E to stitch the wound back up (another 10 stitches). So for a little hole, no bigger than an inch square, it needed 46 stitches. I still have the scar now, so no more wearing short skirts for me!

Around this time, the club had attracted quite a bit of interest in me from higher League clubs and it was rumoured that a move would be imminent. The club had accepted a bid of £120,000 from Port Vale, where Billy Dearden was assistant manager. I had never instigated a move and was really enjoying my football at Mansfield. However, the two clubs had agreed the fee and I was able to go and speak to them. What did I have to lose? If it did not feel right then I would stay, if it was for me Port Vale was to be my new club.

I travelled to Vale Park to meet with Billy, John Rudge (the manager) and their chairman. They showed me round the club and then we sat down to discuss the contract. They offered more than double my wages, a very generous offer, but it did not feel right. Everything abut the club and the area did not seem to be for me. I didn't feel Vale were a much bigger club than Mansfield and with a bit of luck we could be in the same League the next year. Therefore, when I returned to Mansfield I told Vale that I appreciated the offer but felt it was not the right time for me to move. I told Kingy the news and he told the chairman my decision. Kingy was delighted. I am not too sure about Keith Haslam's feelings, although I was to earn him a few more pounds when I did eventually leave!

We were now going to start one of our infamous runs again at an important stage of the season. We lost four out of five in our next few Leagues, the other game being a draw. In this run we also lost against Millwall in the next round of the League Cup. A season that promised so much was threatening to just fizzle out. How could a team that could beat the Premiership holders over two legs be so poor in the League?

Our next game was at a happy hunting ground for the Stags, Glanford Park. Scunthorpe United were always a tough proposition, especially on their own turf, but we went and turned them over in a great game 4–3. Now could I go and get that first FA Cup win to follow on from the success of the League Cup? We drew non-League Northwich Victoria in the first round and eventually came out winning 3–1, scoring two goals myself for the first time in my professional career. We were desperate for a home draw in the next round but had to be content with an away fixture at non-League Halifax Town. For this game we wore, for some strange reason, probably the worst kit ever to be seen in professional football. Whoever designed this kit must have been having a laugh – at our expense! It was lime green and purple! We looked like Quality Street wrappers! We managed to force a replay on an absolute mud heap at The Shay and were quite pleased to get them back to Field Mill. We won the replay against Halifax 2–1 with two more goals from myself, the last coming in the dying minutes of the game. We were now in the third round of the FA Cup and potentially drawn against a big team. The team were drawn against Wolverhampton Wanderers at home, not a bad draw and one that we had a chance of progressing in. We had some important League games before then coming up over the Christmas period, and what a few games they would turn out to be. Goals galore!

Chesterfield were up next and we hammered them 4–2 with two goals coming from the unlikeliest source, our youth team manager Keith Alexander. 'Big Keith' was getting on a bit, but he proved a real handful. The only downside to the victory was that my knee had given way. I had played a lot of games in a short space of time and my knee was giving me a lot of discomfort. What better time than Christmas to miss a few games? We signed a young lad from Doncaster Rovers on loan, who I had met a few years earlier in schools' football when Carre's played Josiah Mason College. He scored a hat-trick in one of those games against Carre's and proved to be equally successful with Mansfield. The man in question was a certain O'Neil Donaldson. I missed the next couple of games but the team certainly did not miss me; Boxing Day at home to Hereford they definitely did not. We hammered Hereford 7–1, the highlights being the debut of Donaldson and a fantastic goal from his own half by Ian Baraclough. Could things get any better than 11 goals in two home games? Just about, winning the next day 5–2 at Scarborough (two games in two days but staggeringly 12 goals). I somehow managed to force my way back into the team, the short break had done my knees a world of good, but I had to settle for centre-back. We saw off Barnet 3–0 but lost against Fulham at Craven Cottage 4–2.

Next up was the big FA Cup tie against Wolves. They played a full strength side and we had stormed into a 2–0 lead by half-time. We were full of confidence and playing some tremendous stuff. However, Wolves came back strongly to beat us 3–2, a big disappointment, but we could take heart from the attacking football we were playing. We won our next two League games scoring six more goals in the process and we were flying. Although losing our next two games away at Preston and Walsall, both by the odd goal, this did not really knock our confidence. We were enjoying playing together and were still playing well. We won our next three games and scored nine more goals in the process, including two more for me at Wigan.

After we had beaten Leeds earlier in the season we had been promised a mid-season trip and, after three straight wins, what a perfect time to recharge the batteries and rewind. The lads wanted to go to Magaluf but that meant us landing in Birmingham on the Friday afternoon before the game against Exeter on the Saturday, something Kingy was not happy about. He was worried about a flight delay before such an important game, but as a squad we stuck together and finally persuaded him to agree to it. We met at Birmingham on the Sunday evening and had a few drinks at the airport, having a laugh and a joke together. When we finally arrived at our hotel in the middle of the night Magaluf was like a ghost town (it was the end of February). Before going to bed, Kingy told us to report downstairs in the reception area of the hotel at 10am the next morning in our training kit ready to for a run. We could not believe it! Here we were to recharge the batteries and Kingy was taking us on a bloody run! We all met in the foyer at 10am and there were a few grumbles and moans before Kingy told us all to follow him. Off we went and we had gone about 30 metres when Kingy veered off into a bar. He was treating us all to breakfast. The cheeky bugger had had it planned all the time, the only stipulation being that we had to have a pint with our breakfasts. That was to be a long first day in Magaluf. We stayed together all day drinking, and we were all the worse for wear by the time the night had come to an end. Magaluf was as much a ghost town as it had been in the middle of the night when we arrived. There were literally a handful of people about. Before going back to the hotel Kingy told us we were definitely training tomorrow and that we were to meet at 11am downstairs. This gave us plenty of time to sleep the effects of the drink off before getting a decent 'sweat on' the next day. We hit our beds around midnight after being in the bars since just after 10 in the morning. Not good.

We all managed to be in the reception area at 11am, most of us looking the worse for wear. It had been a long day the day before, and to be fair I was looking forward to training to get a 'sweat on' and get the beer out of my system. We had a jog down to the beach, put out some sunbeds for goals and started a game. It was embarrassing. I would like to say that it was down to the uneven surface of the beach but that would be lying. The lads were struggling to keep on their feet, some obviously still under the effect of alcohol. One of the worst trainers was Kingy himself, and that was unlike him. Joining him in the competition for the 'yellow jersey' (the smelly, unwashed top that the worst trainer of the week had to wear) was our captain Steve Parkin. I think the two of them had stayed out longer than everybody else the night before and it was showing. Eventually after about 15 minutes of the worst game of football you will ever see, the ball landed at Parky's feet. He had controlled it perfectly, more luck than judgement seeing the state he was in, and promptly bent down, picked the ball up and kicked it into the sea as far as he could. Everybody just stood there and looked at Kingy, not knowing in what way he would react. He burst out laughing and the rest of us followed. It was obviously something that they had concocted the night before over those last few beers. What would we do now? We had lost our one and only ball. We had travelled light on the football front to Magaluf, so it was either going to be a running session or, seeing as it was supposed to be a restful week, an afternoon by the pool. You guessed it – we spent the afternoon lazing round the pool, occasionally having a dip. That was the first hour anyway! After that it was back to the pub for the whole squad. You did not have to drink but you all had to be together. My room partner for the week was one of the scousers in the squad, John Doolan. He was the life and soul of the party and Kingy and John were at each other all week. The banter between them was as good as I have known, but a couple of times it went near the limit. Keith Haslam had gone over with his young family to Magaluf but wisely chose to stay at another hotel, a bit more luxurious, down the road. After our evening meal that day Keith ventured out to our hotel to have a few beers with his players. He obviously had not realised his team were five or six pints further down the line than him and he came in for some right stick, although it was all good-natured. Unbeknown to him, the lads had opened up a slate and it was in his name. When he went to leave the bar a couple of hours later he was a couple of hundred pounds lighter. He did not mind too much and at this time he really enjoyed mixing with the squad. We had drunk a lot, probably too much, but everybody behaved themselves and showed other people at the hotel, outside of our own party, the utmost respect. That was what I enjoyed most about that week. We spent the entire trip together in each other's pockets, but not once was there a cross word between us. The trip had served its purpose. We had had a break away from the normal surroundings of Mansfield, and we had got that togetherness back. All that was left now was to get back to England in one piece on the Friday afternoon, travel back to Mansfield, have a good night's sleep and prepare for the long trip down to Exeter for Saturday's game. The usual 48-hour drinking rule was stretched on that trip (very stretched!) and it was a relief to get to the airport and have a sit down for a couple of hours in the departure lounge before boarding the plane. The nightmare that Andy King was so worried about was about to happen. Delays – not by one hour but by nine!

One of the lads rang home and they told him that it was up on teletext that our flight had been delayed by an hour. Nobody believed him as nothing was showing up on the monitors inside the airport, and we thought he was just doing it to wind Kingy up. He swore blind it was true, but it did not matter much as we would still be back in Mansfield for about 6 o'clock. The hour passed and still there was no news at the airport. The same lad rang home and he came back saying that it was now showing as a three-hour delay. Now we were starting to panic a little, no one more so than Kingy himself. Over the next few hours the news got worse and worse, we were now facing getting on the plane nine hours later than was scheduled and were due to land at 1 o'clock in the morning. (The morning of a vital game at Exeter of all places, at least a five-hour drive from Mansfield on a coach!) The only way round it was for the club to send a coach to Birmingham airport, pick us up and then go straight to Exeter. We eventually arrived at the hotel at half past three, less than 12 hours to kick-off. When we finally had our pre-match meal at 12 o' clock, we assembled as a squad to have our team meeting. Looking at the state of us, Kingy did not know whether to laugh or cry. We were a right state, if only Exeter could have seen us then, less than three hours to kick-off. Kingy announced at our team meeting that he had not decided on what our team was going to be yet and that he would delay naming the team to as late as possible. When he sat us down in the changing room, he asked us to be honest about how we felt. If we said we did not feel fit to play he said it would be treated as a one-off and not held against us. Nobody dare say anything, but I knew for a fact the last thing I wanted to do that afternoon was play football and I would put money on it that every single player in that dressing room felt the same way. I tried to go and have a cold shower in order to wake me up before we went out to warm up, but Kingy said if I needed a shower then I was not fit to play. I have never been in such a quiet dressing room before a game and I think everybody was thinking the same thing, would it be obvious we had not prepared professionally for this game?

The game itself was bad. I think if we had been on top of our game we would have run out comfortable winners but this was not an ordinary football match for us. We were absolutely shattered – although entirely blameless – and it showed. We somehow managed to win the game 3–2 courtesy of a late goal from Iffy Onoura, who had earlier been sick on the pitch as the game was going on. We got into the dressing room after, a very relieved group of players. It had not been obvious to anybody watching, but as a squad we knew we had been lucky to get away with it. There was not a lot of celebrations. Kingy, unusually for him, was also very quiet and we all had a chat on the way home about how it must never happen again. The rest of that long journey home was spent trying to get some much-needed sleep and to prepare for Tuesday's massive home game against Rochdale. We were now fourth in the table and needed to keep our run going if we were to achieve automatic promotion. Chesterfield were in the last promotion spot and, despite having beaten them twice already that season, we were five points behind them. Could we do it?

The Rochdale game turned out to be a bittersweet game for me. Trailing 1–0, I slid in to get the equaliser. Just as I had made contact with the ball sliding it into the net, Rochdale's Shaun Reid (brother of Peter Reid) caught me right on the knee with his studs. It was accidental but I was in agony. I was stretchered off and deep down I knew my season was probably over. My contract was due to run out in the summer and even though Mansfield were going to offer me a new one, everybody knew it was probably the right time for me to leave for pastures new. Had this scuppered that idea? If my knee was as bad as it first appeared, would Mansfield even offer me a new deal? All those thoughts immediately go through your mind in that first hour after you suffer what looks like a serious injury. One thing that was nice, that I do not think happens so much now, is that mutual respect between players. For four seasons now Shaun Reid and I had literally kicked lumps out of each other, not once moaning to the referee. You would pick the other one up and if the referee looked like he was going to book the guilty party, the other one would say 'Leave it ref. It looked worse than it actually was, he must have slipped'. In those days both sets of players would end up in the players' lounge and have a drink together; I think that it is sad that this has gone out of the game. Nowadays you rarely get to know the opposition players, and after a game players just get straight on the bus. I think this is to the detriment of football, especially in the lower Leagues. Anyway, what was nice after the Rochdale game was that Shaun Reid took the time out to come and have a chat with me and wished me all the best in recovering from the injury. It was only an accident but probably twice a week he would ring to see how I was progressing. The day after we went to the hospital to see what the extent of the injury was. It was not good news. I had torn the medial ligaments (the ones on the inside) in my right knee and I would have to be in pot for about six weeks. That was my season over. A season that had promised so much had come to an abrupt end before the finale.

However, Barry Statham, the physio, was to come to the rescue. He worked tirelessly on the computer and on the phone to try and see if there was something that would save me going in a full-length plaster. If I could still do a bit of physical work in the six weeks and get a bit of movement in my legs, there might be a slim chance that if we reached the Play-offs I might be able to play a small part in them. Barry had managed to get his hands on a brace that I would be able to wear after two weeks in pot, so at least I could get that movement in my leg. He spoke to the specialist and he said that after three weeks I could start doing some work in the pool without my brace on. It was such a relief to get that bloody brace off, but in order to get some real physical work done in the pool I saw the return of the infamous bright yellow life jacket. I am not sure now which was worse!

We drew two and won one of our next three games, the win coming against Lincoln City, and saw the team scoring another six goals in the victory. They really missed me – they had scored 18 goals in the three games that I had missed due to injury! April was going to be the make or break month for our season. We were the form team in the League. In our last 17 games we had won 11, drawn three and lost three, scoring an amazing 49 goals and amassing a very impressive 36 points – definitely automatic promotion form.

April was a really disappointing month for us, picking up only seven points out of a possible 18. Our automatic promotion aspirations had gone but we were guaranteed a Play-off position, all that was left to sort out was who we would play against. It was between Chesterfield, Bury or Preston. Chesterfield had finished third, so over the season they had been the best team out of the four of us, but we had beaten them twice and I think if you had asked Chesterfield they would have preferred anybody but us over two legs. We had one last League game to play away at Hartlepool and if we won, our Play-off two-legged semi-final would be against Preston or Bury. If we lost we would play Chesterfield. We did not go out there to deliberately lose but having lost 3–1 we were not disappointed, and Kingy definitely was not disappointed to be facing the Spireites in the Play-offs. Read into that what you will.

I was by no means fully fit, far from it, but I would not have missed the games against Chesterfield for the world. We had just over a week to prepare for the first game, our home tie being first. I had eight days to really work on my fitness to get myself as close to full fitness as possible. While all of the other players rested up for a few days after the long slog of the season, I worked my socks off with Barry in the gym.

The game was on the Sunday morning, and there was a great atmosphere. Chesterfield started the game very strongly and we had the misfortune of Iffy Onoura being injured early in the game. Kingy gambled and threw me up front and after playing up there for about 10 minutes there was a break in play. Nicky Law, an experienced and hard centre-half who knew all the tricks in the book, asked me how my knee was and I told him that it was not too bad but I should not really be playing. He then, totally out of the blue, stamped squarely on my big toe and said 'That will make you forget about your f***ing knee!' For the rest of the game we went toe to toe, both of us giving as good as we got, but again neither of us moaning to the referee. That was how it was in those days. Another incident in the game that showed what Nicky could be like occurred with Simon Ireland. Nicky had got a massive throw in and Chesterfield had used it to great effect over the season. It really was better than a corner. We had done our homework and decided that if we placed somebody right on the touchline in front of where he was taking the throw-in, it would stop his follow through and force him to throw the ball a little higher in the air therefore losing some distance. That would make it easier to defend and stop one of their major attacking threats. It sounded brilliant, could we carry it out? Not exactly. We stood Simon in front of Nicky on the first throw-in and he did not throw it as far. However, he tried to follow through and headbutted Simon, knocking him to the floor. It was plainly deliberate but that was what Nicky was like. Nothing would stop him from trying to win a game – he was an absolute animal on the pitch. I was later a teammate of Nicky's at Chesterfield and he was great to play with. He was a leader and demanded very high standards of his teammates – very much like Steve Parkin was for us. The game ended 1–1 and we were fortunate to get a draw. However, had Chesterfield missed their chance? We were still confident of getting a victory at Saltergate in the second leg. It was all to play for and Wednesday 17 May 1995 will go down in the history of both clubs as a date never to be forgotten, but for totally different reasons.

This was to be my last-ever game for the Stags but obviously I did not realise it at the time, as I was still hoping to have my 'amber and blue swansong' at Wembley in the Play-off Final. We could not have had a better start to the second leg with me scoring after only about two minutes. After the game, Kingy said we had scored too early (?) but for that first half we played some really great stuff. Chesterfield had equalised against the run of play but Steve Wilkinson had restored our lead and we went in at half-time leading 2–1. It was a red-hot night and the two managers could not have looked more different. John Duncan had his customary tracksuit on, a manager's traditional attire, while Kingy had his best suit on complete with designer sunglasses. To wind the Spireites fans up even more he lit the biggest cigar possible, and when the Chesterfield supporters started to give him some stick walking off at half-time he just smiled at them and blew cigar smoke in their direction. This nearly caused a riot and when we came out after half-time the atmosphere was electric. Chesterfield were magnificent in the second half and brought the game towards us. They equalised and both teams had chances to win the game, especially us going close a couple of times in the dying minutes of normal time. However, disaster was not far away!

We had got caught up in the heat of the game and as a squad we lost our discipline. Not long into extra-time, we were reduced to nine men with Mark Peters and Kevin Lampkin sent off. We now had no chance. Chesterfield were well on top, playing hard but in a very disciplined manner. It should have been the other way around. If the scores had remained level at the end of extra-time we would have been going to Wembley for the Play-off Final courtesy of the away goals rule. Instead, we wanted to win the game by scoring loads of goals as we had done all season, playing attractive football along the way. Wrong time, wrong place. Chesterfield murdered us in extra-time to go on to win the game comfortably 5–2. I had inexplicably handled the ball to concede a penalty which Nicky Law converted to make it 3–2. Over the course of the season, Chesterfield thoroughly deserved to go to Wembley and over the two legs they had 'bullied' us. They went on to clinch promotion at the Twin Towers beating Bury 2–0 and all that was left now was for me to sort out my future.

I had managed to be selected for the Division Three select team at the PFA awards, a great honour which was voted for by your fellow professionals in the League that season. I had managed to win the club's Player of the Season a couple of seasons during my time at the Stags but I felt this was a big achievement for me and a great way to end a great season. I had decided that the Chesterfield game was going to be my last in the amber and blue but I had no idea where my career path was heading. I was about to have a couple of massive surprises, both good, one of them coming out of the blue!

Chapter Fifteen
Me and Becks

Mansfield had offered me a new contract, but they knew I was on my way out. They had done it out of courtesy for the service I had provided them over the previous four years, even though the offer they made would have put me still nowhere near being the top earner at the club. I have never been in football for the money, and it's a good job I was not when you are playing for Mansfield Town! My first contract in that promotion season of 1991–92 was a paltry £120 a week, and when I left Mansfield I was on £300 a week. I appreciated the help Mansfield had given me, they had given me my big chance in football, and I had repaid them with 29 goals in about 150 games. I had loved my time with the Stags, but it was now time to move on to a bigger stage. There were rumours of interest from bigger clubs, a return to Forest, a move to Luton and talk of a move to Sheffield Wednesday but there was no definite bid made. I was not unduly concerned at this stage, I was sure something would happen and it was just a matter of being patient. All I was interested in was having a well-earned break and giving my knees a much-needed rest. I was thinking about going away for a break with a few of the lads but I would just play it by ear. My previous experiences of going away with the lads on holiday were that they never went according to plan!

Towards the end of every season, the talk in Brenda and Colin's was about us all going away somewhere abroad. Our first venture away was to the then buzzing resort of Kavoz. For the first few days it was heaven. The eight of us shared two bedrooms, four in each and it was pure bliss. It was red-hot and so relaxing (during the day!), just what the doctor ordered at the end of a long football season. We had booked the holiday for two weeks and on about the sixth night I walked back to the apartments after a night out. I was the first back and did not even put the light on, instead just getting straight into bed. I am not sure why but I sensed something was wrong, the room did not feel right. Had I had one too many? I shot up in bed, the room seemed empty enough. It was empty! Not only was I alone but the bags, suitcases and clothes had all gone! I rushed upstairs but their room was fine. Out of the eight lads who went, four of us (me included) had not got anything left apart from the clothes he was in. I went back down the street where the lads were still in all the pubs and clubs and told them about our break-in. I do not know whether it was the drink but they did not seem that bothered. For the rest of the holiday the 'clothes-less four' borrowed off the others and we enjoyed the rest of the trip. That was our first misfortune.

The year after, eight had become three. Myself, Darren Ward and Alex Sykes decided we would go on a last minute holiday. The idea was that we would all go to Sleaford with our suitcases packed, go to the travel agent in the afternoon, book a holiday for the next day, have a night out in Sleaford and then travel to the airport for our holiday the morning after. Sounds easy! It did not quite work out that way. We went into the travel agents and it was a choice of two holidays. The first choice was a fortnight in named accommodation in Gran Canaria. The second choice was un-named which meant we could end up in the lively resort of Kos or a quiet fishing island called Kalymnos. Wardy and I wanted the guarantee of a lively holiday but Sykesy was not so sure. He would rather pay a lot less and take a chance. The travel agent talked him into it saying he had booked this holiday hundreds of times and never knew of anybody going to Kalymnos. Sykesy pleaded with us to go with the cheaper option and reluctantly we agreed. We set off for Newcastle the next day, got to the airport and got into the holiday spirit. We had a couple of beers in the bar and then a couple more on the plane, and when we arrived at the Greek airport Sykesy was a little worried; would his gamble pay off? We waited for our bags and then the moment of truth arrived. The travel rep came up to us and asked us what name our holiday was under. 'Holland' I replied. She looked down her list and it was like it was in slow motion. Eventually she said 'You need to be on Bus G, going to Kos Town'. I have never seen anybody so relieved and happy as Alex Sykes at that moment. He was dancing about saying 'I told you, I bloody told you! You should be thanking me. I have saved you £300!!'

We boarded Bus G and it was like a party bus. The music was blaring out and we could not believe our luck. Sykesy was absolutely buzzing and did not look the slightest bit bothered when the same travel rep came down the bus. 'Mr Holland,' she said, 'I have made a mistake. You are on Bus J going to Kalymnos.' 'Yeah, good one Sykesy', I laughed. I thought he had had a quiet word with her to play a practical joke on me and Wardy. I looked at Sykesy and immediately realised this was not a joke. He was white! We had to leave and try and find Bus J. Much to the amusement of everybody on the 'party bus', we waited next to the road while they went past us. The three of us had not said a word. Sykesy was still white. It got worse! A mini bus arrived and took us about two miles to a harbour where we were dropped off and told to wait, on our own, for the boat to Kalymnos. The boat arrived after about an hour, well I say boat it was more like a little fishing vessel. We did not know whether to laugh or cry! The deck of the boat was wet through and the sea was choppy. By the time we arrived we were all as white as Alex. The place was deserted and the beach was a real sight with broken sunbeds and seaweed everywhere. This was like 'holiday hell'! We made the most of the two weeks but I can remember actually babysitting for a couple so that they could go out for a romantic meal. Not the holiday I thought we would be having!

Therefore, I was reluctant to book somewhere the next year, due to my past experiences and not yet knowing where my future lay. I am glad I did not. I was at my mum and dad's when I got a phone call out of the blue. Mum shouted it was Andy King on the phone, and I went upstairs to take the call. I thought he would be keeping me up to date with any interest from other clubs, but he had rung to say I had been selected for the England Under-21 squad to play in the Toulon tournament. I told him to stop messing about (not quite as polite!), but he swore it was true. He was as excited as me. He read me the letter and it started to sound a bit more believable. I was in a bit of a daze and he congratulated me on what, for a Division Three player, was a massive surprise and achievement. You never expect to be selected for a national team while playing in the lower Leagues, but it just shows you never know who is watching, something I always preach to young footballers. Kingy said he would post the letter to my parents' house, but he gave me some sound advice before putting the phone down. He said I was now in the shop window and that I would be playing on the international stage with better players but also against much better players as well. He told me to enjoy the next couple of days, but to come down to the ground and do a bit of training with him. I really appreciated that, after all he was on his holidays and he knew that the following season I would no longer be his player, but, typical of the man, he did this out of his love for football and Andy if you are reading this, I really appreciate it. (And as you kept saying, I was never as good as you anyway!)

I rang everybody I could think of. 'Who else is in the squad?' they all asked. I could not tell them and I was not bothered. All I wanted was for that letter to drop on the mat and to find out the arrangements. The following morning it arrived, with the three lions badge on the envelope. In the squad were Dean Richards, David Beckham and Phil Neville among others and we would be playing in a group which comprised of Brazil, Malaysia and Angola. BRAZIL! I had to report to a hotel near Heathrow airport at 4pm on 3 June, and I can remember making that journey feeling very nervous and unsure of what to expect. Could I really expect to compete against these countries, deep down I was worried about whether I should really be going there at all. All the other players in the squad were from big clubs, how would they feel playing with somebody from a club that they did not know anything about? I need not have worried!

I arrived at the hotel feeling very, very nervous. I did not have a clue what to expect. I was about two hours early, but there was absolutely no chance of me getting off on the wrong foot by being late. There were a few FA people milling about and a chap with a clipboard came up to me and asked my name (I bet he did not have to ask Beckham). I was getting more and more nervous by the second and he told me my room number and that my 'roomie' was going to be Dean Richards, a footballer who had just moved to Wolverhampton Wanderers for £1.85 million. I can remember getting to the room and thinking there was no chance Dean would have a clue who I was. After about an hour Dean came in and I could not believe the size of him. He was 6ft 2in of pure muscle. He was a really nice bloke and we went out for our evening meal where we met the rest of the squad and all the members of staff. There seemed to be more officials than players! Ray Harford (ex-Blackburn manager) was the manager, his assistant was Ray Lewington (assistant manager at Fulham), Peter Bonetti was the goalkeeper coach and the physio was Dave Galley (ex-Liverpool, now at Wigan). Clare Tomlinson (ex-Sky Sports) was the FA Media Officer at the time and she was the person who you had to get permission from if any member of the press wanted to speak to you. It was very professional. We flew out to France on the Sunday and I was actually sat between Dean and Beckham, who seemed very level-headed for all the hype around him at the time. I roomed with Dean again and we had our first training session on the Sunday evening. I was absolutely awful. The pace of the training was frightening and I was out of my depth, I have never felt so out of place on a football field. I can remember Nicky Forster being so quick, they all looked the part while all I could think of was what the squad would be thinking 'What the hell is he doing here?'

I got back to my room and felt so low. I think Dean realised this and tried to lighten the mood a bit. Ray Lewington pulled me to one side after the evening meal that night and asked me how I felt. I told him and he said, 'You are here on merit. You know what your game is all about, don't try and be somebody else. Train as you play. If there is a ball there to be won, go in and win it'. That little chat with Ray changed my mindset and I could not wait to redeem myself the next day, the day before the first game which was against Brazil of all teams. I was like a man possessed the following day, really getting stuck in and upsetting a few squad members with some hard tackles. After one such tackle on Forster I can remember him giving me a bit of a mouthful, but Lewington told him to get on with it. I just wanted to play a part against Brazil, even if it was for a couple of minutes, to say I had played against probably the most well-known footballing nation in world football.

We were to train on the morning of the Brazil game, just to run through some team shape and a few set plays. Before the session started we sat down and Ray Harford named the team. I was to start in the centre of midfield playing alongside Beckham. I had made the team.

I have never felt as proud on a football pitch as I did that night on the 6 June 1995. There I was, representing my country against Brazil. I was determined to enjoy the occasion. We started like world beaters and after about five minutes we won a corner that Beckham swung in. I met it perfectly and crashed a header against the cross bar. That was as close as we came to scoring, as for the remaining 80 minutes or so we were given a lesson on how to play football. They were unbelievable and passed the ball around for fun. We eventually lost the game 2–0 but it was an honour to be on that pitch that night. Juninho and Leonardo were the stars on show for Brazil, but technically they were all head and shoulders above us. I had thoroughly enjoyed my Under-21 debut and to play alongside such great players was a dream come true. You could tell at this time that Beckham was a quality player and had a great future in the game but you could not see the 'superstar' in him that would make him one of the most recognisable males in the world (if not the most) over the next decade. He was just one of the lads.

We now had to win our next two games to qualify from the group and reach a place in the last four. We did this comfortably, beating Malaysia 2–0 and Angola 1–0 respectively, and we were to face France in the semi-finals. I had settled into the squad really well and played 90 minutes in both games. I was the eldest in the squad, nearing my 22nd birthday, and I was put in charge of the money when Ray Harford decided to let the squad go out for an hour one evening after our meal. This was the only time we were allowed out of the hotel and we went down to the harbour area in Toulon. All the lads sat down outside a bar and the waitress came over. The lads had a beer but only half a pint. After we had all finished, I asked if anybody else wanted another one. Beckham said he would have a pint but no one else was bothered. So my most famous story about having a pint with Beckham in a bar overlooking the harbour in Toulon is true, but there were also 20 other footballers there which I sometimes forget to mention! Nevertheless it is a story to tell the grandkids one day. I doubt somehow whether David Beckham will be telling the same story about having a drink with Paul Holland, but never mind.

On the afternoon of the France game I was laid in my room when Andy King rang. He said that a club had made a bid for me which the club had accepted, and that the manager was flying out to watch me in the game that night and wanted to chat to me after about a possible move. I was desperate to find out who the club were but Kingy would not tell me.

I lined up in midfield, again with Beckham, and after about 10 minutes I slipped on the wet surface. I felt a twinge in my groin but obviously I wanted to carry on. However, it got worse very quickly and I had to give way. My last ever England appearance. A young French player ran the show that night, a young man called Robert Pires, and he masterminded a 2–0 victory.

I sat in the dressing room after the game thinking that the manager who was interested in signing me might be on his way back to England having not seen a lot. Ray Harford sat us all down and thanked us for our efforts and wished us all the best in our careers. The lads all showered and I waited for them, having already got washed and changed, when Ray came in and said somebody wanted to see me at the end of the tunnel. I went out and saw the mystery manager waiting there. Dave Bassett, the Sheffield United manager was there along with his secretary. He said he would like to have a chat but somewhere private, so we went out to the car he had hired. It was absolutely throwing it down and there I was discussing a £250,000 move to Sheffield United in the front seat of a hired Nissan Micra in a car park in Cannes. I had asked Ray Harford to come out and listen to what Harry (Dave Bassett) had to say, in order that I did not miss anything of importance. There was not much of a discussion. Bassett said that this was what he was offering and that I would not get a penny more. I was not even listening to the money on offer, I just wanted to play for a big club. We shook hands on the deal and it was agreed that night I was to play for Sheffield United.

The lads were sat on the team bus waiting to get back to the hotel and when I got on they all cheered and clapped and shook my hand. I had started out the trip as a Division Three player and ended it as a Division One player. I had agreed to travel to Sheffield a few days later to officially sign, what I had not banked on was the sheer size of Sheffield United FC. I could not wait to get started!

Chapter Sixteen
Sharpening the Blades

I travelled down to Sheffield to sign for the Blades on the 14 June 1995. The size of the stadium and the professionalism intimidated me a great deal. I was met by Andy Pack, the media officer, and he immediately made me feel at home. It was his job to give me a tour of the ground and to show me the club's training facilities. I could not believe they were making such a fuss of me, even going as far to show me nice areas to live in. All morning he kept mentioning the afternoon's press conference and that they were going to make quite a big thing of it because I was likely to be the only signing that summer. When we went back to the ground at dinner time I went in and met the chairman, Reg Brealey, and discussed the contract. I was not particularly bothered about the money side of things as I just wanted the chance to pit myself against better teams and better players. I signed the contract and then the afternoon was spent doing interviews and having photographs taken in various Blades paraphernalia. I could not get over the sheer number of press people there; I was not used to it. The Mansfield press I had got to know personally and would consider people like John Lomas (*Mansfield Chad*) and Simon Mapletoft (ex-*Notts Evening Post*) as friends. Before leaving Bramall Lane I had a quick meeting with Dave Bassett, or Harry as he demanded to be called (not gaffer or boss!), and he told me in no uncertain terms that now that 'all the shit' was out of the way the important stuff was soon to start. He said a letter would be sent out letting me know the arrangements for the start of pre-season training and the tour of Norway which had been arranged for a couple of weeks into the schedule. I left Bramall Lane that day feeling 10 feet tall. I had signed for a big football club, a very big club, and I could not wait to get started. One thing I was determined to do was have a couple of weeks away on holiday to rest up for what was sure to be a testing pre-season.

I can remember feeling as nervous as I had ever been as I travelled into Sheffield for that first day of pre-season training. Not so much nervous about the training itself but about meeting my new teammates, many of them established premiership players who had been involved a year earlier in their relegation from the Premier League. I had seen many of them before on television, either playing for United or plying their trade for their respective countries, but nothing can prepare you for that first morning at work, whether it is in football or in any job. I arrived really early and was the first player in the changing room. Players arrived over the next hour or so and many came over and introduced themselves which is always a help – you never know which way is best to tackle your first day in a new dressing room, you do not want to come over too cocky and confident but on the other hand you do not want to come over as shy and intimidated. Changing rooms are often very cruel places and first impressions count for a lot. I had been warned by Harry that there was quite a lot of unrest in the dressing room and that a lot of senior players were unhappy with new faces coming in. Cheers! One thing that I could not believe was the amount of players in the first-team squad. At Mansfield I had been used to a squad of roughly 20 but in the meeting with Harry on that first morning there were 46 professional players! A couple of United players who I really admired having watched a lot of their games were Alan Kelly, the Republic of Ireland goalkeeper, and Glyn Hodges, the experienced Welsh midfielder. I can remember being in awe of them when I was introduced – I had only shown promise in the lowest League of all while they had played at the top level, both domestically and internationally. However, they were great with me and I really hit it off with them from day one. Another familiar face in the dressing room that morning was Billy Mercer, the ex-Rotherham United goalkeeper who had moved to Bramall Lane the previous season. Billy was a great lad and I had had a few drinks with him a few years earlier in Gran Canaria when Rotherham and Mansfield were celebrating their respective promotions. Little did we know at that time that we were to spend the rest of our playing careers at the same clubs. We went on to play together at Sheffield United, Chesterfield and Bristol City. If that sounds strange, something a bit stranger still is that we both retired due to injury within a couple of months of each other. We were great friends on and off the pitch and we still are to this day. We have been through many ups and probably even more downs in our careers but we have always been there for each other.

One thing that was new to the squad for that pre-season was the introduction of a sports scientist, brought in to take pre-season training. His job was to make sure the lads were working to their optimum and not working too hard or not doing enough physical work. Every single player had a watch and chest band that measured your pulse rate which meant that Jez (the sports scientist) could check each player individually and see where they were fitness-wise. He was from the new school of thought which believed that you did not have to do the hard slog of long distance runs to get your fitness up, but that it should be done using all the new scientific methods. That pre-season we did not do a run above 15 minutes. I can understand all the new methods and I must admit it was nice not to have to do those mind-numbing five or six-mile runs, but I do not think that pre-season was anywhere near hard enough. I had been used to working my nuts off in pre-season at Mansfield and, even though I hated those long runs, you certainly felt the benefit of them come the first game of the season. However, who was I to argue with the people in the know. Another massive difference in the pre-season was the advice given by the specialist staff in the amount of fluids and food required to refuel the body after training sessions. Water, water and more water was the 'in fluid' while the food was hundreds and hundreds of boxes of Jaffa cakes. I have never seen anything like it. I always enjoyed the odd Jaffa cake before but by the end of my spell at Bramall Lane, I was bloody sick of the sight of that blue and orange box.

Usually at a football club you have your own little driving school where you have three or four lads who travel in to the ground together and then go on to wherever you are training that day. There is usually a lot of banter flying around within the group about whose turn it is to drive and whose turn it is for the sandwiches and the like. That is one thing that you dread on your first day at a club. You have driven on your own into the club and everybody else seems to have already got their 'driving school' sorted and you feel the odd one out. That is when the captain or one of the senior professionals usually comes to the fore and sorts the 'new boy' out. Glyn Hodges told me to jump in with him and when we went out to the car park I could not get over the class of car there. I was the first to arrive so when I arrived in my J-reg Escort there were no other cars in the car park. It was different now with all the new BMWs and Mercedes everywhere, not just the senior pros owning these but also some of the first-year pros. That seemed strange to me, a little bit 'big time' if you like. There was one clapped-out Mercedes Estate that looked a little bit out of place next to all the other cars. That was Glyn's second car. He did not want to put miles on his 'first' car so he bought this car that had a remarkable resemblance to the car out of *Ghostbusters*. In Glyn's car school there was a player called David Tuttle, a Cockney centre-half who looked a lot older than he actually was, and the Norwegian legend Jostein Flo. They soon made me feel at home and it did not take me long to work out that Tutts (Dave Tuttle) was the joker in the squad, but he also seemed to be the one who was at the butt of everybody else's jokes. He loved it! As long as he was at the centre of everything he was not bothered. We all got talking and I found out that both Glyn and Tutts lived not far from me so they said I could travel in with them which was a relief to me. It was nice that they had taken an interest in their new signing; it would have been easy for them with the size of the squad to have left it for someone else. Being such a big squad, it was impossible to talk to everybody on that first day but one thing that I could sense was that there were little cliques everywhere. There did not seem to be that togetherness that I had been used to at Mansfield but that was impossible due to the vast size of the squad. One player who looked more miserable than most was Simon Tracey, the goalkeeper who I later worked with at Mansfield. (He never changed!) I think he was fed up with his limited opportunities at the club, due in the main to Alan Kelly being a world-class goalkeeper, and he was not going to be the one who showed the new boy the ropes. There were a few unhappy faces, as you get in any dressing room when you are not playing, but you can still welcome new lads to the club. I obviously got to know Simon a lot more over the years and even though we never really hit it off, every man to himself. Alan and Glyn could not have been more different. They could remember themselves how difficult it was to be the new boy at a club, especially when you have come from the lower Leagues. People don't know what you have done in the past, and you have to earn their respect straight away. Sink or swim comes to mind as does the phrase 'a little fish in a big pond' rather than 'a big fish in a little pond'.

That first session was really light, a big surprise to what I was used to. I believe George Foster did not see it as a good first day of pre-season training unless he had made a couple of players sick due to the sheer hard physical work he made us do. All we had done was a 15-minute run at our own pace and a few stretches. Jostein did not seem to mind this, and although his English was not brilliant he put himself out to come over and introduce himself and welcome me to the club. We climbed back into the Ghostbuster van to take us back to the ground. It was a red-hot day and the windows were open. I could smell smoke coming into the car and wondered where it was coming form. I looked over and quickly found out the answer. There was Jostein puffing away on a cigarette. We had not even got out of the training ground's car park. He gave me a wink and carried on. After another couple of cigarettes we got back to the ground and were given our instructions to report to Don Valley Stadium at 5 o' clock that day. That raised a few eyebrows, but when you are the new lad you just keep your head down and get on with it. We would be doing our weights and then be given our own personalised weights programmes: very professional. One thing I was keen to work on was to strengthen my shoulders, particularly my right shoulder which used to dislocate every time I landed awkwardly. The ligaments were that loose that I used to put it back in place myself. Barry Statham, the physio at Mansfield, had shown me how to do it myself, and I had lost count of the number of times I had gone behind the goal in front of the North Stand at Field Mill to crunch it back in. I was determined to get it strengthened so that I did not require yet more surgery to tighten the lax ligaments.

The first week of pre-season passed fairly quickly and with not too much hard work! The second week was to be spent on a break in Norway, although break might be the wrong word. It was to consist of training, training and more training. If it was not training, it was games. I think we had about four games in nine days. The squad had been trimmed down to about 20 professionals travelling so there were many unhappy footballers left in Sheffield, among them Simon Tracey and John Gannon. I went on to work with Ganns at Mansfield (as with Simon) and at that time at Sheffield I think there was a bit of rivalry between us, not nasty stuff but Harry had bought me in to probably provide competition in the same position as Ganns. I travelled to Norway and Ganns did not. I am not sure that went down too well at the time but we never had any problems. I thought Ganns was a quality player and I would have loved to have had the chance to play alongside him regularly but that was never the case. He had a really dry sense of humour, and was really quiet until you got to know him. Later, when we worked together at Mansfield, we had our differences, but when you are working with someone you are bound to have those. I have not spoken to John since he left Mansfield, but that is down to other events as you will read later. I hope one day we can shake hands and put the past behind us, as a lot of it was unnecessary and everybody was to blame. However, back to the story…there I was sat in the airport ready to go to Norway, a first visit to Scandinavia, and still not sure who was to be my roommate for the next nine days. It was to be Tutts. I have never met anybody with such peculiar living habits in all of my life and I would put money on nobody else having done so either. He is a strange guy!

Chapter Seventeen
Casper

David Tuttle was an absolute legend but also an absolute nutter! Tutts is one of the funniest people I have ever met but the funny thing is he does not even try to be. He comes over as, in the nicest way possible, not the brightest but I am sure it is all an act. On the flight to Oslo Harry announced who would be rooming with who. When Tutt's name was read out, all the lads were on tenterhooks. It was not that Tutts was disliked, far from it, but his room antics were of legendary status. I did not know quite why they were, but I was soon to find out. When my name got read out as Tutt's roommate there was uproar on the plane and cries of 'Unlucky Dutch' and 'Make sure you sleep with one eye open!' The 'Dutch' shout was an unusual one for me. All through my Mansfield career, my nickname had been 'Jools' after Jools Holland, the famous jazz musician. However, from day one at Sheffield it was to be Dutch for obvious reasons, even though it is amazing how many people over the years have asked. We landed in Oslo and then boarded the smallest plane I had ever seen to take us to Northern Norway to a town called Trondheim. The hotel was nice and Tutts and I soon settled down in the room and I wondered what all the fuss had been about. He seemed fine. There was even a cup of tea waiting when I got out of the shower. We went down for our evening meal and a quick team meeting to find out what the arrangements for the next day were. We were told we had to be up and ready to train at 7.30am sharp so an early night was in store for the whole squad. That was when the legend that surrounded Tutt's nightly antics came to light.

Tutts can talk! For an hour or so we talked, or should I say he talked? The stories he told were hilarious, from jumping out of a toilet in a Superman outfit to meet his wife's work colleagues for the first time, to going in the kitchen where he and his wife were entertaining (having a dinner party for a couple who were really into their classical music) and coming out in an inflatable Pavarotti costume. The stories were fascinating but I wanted to get some sleep ready for an early start the next morning. I said 'Goodnight' and switched my light off. I closed my eyes but I could still hear Tutts fumbling around in his suitcase for something. Nothing too unusual there then. Then I heard a few short bursts of air as if he was blowing something up. I shot up in bed and found myself coughing and spluttering. I struggled to open my eyes but could just about make out a figure – a white outline that resembled a ghost exactly in the shape of Tutts. I reached for the light and could not believe what was in front of my eyes. There he stood stark naked (he was six foot three but by no means a muscle man) covered from head to toe in talcum powder about a cm thick on his body. I asked him what the bloody hell he was doing, trying my hardest not to laugh. He replied saying he could not go to sleep unless he was covered in Johnson's Baby Powder as it helped him relax. He opened his suitcase and without a word of a lie, there were at least 10 big talcum powder containers in it. Through my tears, I asked him how long he had been doing it and he said for at least 20 years. Johnson's have got a lot to thank Tutts for. Not only Johnson's but also Vic's Rub Vapours. I also found out that before every single training session and every single game he took part in he would cover both legs, from groin to toe, in Vic's. His reason – to make his legs breathe. I had heard it all. The room was like a thick fog and literally everything was covered in talc. I somehow managed to get to sleep, and when I went down to breakfast the following morning all eyes were on the door. As soon as I entered the whole place erupted. They were obviously all aware of the talc routine and it was always funny when a new lad joined the club to see his face after one night with Tutts. It was a good way of breaking the ice (or clearing the smog) with the group. It is always a help I think to go on a pre-season trip as it gets the new lads involved and you get to know each other quickly. The training was going well and the first game of the trip ended in victory although it has to be said the opposition were very poor. I played for about an hour and did alright, so it was nice to get that first game out of the way and show your new teammates what your game was all about. In the dressing room after the game Harry sat us all down and said that when we got back to the hotel the time was our own and if we wanted to go out and have a few beers that was fine, although there was to be a curfew of midnight. That was fine. The majority of the lads agreed to meet in the reception of the hotel at about 8pm so I thought it would be a good opportunity to get to know some of my new teammates over a few pints when everybody was relaxed and the 'ball was away'. Tutts and I were the first down to the bar followed by a few others so I said I would buy the first round. Oh my god! I ordered one pizza for six and six pints of lager expecting it to be around £20. The waiter came back and put the bill on the table. I looked at it and could not believe my eyes – £58! I tried not to look surprised, as if I knew it would be that much. The last thing you want your new mates to think is that you are a tight arse. We soon left the hotel and went to a few bars around the hotel. I could not believe the attention Jostein was getting. He was a national hero and everywhere we went he was surrounded by fans. The press soon found out and every bar we came out of, there were cameras flashing at Jostein. He did not seem a bit bothered as he came out of each bar, a bottle of beer in one hand and a cigarette in the other. Tutts was on form as usual. He had given his first pint away halfway down, citing the reason that 'he felt himself going' but the way he was acting you would have thought he had had five or six pints. I am always amazed how people can act so relaxed and not be frightened to make a fool of themselves when they have not had a drink. I am always relaxed without a pint but not prepared to make a fool of myself without one! I have my limits.

The one thing that amazed me about Trondheim was that at the time of the year we were there (July), it was 24-hour sunlight. It was really strange coming out of bars at 11 o'clock at night into brilliant sunshine. We ended up going into a night club around 11, a little bit pointless I thought because we had to be back at the hotel in less than an hour. After a couple more pints I was in a predicament. It was about 11.45 and it was about a 10-minute walk back to the hotel. There was no way the six or seven lads who were left were going to be back in the hotel in time so they had decided that if they all stuck together and went back there all together a bit later, they would still get a rollicking but it would be better a group roasting rather than an individual one. Hence my predicament. It was my first night out with them. Did I stay with the lads and risk my first tongue lashing by Harry (which were legendary) or risk losing face with the few lads left? I decided as I had only just joined the club that I better get back before the curfew. I did my usual trick: I left my pint and said that I was going to the toilet and quickly made for the exit when they were not looking. I could make my excuses the next day. Outside it was still brilliant sunshine so there was no way you could sneak back into the hotel. I got back into the reception area with about a minute to spare. I expected there to be one of the coaching staff there ticking the lads in as they got back but no one was in sight. The staff had gone out for a quiet meal so they must have been tucked up in their beds, or so I thought. Tutts had already gone back to the room and was fast asleep, again looking like Casper, and the room resembled a scene from a Christmas Wonderland with a light sprinkling of white powder over every possible surface.

At breakfast the next morning I found myself getting a bit of good-natured stick about leaving the lads in the club. They said they were only having a drink to help me get to know each of them better. The excuses footballers make to have a night out! It made me laugh when they said that they tried to sneak back into the hotel at about 3am, three hours late, all of them keeping look out for one another. When they looked behind them, down the road they had just come, about 300 yards behind them were the members of staff stumbling about, obviously the worse for drink. That was what life was like at the Blades. Work hard, play hard was the name of the game.

The rest of the trip passed by, the games were won and I felt much better as I settled well into the routine both on and off the pitch. Having got back to England, the final Saturday of pre-season was a game against United's biggest rivals Sheffield Wednesday. A chance to play in the Sheffield Steel Derby was a big thing for me and as we ran out the atmosphere was electric. Harry had decided to play with three centre halves for the first time in pre-season, something the lads found a bit odd especially with it being our last game before the new season kicked-off. I found myself playing as the central man in the back three, a position I enjoyed playing as I thought it was a breeze. Anybody with half a football brain and an ability to organise people on a football pitch should be able to play there. We ended up getting beaten but Wednesday were a very good team at that time. I managed to get the Man of the Match award and even though we had been beaten, optimism was still high at the club as it is at every club before a new season. However, with what I had seen and with the players at Harry's disposal, people believed, and I believed, that promotion was something that could easily be achieved. On paper we had by far the strongest squad in the division. I could not wait for the new season to get under way, with the chance at the end of it of clinching promotion and achieving my dream of playing at the highest level in the Premier League against the likes of Manchester United and Liverpool. How wrong we all were!

Chapter Eighteen
Chesterfield Beckons

The first game of the season was a tough one away at Watford. As was usual in every season the first game is always played in red-hot sunshine, but this day was hotter than I have ever known on a football field. The temperatures were in the mid-90s but it felt even hotter than that. Pre-season friendlies are very useful in getting you prepared, but there is nothing like that first game of the season for getting the adrenalin going, especially if it is your debut. There is no better feeling as a footballer knowing that you have got pre-season training out of the way and the real business of League football is about to get underway. I felt fine fitness-wise but you can never tell how fit you are in terms of playing until that first game. I had a nagging doubt in the back of my mind that as a squad we had not done enough work fitness-wise through pre-season but we would soon find out. Jez, the sports scientist, was in the dressing room before the game saying how important it was to get our fluids in. The amount he was asking us to drink was unbelievable, at least three litres of water in that last hour before the game. Stupidly I did not feel comfortable doing this as I would feel bloated and too full with all that water floating around in my body. I admit to tipping some of my water away, having pretended to have drunk the suggested amount of water. Was I ever to pay for this!

The game started and we were well on top in the early stages. However, Watford scored against the run of play and to make matters worse they were starting to get a real foothold in the game. We were hanging on until we equalised again against the run of play (it is amazing how many times that happens in football). The game was being played at a frenetic pace with not much actual football being played, but no quarter being asked for and no quarter being given. This is what football was all about, and no amount of pre-season friendlies can prepare you for that. I was doing okay, working hard and getting my fair share of tackles in (most of them fair!) but I had the worst headache ever. I felt red-hot, as if I was overheating, but I was shivering as if I was freezing. We conceded again to go in at half-time trailing 2–1. Harry went mad at half-time and told Jez, who was handing out the customary bottles of water, to leave, but nowhere near as politely as that. After the roasting I went to the toilets and proceeded to be sick. I felt shocking but there was no way I wanted to come off. Derek French (Frenchy) the physio came through and said that I had better come off, but I told him not to say anything. There was no way I wanted people to think of me as a bottling out, so Frenchy went and filled a big towel full of ice and put it over my head just to try and get my temperature down a little. For the rest of the interval I stayed in the toilet on my own, being sick a few more times. I should have come off but you can get stuck with the reputation of throwing it in when things get a bit tough if you give in, and there was no way that was going to happen. I was shaking violently but managed to get out on the field for the second half without anybody apart from Frenchy knowing about how rough I felt. It did not last long. Midway through the second half I was brought off and for the first time on a football field I was relieved to be substituted. We ended up losing the game 2–1 and after the game Frenchy called for Watford's club doctor to give me the once over. He said I had got severe dehydration and sunstroke and that I should not have even contemplated going out for the second half. I joked that Frenchy had forced me to, but after the glucose drinks and sachets he gave me I was soon feeling a lot better. I was disappointed to have lost the game but delighted to have made my debut for United.

The season had not started well and we also lost our next game at home to Tranmere Rovers with John Aldridge in outstanding form. Surely this was an early season blip and we would be all right in our next game away at Oldham Athletic. Things failed to improve in this game on a club or a personal level. Brian Gayle got sent off early on and I landed awkwardly on the dodgy shoulder and dislocated it again for the umpteenth time. This time felt a little worse than the times before so there was no chance of continuing. We lost the game and also lost the next two games, which I missed due to the shoulder, so after five games and five losses we were rooted to the bottom of the League with no points on the board. Unacceptable and definitely not what was expected, and the fans were not happy.

I came back as substitute for the Norwich game, our sixth of the season. The first half was a fairly tepid affair until the half-time whistle went and then all hell broke loose in the players' tunnel. There were punches being thrown and it resulted in Bryan Gunn, the Norwich goalkeeper, being sent off at half-time. I had never seen anything like it before. One thing Harry instilled in all of his players was that if one of your players was involved in an altercation you all waded in with everything you had got. Whether you agreed with this or not, it did not matter. If you wanted to be in Harry's team you did it. Simple. If you would not, you did not play.

We went on to win the game 2–1, would this kick-start our season? It certainly looked like it had done as we followed up this victory with another home win against Charlton Athletic 2–0. We had turned the corner and everyone at the club was looking forward to our televised local derby against Barnsley, always a tough place to go at the best of times, but when you are struggling at the wrong end of the table and it is a local derby it makes it even more so. I had come on in the second half against both Norwich and Charlton and done okay so I was hoping for a starting place against the Tykes (Barnsley) but had to settle for a place on the bench again. I was not too disheartened, I was just pleased to be involved in any capacity, whatever it was. We were dreadful first half and found ourselves 2–0 down at half-time. The fans were not happy and they let us know in no uncertain terms. I got the shout that I was coming on and I thought at the time what a great chance to make a difference and impress a few people. I had my best game for United and we managed to come back and force a 2–2 draw. A good away point especially as we had done it from 2–0 down.

Harry totally changed the team for our next League Cup tie at home to Bury, and it showed. We were awful. We managed to scrape a 2–1 victory, but Harry let us have it both barrels blazing. He had the whole squad in the next day to watch the video of the entire game. Not good viewing! Had I done enough to keep my place against Huddersfield for our next game, again away, again televised and again a local derby? I probably deserved a chance to start after my performance in the Barnsley game the previous weekend but I had not done myself many favours against Bury, but neither had many others. When the team got read out on the Saturday (it was a Sunday game) I had got my place back: I was starting.

The Huddersfield game was a typical local derby, a lot of effort and blood and guts but not much football played. My type of game probably. Midway through the first half, I went to challenge for a header with Simon Bullock, Huddersfield's midfielder. Simon's playing style was very similar to that of mine; he was very physical and did not give or ask for any quarter. I always enjoyed going up against players like that, because there was never any moaning to the referee or anything underhand going on (not usually anyway!) It was just two men battling to come out on top in their respective tussle. Anyway, we went up for this header, Simon trying to flick the ball backwards and me trying to head it forwards. He got the flick, and flicked his head back forcibly straight into the lower half of my face. There was blood everywhere. My nose was splattered across my face (yet again) but it was my mouth that was the worst hit. I had bit my tongue and both lips with my teeth somehow going through all three. The referee called Frenchy on and, as he went about his job of clearing the blood up, he was killing himself laughing saying that I looked like Bubba out of Forrest Gump. You never got a lot of sympathy out of Frenchy. I soon got cleaned up and the game carried on. My lips were becoming bigger and bigger as the second half went on and it felt as if my bottom lip was trailing along the ground ('Nothing new there' I can hear Clare saying!) This did not matter in the end as we held on to get a tremendous 2–0 victory, with Jostein getting on the score sheet. I loved playing with Jostein because he knew exactly where you were making your runs and more often than not found you with a deft little flick off his forehead. The optimism was back and the Blades were back on the way up the table. However, the little looks I did have had definitely taken a turn for the worse as I left the ground that evening. I looked as if I had gone 10 rounds with Tyson, not like I had just played in a football match. I would have liked to say that my couple of celebratory pints went down well that night, they should have done after a fantastic away victory, but with my tongue and lips how they were it was hard going. I never thought I would hear myself saying that!

We had now climbed off the bottom of the table, had had our early season blip in form (earlier the better!) and confidence was high. Not for long! We drew our next game at home to Ipswich, not a massive disaster, but the game after was the return leg of our League Cup tie away at Bury. Harry gave the youngsters, me included, the chance to redeem ourselves after our awful showing in the first leg. We still went into the game leading 2–1 but we were even worse that night at Gigg Lane. With a couple of minutes to go, we found ourselves trailing 4–1. A horrible performance and even though I scored in the final minutes to make it 4–2 I did not feel like celebrating. I had scored my first goal for United, it had been a long time coming, and as we went back into the changing rooms after the game Harry was there waiting. 'Roasting', 'telling off', 'rollicking' – the words do not do it justice. He went absolutely berserk. I had never seen anything like it. He tore strips off everybody, saying we were not fit to wear the shirt and he was right. We were awful and deserved every minute of it. People were saying that season that Harry had lost his desire to be successful at United; they should have been in that dressing room at Bury that night. He was still passionate all right!

The senior pros came back into the squad for the next game, and I could not have been too bad at Bury as I kept myself in the team for the upcoming weekend against Derby.

It went from bad to worse. We lost our next four League games (two at home, two away) to leave us one position off the foot of the table. However, I felt as if my performances were getting a little bit better, as I adjusted to the pace of the play in the higher League. I had managed to score my second goal for the Blades in the 2–1 defeat at Southend, but at least I had started scoring again. Little did I know that was to be my last goal for United. The fans were starting to call for Harry's head and there were rumours of an imminent takeover (sounding familiar) and people believed that the next two games would make or break Harry's time at Bramall Lane. We thumped Portsmouth 4–1 and followed it up with a good 3–2 victory at Port Vale. I was sub for the game at Vale Park along with a lad who was probably the person with the smallest amount of common sense (and that is being polite) I have ever met, Tony Battersby, a young centre-forward who had great potential and a great physique. I had only known Tony for a couple of months but he had already provided me with three great stories to tell in later life. The first centred around the carousel at the airport in Norway. There we were, all the squad, waiting for our bags at Oslo. One by one everybody got their bags off, until there was only one bag left. 'That has to be your's Batts' the lads remonstrated. 'It's not! Mine was a brand new suitcase, and even though it looks a lot like that one, it definitely isn't mine. That's got marks all over it'. The lads left it for a few minutes, and still there was no sign of any more bags on the belt. Eventually we took the bag off and opened it up in front of Tony. 'There, I told you' he said, 'They are not my towels on top'. We took the towels away and sure enough there was Tony's stuff. His mum had packed his suitcase and put a couple of new towels on the top! The second story happened when we were waiting on the team bus at Bramall Lane to go to an away game. It was usual for the younger pros to help load the kit skips underneath the bus. Batts was helping Greavsie (the kit man) and as we set off, Greavsie shouted to Batts and asked whether he had put the skip with all the boots and pads on. 'Just as you told me Greavsie, I put it under the bus.' All of a sudden the bus screeched to a halt. Luckily the bus driver had looked in his mirrors and seen something left on the floor. He reversed all the way back; Greavsie jumped out and found the skip with all the boots left in the middle of the car park. He got back on the bus (if we had got to the game and there were no boots Greavsie would most probably have lost his job) and went for Batts. 'I told you to put the boots under the bus!' 'I did. Just like you asked'. Batts had put the boots under the bus all right. Not in the compartments but on the car park under the bus! The whole bus erupted in laughter.

Anyway, Batts and I went for a warm up midway through the first half. Anyone who knows Vale Park knows that the actual pitch is massive, one of the biggest, if not the biggest, in the Football League. It is so wide that you could turn the pitch round 90 degrees and there would be enough grass to have a pitch running the other way. Obviously I was disappointed to be on the bench, but you have to get on with it. Making conversation, I said to Batts as we jogged along the touchline that it might be a good game to be subs because of the size of the pitch. 'Good one Dutch', he said. 'You can't trick me. I'm not stupid. I do know that all pitches have to be the same size.' I didn't even bother arguing. What was the point? If a professional footballer does not know that all pitches are not the same size then what chance have you got? Batts was a really nice lad but not the sharpest tool in the box. Later, somebody told me that he was in a car school of four at his new club and what did he go and do…buy a two-seater car!

One thing I was really enjoying at United was the free golf we were allowed at Bondhay Golf club near Worksop. All of my days off were spent there and we had a regular four-ball going. It consisted of Billy Mercer and I taking on Paul Rogers and Carl Veart, the Australian centre-forward. It was always a tense affair, usually going down to the final hole. Carl was a really quiet lad, who never got flustered on the pitch and was very level-headed. You simply could not put him off. He was very focused, even at golf, but one day this would slip and a side of Carl that nobody had ever seen before came to the fore. He missed a putt and in anger, threw his putter across the green. We could not believe it but Paul Rogers certainly felt Carl's anger. Carl had not looked where he was throwing his putter and it hit Paul straight on his kneecap. It was lucky we were on the 18th green as Paul hobbled into the clubhouse to put ice on his now red and swollen knee. We had a little laugh about it but Paul's record of never having missed a training session or a game through injury would be in jeopardy, not because of an errant kick in training but from the putter of an angry Australian. Classic! For the record, Paul's knee got worse overnight and he missed about a week's training and one game. Nobody ever found out how he did it until now – apart from the Bondhay four-ball.

I got myself back into the starting XI for the next game away at Sunderland at their old ground Roker Park. What an atmosphere! It was electric. However, my own bravery was the undoing of me yet again. I was up against a really physical player in Kevin Ball. We were both giving it as good as we got and when a ball bounced in between us, both about five yards away from the ball, we both went into the challenge full-hearted.

However, whereas I went in fairly, Ball went straight over the ball and caught me right on the inside of the knee. It was a horror challenge. Nowadays it would be a straight red card, no doubt, but back then it was occasionally the done thing, especially from these older pros. I have never gone in deliberately to hurt anybody in my life, not where it could end up in a career-threatening injury. However, Ball did me, well and truly. Yet again in a football game, I was writhing about on the floor in agony. I got stretchered off, again a victim of my own honesty. As I lay on the treatment table, the lads started to come in at half-time and ask how I was. They knew I had been done so they were full of sympathy. Not Harry. He came in and went mad asking when was I going to grow up and stop being so honest. He said not everybody was as honest as me and that was why I kept getting injured. He did not say if he goes over the top you should go even higher, but that is basically what he meant. I think Harry was getting as frustrated as I was, with me continually getting injured, and we both knew that this latest injury could keep me out for a few weeks. I kept getting back into the team, finding my feet, reaching a decent level of form and then I would get injured again. We went on to lose the game and lost three out of the next four, culminating in a 2–0 home defeat against Huddersfield. This was to be Harry's last game in charge at United. I had managed to get back fit enough to be on the bench in his last game, but as a squad we had let Harry down badly. I think it was Tuesday when he came and told the lads before training that he had been sacked. He thanked everybody for their efforts but deep down you could see he was hurting. Howard Kendall was appointed as manager and brought in with him Adrian Heath and Viv Busby. They quickly stamped their authority on the club by saying that we were going to completely change the style of play and the training. It was going to be total football. We were going to pass our way out of trouble. We were second from bottom, but not adrift, and there was a new-found optimism at the club that you often find when a new manager comes into a club. Our first game was to be away at Portman Road, the home of Ipswich Town. I had never played there before but I thought it was a great set-up and the playing surface was as good as any I have ever played on – definitely better than Old Trafford and Wembley. We were given our instructions and our game plan was to go out and pass the ball to death. We drew the game 1–1 and drew our next game as well, also away, this time at Stoke City. I had loved the games and felt more at home than I had ever done before at United. I was enjoying the style of play but the only concern was that we had not won the games and we were going into the busy Christmas period still at the wrong end of the table. However, the training was really relaxed and we were full of confidence going into the Boxing Day home game against Birmingham City.

One thing that Kendall brought in was a different approach – he was always doing different from the norm. One such thing he apparently did all the time at Everton, was to spend the night before a home game at a hotel. Nothing wrong there. A very professional approach you may say, but this was Christmas night. I had not been used to this before: I had trained early on Christmas morning but never stayed away for

Christmas night. It was not a big thing for me but some of the lads who had families were a little bit put out. We had to meet at Bramall Lane at 4 o' clock, train on the main pitch and have a light evening meal before going to bed. I was looking forward to the game but got the shock of my life in the team meeting on Boxing Day morning.

The squad comprised of 17, obviously the 11 starters, five substitutes and one more who went just in case anyone fell ill. I felt I had done okay in the two games since the change of manager, but even though I knew I was not guaranteed a starting place I expected to be in the 16. I was wrong. He read the starting XI and then the substitutes and my name was not among those read out. It was the first time in my career I had ever been dropped from a squad and, luckily, it never happened to me again throughout my playing career. I know a lot of players who have to suffer this situation many times throughout their careers but when you are not used to it it is heart-wrenching. I did not know what to do. I was numb. I did not make a big fuss, that was not my style. I was absolutely fuming though. More so that no one had come up to me either before or after and given me a reason. That was why, years later, when I went on to manage the games at the end of the 2007–08 season I always spoke with the players who I had decided to drop from the team and gave them my reasons before they heard it in the team meeting. Many of you might not agree with this and you may think that the manager should not have to explain his decision to the players but I remember how I felt that Boxing Day in 1995. What a way to spend Christmas Day and Boxing Day. My dad had travelled to watch me play so I had a good chat with him during the game. He put things into perspective, as he always did and still does, and told me I had two choices. Either sit and sulk about it or work even harder and prove Kendall wrong. The choice was soon to be taken out of my hands. Kendall called me into his office and we sat down and had a chat. It was not heated, far from it, but he explained his decision and I could accept what he had to say. He said that the club was in the mire and that he needed people at the club with a proven track record at this level, who could come in and do a job straight away rather than someone with a lot of potential who might do it but might not. I could understand where he was coming from but it was then that he dropped the bombshell. He said he was more than happy for me to stay at the club and play in the reserves and try and force my way into the team, as he was bringing a couple of experienced midfielders into the club namely Gordon Cowan. My other option would be to go to another club and play first-team football. I said that I backed my own ability and I felt I could force my way back into the team. He changed tack a little bit then and said a club had shown an interest in me and that the club had already agreed a fee of around £150,000. In little more than six months my value had dropped by £100,000. I had played nowhere near my full potential at United, due to injuries and a lack of confidence in my new surroundings. However, I had enjoyed my time there and felt I had some more to offer the Blades. When he told me who the club was that had bid for me I nearly choked: Chesterfield FC, Mansfield's biggest rivals and the fans who most hated me. However, I respected their manager John Duncan and his assistant

Kevin Randall, who I knew from my time at Mansfield, and so I said I would go down and speak to them. I had two and a half years left on my contract at United and I felt there was a lot of unfinished business ahead of me at The Lane. I even asked whether I could go back on loan to Mansfield and that was quickly squashed as you can not go back on loan to the club that has sold you for at least a year. Whether that was true or not I do not know, but I was getting more and more suspicious that it was not really my choice, and that Kendall did not fancy me and wanted me out. Looking back I made the wrong choice – not going to Chesterfield but me making the choice. As I said, I had two and a half years left on my contract, and if my suspicions were correct I should have waited a little to be pushed. If it was their choice they would have had to offer me a settlement on my contract. Not for the whole contract but for a portion of it. I could have probably walked away from United with a nice cheque of around £80–£100k and gone straight to Chesterfield on the same money, but that was not my style. If United did not want me I wanted out and I would go somewhere where they wanted me. If Chesterfield wanted me, I would go. I said I did not need to think about it, my decision had been made. I shook Kendall's hand and wished him all the best. There were not any hard feelings but I bet when I left his office, he could not believe his luck. They had got £150k for me, saved my wages for two and a half years and not had to fork out for a pay-off of approximately £80k. I left United that day with my pride intact but looking back I was bloody stupid! I went to Chesterfield, a smaller club on a par with Mansfield, but they had been promoted the previous season after beating us and Bury in the Play-offs and they were currently lying fifth in the League above.

It was a fresh start, a fresh challenge to try and get the fans, who had hated me for the last four or five years, on my side. The only way I would do this was to be a success on the pitch.

It took time but eventually it happened. I was to have nearly four great years at Saltergate, culminating in an FA Cup semi-final. We were not a great team but the strength of mind and character in the team at that time were by far the best I ever played in. We were horrible to play against but boy did we stick together. A lot of clubs could learn from Chesterfield and the club's attitude in the late 90s. It was that good!

Chapter Nineteen
My Left Foot

I can remember my first training session as if it was yesterday. It was on Sunday 7 January 1996 at some pitches near Langer Lane in Chesterfield. I did not feel as bad as I did on my first day at United as there were so many familiar faces in the Chesterfield dressing room from my time at Mansfield and most of the others I knew from my time playing against Chesterfield over the years. The training pitch was crap, the balls were crap, the training kit was crap but not once did I hear anybody moan. That is what impressed me most about my early days at Chesterfield – everybody just got on with it. I could not have imagined the players at Sheffield United putting up with it and that told me oceans. I had only been at Chesterfield for one session and honestly I could tell that the spirit was a hundred times better than that at United. The squad at United were far superior in technical ability but nowhere near as strong mentally or physically. I can honestly say that in a one-off game I would have fancied my new club against the club I had just left just because of their passion for the game and their desire not to let their teammates down.

I could not play in the first game at Blackpool in the Associate Members Cup because I had not signed in time. However, I travelled up with the rest of the squad and within a week I felt at home. There was a mutual respect between all the players and between the staff and players. You were treated like adults and as long as you were doing the business on the pitch, that was all that mattered. After all that was what you were paid for. An example of this was at the pre-match meal. Everybody was eating their usual healthy stuff, and then the waiter came out and asked who the bacon sandwich was for. A bacon sandwich three hours before a game? I could not believe it. Nicky Law, the captain (the one who had stamped on my foot less than a year earlier) said it was his and gave me a wink, 'Not bad here, is it Joolsie?' However, this nickname caused a bit of a problem. Here I was back at a club where the people I already knew, knew me as Jools but there was already somebody in the squad called Joolsie – Mark Jules. Obviously there was no way I could be called Jools anymore and the lads were thinking of a new nickname when Billy Mercer, my old United teammate, looked up from his food and said, 'It has to be Dutch'. It has stuck ever since.

The game against Blackpool was not a classic. Chesterfield were under pressure for much of the game but went on to win 1–0. I came into the starting XI for the away game at Carlisle where we earned a creditable 1–1 scoreline. One thing that was clear from the outset at Chesterfield was the amount of team shape you did. We did it for hours; everything was accounted for and every eventuality covered. It was good preparation but god was it boring! This is known as shadow play (an XI v XI with no contact and done at walking pace) and from day one I knew I was never going to be allowed the freedom that I was given at Mansfield and that therefore I was never going to be able to score the goals I did at Mansfield. However, if it was for the good of the team who was I to disagree? I could not argue with the results. We won our next five games to move up to fifth in the table. We were so resilient it was frightening. You backed each other up whatever was happening. However, in the third game the injury jinx struck again. I had endured only a little trouble with my shoulder since I dislocated it in August for Sheffield United against Oldham Athletic, so when I was having this decent run at Chesterfield my dodgy shoulder and my dodgy right knee were the last thing on my mind. Wycombe were the opponents and they had an absolute 'man mountain' playing at the back for them in the shape of Terry Evans, who was 6ft 5in of pure muscle (he is their physio now). The ball fell between us and we both went flying in for it. I got there just before him and he caught me, sending me through the air over the top of his shoulders. As I arched down towards the floor it was like slow motion; I can remember thinking that if I landed on my right shoulder from this height I was in serious trouble. I managed to twist my body so that I would land on my left hand side, but ended up dislocating my left shoulder. Agony. It was thought that I may have broken my collar bone as well so it did not look good. However, upon inspection the news was a bit better. I had dislocated my shoulder but just badly stretched the ligaments. This meant I now had two dodgy shoulders and a dodgy knee at the age of 22.

As I said, we won the next two games but we lost heavily at Wrexham, all of which I missed. I came back for the home game against Brighton where I scored my first goal for the Spireites. The next game was away at Hull on a cold Tuesday night and it was the coldest night I had ever played on. For some reason I played out on the wing, which was not my strongest position by a long way. John Duncan, the manager, had an idea that they would aim everything out at me to win my headers against their small full-back. I definitely headed the ball more in that game than I kicked it. Not one of my best or more enjoyable games, not by a long way.

The rest of March was an up and down month with a couple of good results but also a couple of bad ones. The League that year was one where anybody could beat anybody on any given day. Come the end of March we were still in with a shout of the Play-offs and our next game was a massive one against Blackpool, the League leaders. I think this was the game that endeared me to the Chesterfield faithful. Not to blow my own trumpet, but I had a great game and ended up scoring the winner in a 1–0 victory. It was the best goal of my career. It later made the goal of the season competition for the whole of the Midlands area and I was lucky enough to win. The goal itself was a bit lucky. I managed to flick the ball over a couple of defenders at the same time as keeping the ball off of the floor. I found myself about 20 odd yards out and smashed it on the volley with my left foot. Those people who have seen my left foot will be amazed. It could have ended up anywhere. It whistled into the top corner. I ran to the Kop and I think they could see what that goal meant to me. It was as if I had been forgiven in an instant. For the rest of my time at Chesterfield I had a great relationship with the Chesterfield public. I think wherever you play and whoever you play for, you can win a set of fans over with plain hard work.

However, things went badly from then on. In our next six games we failed to win a game. We drew three and lost three. We had found ourselves in 10th place with three games to go, two away from home and Notts County at home on the final day of the season in what could potentially be an absolutely massive game. We let ourselves down in the first of the trilogy away at Bournemouth. We deservedly got beaten 2–0 and now it was very much out of our hands. We beat York away 1–0 and then beat County 1–0 on the final day. We had finished the season on a high but missed out on the Play-offs by a point. We were disappointed to miss out but the club could be proud of their first season in the higher League. I had loved my time since Christmas; it was a real close-knit club with a great work ethic. The fans had been behind the club all season and they were very realistic in their ideas of what a successful season was. My season could not have been more different. Starting off with a big club where the spirit was not great and where I never really felt at home, and ending at a small club where the spirit was second to none and where I definitely felt comfortable. Bring on the new season.

Chapter Twenty
The Cup Run

This season was the highlight of my career at club level mainly due to our tremendous FA Cup adventure. It was unbelievable but things like that seemed a long way away when we started pre-season training in July 1996. After the easiest pre-season I had ever done the previous year at Sheffield United this was certainly the hardest, but yet again nobody moaned, well, apart from me. That was my way of getting through it. The first day was such an example. When the George and Dragon run was mentioned I did not know what to expect but I could see from the looks on the other faces that it was not good news. The George and Dragon run sounded very simple: you ran from the ground to a pub in Old Brampton called the George and Dragon and back to the ground. Simple! Not at all! As on the first day of every season, the temperature is always red-hot and this was no exception. I had learnt my lesson from the first game of the previous season at Watford and I must have had at least three litres of water before training on that morning. There was no way that was ever going to happen to me again. Another lesson I had learnt from way back courtesy of Fordy at Mansfield was that no prizes are won on the first day of pre-season training and it is supposed to be a gradual build-up in your fitness so that by the time the first game of the season comes round you are at your optimum (or that is what I told everyone!) I did my usual in long distance running – just enough. I hated it. I could see the point in getting your base stamina level up but how bloody boring it was. The run was probably about six miles so it was not too bad. After we all started getting back to the ground and Kevin Randall was taking the times it soon came to light that we were one down on our numbers. Mark Jules, our full-back, was missing. Julesy was as quick as anybody at the club over 50 to a 100 yards but long distance running was not his forte. We were having a bit of a laugh at his expense as a couple of minutes passed saying that he must have had a good summer and too many San Miguels. Five minutes passed. Then 10, 15, where was he? We soon found out. The club got a phone call from the hospital saying that somebody in a Chesterfield training kit had just been dropped off. He had collapsed at the side of the road due to dehydration, a car had picked him up and driven him to the nearest hospital. Once we found out he was okay we could not wait for him to get back to the ground so the mickey-taking could start. A couple of hours later he walked in a bit sheepish. He got slaughtered!

Pre-season had gone well and we were looking forward to the start of the season. Our first game was away at Blackpool. It was still August so the fans decided to make a weekend of it, after all it was bound to be red-hot – it was the first game of the season.

True to form it was boiling and the game was a typical first game of a season with both sides playing cautiously, frightened of making mistakes. It was a tense affair and our favourite scoreline of 1–0 was achieved courtesy of a goal by yours truly. Blackpool was becoming a lucky team for me!

Obviously this season would be remembered for our famous Cup run, but it was not going to be in the League Cup. We were dumped out by Stockport over two legs with them winning both games 2–1. Whenever we played Stockport we always had a chuckle to ourselves as a squad. The preparation as always was meticulous. John and Kevin always had the opposition watched and ran through their players one by one. When it got to their midfielder, Chris Marsden, we knew what was coming. Kev always said the same about Marsden, 'He is overrated. He is just a Pontins League player' (reserve-team player). Every single game against us he was head and shoulders above anybody on the pitch; he always murdered us. Kev said it again before both games and both games Marsden got Man of the Match. Back to the League, after our great win at Blackpool we came back down to earth with a bad result at home to Bury losing 2–1. However, normal order was soon resumed with a 1–0 home win against Walsall which was followed by one of the strangest games I have ever been involved in. We went down to Gillingham, always a hard place to go, well prepared as normal but with very much a plan in mind. I have never played in, or seen, such a one-sided game. We were awful and they played like Brazil. They must have hit the woodwork 10 times. There were goalmouth scrambles, clearances off the line, last-ditch tackles, everything. It was comical. Their players were gobsmacked, we were just laughing. We could not believe our luck, and what happened? With a minute remaining, on one of our few attacks we managed to force a throw-in near the corner flag. I can remember Kev Randall screaming across the pitch for us to take a short one and keep it in the corner. Whoever took the throw-in obviously did not hear the instruction and launched it into the box. The ball dropped and was smacked in by Jon Howard. Somehow we had snatched a 1–0 victory from nowhere even though there was still enough time for Gillingham to hit the woodwork for the umpteenth time. When the final whistle went Gillingham slumped to the ground. They were devastated. I have never felt so embarrassed after winning a match. We have all seen games where you win but you do not really deserve it, but unless you were actually at this game you would not believe how one-sided it was. We did not even celebrate at the final whistle; it would have been rude to. Instead we just went and picked the Gillingham players off the floor and apologised to them. It was that bad! I had a beer after the game with Iffy Onoura, who I had played with at Mansfield, and he was crestfallen. He said he alone had hit the woodwork four times. I could not help but laugh. I remembered what my dad always says, 'It's a lot bloody harder to hit the woodwork, than the goal!'

By the end of September we had had a mixed start to the season and found ourselves in seventh position, not bad considering we had already lost three games, excluding the two games against Stockport. On the other hand we had won five games all by the 1–0 scoreline. We had played 11 games in all competitions and had kept five clean sheets – not a bad ratio. It showed how much work we did in stopping the opposition play and on our defensive shape. It was as boring as hell in training but it was reaping dividends. Our League form continued very much in the same vein and in the next nine games we won four, lost three and drew two which left us in eighth place, just outside the Play-offs by one point. There were differing views on our next game, a televised FA Cup game against Bury at home. One train of thought was that our FA Cup run would be a distraction and that all our efforts should be concentrated on securing a Play-off place, while other people thought the FA Cup would be a respite from the pressures of League football and should be enjoyed. Either way there was no real chance of us progressing into the latter stages of the competition. How many times have a lower League team even reached the semi-final of the FA Cup? Hardly ever. One or two times at the most probably. Chesterfield were not renowned as a Cup team, so hopes were not particularly high as we entered our first game of the competition. Realistically all we were hoping for was to reach the third round and draw one of the big boys. How wrong we all were, for this was to be the start of probably the best underdog story in the history of the FA Cup.

The run did not begin spectacularly as we did our usual and won 1–0, with a typical gritty display against a decent Bury team. We never created a lot of chances but we restricted the opposition to very few, often long-range shots. We were a very resilient team and our motto was to stay in games for as long as we could, frustrate the opposition and wait for a mistake or a set play. We were a big team and therefore a big threat to other teams at set plays. We seemed to do hours and hours of the same shadow play and practising the same set plays until it had all become second nature. You could not have got two more contrasting managers than Andy King and John Duncan in personality, their methods of training and their principles of how the game should be played but both were great managers: Andy King's extravagant open style of play versus John Duncan's meticulous approach to every game.

Our next League game was away at Plymouth. It was mid-November but there were massive amounts of snow on the morning of the game. If the game was at Saltergate (Chesterfield's home) there would have been no chance of the game going ahead, and as I set off in what I thought was plenty of time to report for the journey I was waiting for a phone call to say the game had been called off. It had to be! A 10-mile journey that would have normally taken me 15 to 20 minutes at the most took me one and a half hours. It was horrendous. When I finally arrived at the ground I found myself only one of four people there. Everybody was having the same problem. Eventually when everybody arrived, we rang Plymouth one more time just to check whether the game was still on before we set off. They said it was brilliant November sunshine and not a single snowflake in sight. We set off and soon realised that there was no way that we would be able to make our pre-match meal which was booked as usual three hours before kick-off. We would have to make do with what we had with us on the coach –

far from ideal. As we approached Bristol we still had yet to see grass due to the volume of the snow. Surely there was snow at Plymouth. However, true to their word, about half an hour from Plymouth the weather improved and by the time we arrived at Home Park (Plymouth's ground), exactly an hour before kick-off, the conditions were perfect. Totally the opposite from our preparation. What did we do? We murdered them and won 3–0. No other team that I played in would have done that, not after the day we had endured.

To make the journey home a bit sweeter, I scored a goal – well I say goal in the loosest terms, because it was the softest goal of my life. I hit the ball from the edge of the box and it literally rolled towards Bruce Grobbelaar, the former Liverpool goalkeeper. How he failed to save it I do not know, but somehow it slipped from his grasp and rolled over the line stopping after about two inches. Grobbelaar did not even make an effort to redeem his mistake and simply watched it roll over the line and stop. The whole ground went quiet, it was really surreal. However a goal is a goal, no matter how it goes in, but it does make you think. I shall say no more!

We got four points from our next two League games before our next FA Cup tie. In the second we were drawn at home to Scarborough and we went through comfortably 2–0. Again it was not spectacular, but we did enough and kept another clean sheet. We were now in the draw for the third round which is always nice for fans and players alike as it gives you all the chance to potentially pit yourselves against one of the big boys. It is great to watch the draw whether you are a player or fan, it's so exciting willing your ball to appear alongside Man Utd or Liverpool. We did draw a bigger club but only a bigger club in our own League: Bristol City at home. A tough draw, but at least it was at home.

Our lead up to Christmas was not particularly impressive, with a draw and a loss, but with a busy Christmas period ahead of us we were still hoping for a good push to cement a place in the Play-offs. Christmas is a hard time for a footballer because you have to be careful what you eat and you can not have a drink, but you accept it at the end of the day as it is your job and you are well paid. What is frustrating, however, is when you are careful on Christmas Day and then your Boxing Day game is called off! That Christmas and New Year period was far from busy. Due to the weather we did not have a game from the 21 December to the 11 January. It was nice to have a bit of a break mid-season to recharge the batteries especially for me as I was now struggling with an injury that was diagnosed as a double hernia that would soon need surgery to rectify. Looking back this rest period would have been the ideal time to have had it done because you can be back playing within three weeks of surgery, but with the games not being called off until the last minute it was not realised until too late. One such game that fell victim to the weather was our New Year's Day fixture away at Burnley. Burnley had not had a game called off over the festive period and would therefore have the edge over us. We arrived at Turf Moor to find the playing surface rock hard due to frost. Burnley were desperate to get the game on whereas we were not so keen. Basically we wanted a nice home game to get ourselves back into it rather than a tough away fixture at Turf Moor. We were trying to bend the referee's ear as he was doing his pre-match inspection, saying that it was dangerous and unfit to play. Eventually we persuaded him to get one of Burnley's youth-team players to put his boots on and try running, turning and stopping. Little did the referee know that we had already had a quiet word with the lad and gently persuaded him that when he went to turn, he was to basically fall flat on his arse. We were all watching intently as he increased his pace waiting for the referees whistle to blow which was the sign for him to change direction. When the whistle went, it was hilarious. Down he went as if a sniper had shot him. It was a little too exaggerated but it had the desired effect as the officials promptly called the game off!

We had not had a game for about three weeks as our FA Cup tie was also called off. Therefore we had two home games in the space of four days against both of the Bristol clubs, one in the League and our rearranged Cup game against City. Yet again we surpassed ourselves winning both games and keeping two more clean sheets in the process. Our Cup win against City emphasised the different mentalities between the two clubs perfectly. It was a freezing cold night and you could see they did not fancy it. Saltergate was, and still is, a horrible place for away teams to visit. The changing room is horrible and cramped, nothing like City were used to. On paper they were streets ahead of us ability wise, but they did not have our mental strength and togetherness. Put simply, we bullied them. We played a horrible game but it worked perfectly. All they wanted to do was get back on to the bus and get home. We won 2–0 and I do not think they even had a shot on goal all night. We already knew by this time that the winners would face Bolton Wanderers away at Burnden Park. Something to look forward to!

We were seventh in the League at this stage, level on points with the team in the last Play-off position. We had three difficult away games on the spin and we decided as a squad that we would be happy with three draws or three points. We went one better, winning one, drawing one and losing the other. We went into our fourth-round FA Cup game against Bolton on the back of a great away win at Preston, so we travelled to the North West full of confidence. On a memorable night for Chesterfield, and in particular for a young Kevin Davies who is still playing for Bolton, we won 3–2 with Kev scoring a hat-trick. We were in dreamland. We were now in the fifth round and the draw was kind to us: Nottingham Forest at home. A tough game but a winnable one. We had a chance of reaching the quarter-finals of the FA Cup!

We only had one game before the Forest tie and that was a home game against Wrexham, very much a low-key game with everybody looking forward to the FA Cup. It was to be a bad game for us, not result-wise but for the team as a whole. We drew the game 0–0 (another clean sheet) but we were hit by injuries and subsequent suspensions leaving us decimated for the Forest game. We were left without our usual centre-half pairing of skipper Sean Dyche and Mark Williams who had both been superb all season, along with a few other players. By this time I should not have been playing as I was struggling with my double hernia. I was fine during the first half in games, but then I would stiffen up over half-time and would virtually not be able to move in the second half (nothing new there many people would say!) John Duncan, however, was left with no choice – I had to play! I found myself in the centre of a back three, a position, as I mentioned previously, I found easy. I was relieved to be playing there because I would not have lasted the game in midfield. Playing alongside me was Jamie Hewitt (my best mate at Chesterfield) and Darren Carr, one of the hardest centre-halves I have ever seen. Darren had hardly played any games due to the form of Dychey and Bomber (Mark Williams) so our back three consisted of two players playing out of position and one who had not played a lot of games. It did not matter. It was by far our easiest game of not only our Cup run, but of our whole season. We breezed it and their front three of Dean Saunders, Bryan Roy and Kevin Campbell caused us no problems at all. We won the game – yes, you guessed it, 1–0, courtesy of a Tom Curtis penalty. Now the hype started and ultimately our Cup run was to scupper our chances of reaching the Play-offs. The cameras were everywhere. The rest of our League season dwindled away and we ended up falling from sixth before the Forest game to a disappointing 13th by the middle of April. We rallied a little, winning four out of our final six games, and finishing the season in 10th place five points outside of the Play-offs. There is no doubt that if it was not for our Cup run and the size of our squad we would have definitely reached the Play-offs and who knows what would have happened. I can tell you one thing, not one Chesterfield supporter or anyone connected with the club would have swapped the Cup run for a chance of promotion. It was unbelievable and worthy of its own chapter in the book. So here goes, it makes great reading and was a great time to be associated with the Spireites.

Chapter Twenty-One

A Day to Remember

I t was all starting to happen. Straight after the full-time whistle against Forest all that anybody was talking about was the FA Cup. No matter how hard we tried to forget it, it was impossible. All the talk from the players and staff at the club about taking one game at a time and that the League was still our main priority was rubbish. Our thoughts were purely FA Cup. I do not think I even played in another League game that season after the Forest game. I was desperately in need of the operation to cure the double hernia but there was no way I was going to miss the chance to play in the FA Cup quarter-final, no matter who it was against. The cameras were in the dressing room after the game, and there was champagne everywhere. The lads were buzzing and were eagerly awaiting the draw to see who we would play in the quarter finals. The options were Derby, Middlesbrough, Wimbledon, Chelsea and Sheffield Wednesday of the Premier League, Portsmouth of the First Division or Wrexham of our League. Did we want an away game at one of the Premier League teams or did we want the game that would be the easiest on paper – Wrexham at home. The worst possible draw for us would have been Wrexham away. The waiting was soon over and we had drawn Wrexham at home. Were we to be happy or disappointed? Someone said 'Think of Wrexham. That is the one draw they didn't want!' From the moment that was said we were confident. There was no way Wrexham would relish coming to Saltergate. We all went out into Chesterfield that night and had a great time.

I do not think any of the players bought another drink from after the Forest game until the end of the season. The town had come alive and all that everyone was talking about was the FA Cup. It had given everybody a much-needed boost. We were now becoming national news and Tom Curtis was invited to be a guest on *The Frank Skinner Show*. Frank wanted Tom on there to take the mickey out of Chesterfield – in a good-natured way of course. He asked Tom whether we were used to success and having champagne and before Tom could reply he showed a clip of me struggling to open a bottle of champagne. It showed me biting the paper off, not the done way! That little clip showed what we were all about as a group of players – not a bit cultured and a lot rough and ready! Because of all the interest from the media we had an agency working on our behalf dealing with our media interests to allow us more time to concentrate on our football. This worked in the sense that it raised a bit of money for the squad but meant us having to do even more interviews and appearances if the agency saw a quick way of making a buck. We appeared on the BBC's *They Think it's All Over*, among other programmes. Obviously it was all good for the club and the town itself, but we still had to go out and play a few League games before probably the biggest game of all our careers against Wrexham. I was in the stands as a spectator for our home game against Plymouth, and I half expected to be bored out of my skin (I hated watching). How wrong I was. It was not the football that this game would be remembered for but a 22-man brawl that I have never seen the likes of. It was mayhem. The game had been pretty much a low-key affair until the ball was floated aimlessly into the Plymouth box. It would have landed about 15 yards from their goal if it had bounced but Plymouth had no ordinary 'keeper in goal. That man Grobbelaar was the man in question again. Off his line he raced like a mad man, no other 'keeper would have been interested in going for the ball. What he did not realise was that Darren Carr also had his eye on the ball and no one was going to get in his way. Something had to give! Darren caught Grobbelaar full pelt in mid-air knocking the 'keeper out cold. All hell broke loose. Fists were being thrown, players were in the net fighting. It was like a pub scene. The referee could easily have sent the majority of the players off. That fight and a few choice tackles in the remainder of the game saw the game finish five men short. Three Plymouth players were sent off and Darren Carr and Kevin Davies of Chesterfield were dismissed as well. We did not realise it at the time but that meant both of them having to miss the upcoming Wrexham quarter-final. Losing both players for that game was a massive blow with having such a small squad, but especially losing Kevin who was our key attacking player and a massive influence on the way we looked to play. All of a sudden Wrexham would have been fancying their chances a little bit more now. One thing I remember about that game was Jamie Hewitt running from the halfway line when the fight started. It looked as if he had singled somebody out and was going to throw the biggest punch Saltergate had ever seen. He got into the box and promptly kicked one of the Plymouth players' bottoms. It was playground stuff as he then ran away. He did not hear the end of it for a long time after. Whenever there looked to be a bit of bother in a game, Jamie would be shouted to sort it out!

The Wrexham game was to be played on a Sunday at dinner time. I hated early kick-offs, to me it did not seem right and I hated playing on a Sunday even more. The atmosphere was electric and hopes were high for a Chesterfield victory that would see us in the semi-finals of the FA Cup. The semi-finals of the FA Cup – it did not ring true. Wrexham came out fighting from the first whistle and how we did not concede in that first half I will never know as they absolutely bombarded us. We went in at half-time 0–0, very lucky to still be on level terms. Not a lot was said at half-time. A lot of managers would have been trying to change things around after seeing their team so outplayed but not John Duncan. He was coolness personified, on the outside anyway, and said we would have our spell on top and we would have to make the most of it when it came about. We were told to keep our shape (it was well and truly stamped into us by then!) and be patient. Sure enough it came. The game was turning into a very nervy affair with nobody wanting to make the mistake that would see the dreams of their club dashed. Chris Beaumont was to be the hero. He had not played a lot for us, but he was a great lad and I was delighted that he was the hero for the day. He scored the all important goal and we then sat back and hung on. The last few minutes seemed to go on forever as Wrexham threw everything they had at us.

It was hard on Wrexham as they definitely deserved something out of the game. How many times did we say that about the opposition that season? The final whistle blew and it was all over. Chris's goal had secured us our place in the semi-final. The fans invaded the pitch as they had done in the previous round against Forest; we were carried shoulder high off the pitch and once again the champagne flowed in the dressing room. I would like to say I had practised my technique in opening a champagne bottle but I had not. I think we stayed in the dressing room for about an hour as a squad having a few drinks and trying to savour the moment. This would probably be the only time in our careers we would be in this position and we were determined to make the most of it. With getting to the semi-final we had received some good bonuses but I can honestly say that this was not the driving force behind our success, we were honest professionals who worked for each other and did not want to let each other down – the best team spirit I have ever been involved in. We watched the draw live on TV; it was to be Middlesbrough, Chelsea or Wimbledon. As a squad we knew that the semi-final would realistically be our Cup Final. We had ridden our luck in getting this far, especially against Wrexham, and against Premier League opposition we would surely be found out this time. We were desperate to be drawn against Middlesbrough with their brilliant foreign imports such as Juninho, Ravenelli and Emerson starring for them. When the draw was made and we had got our wish we went mad. The first question we all asked was 'Where will it be played?' I was praying it would be at Old Trafford as I had promised myself at a young age that I would play at Old Trafford, home of my beloved Manchester United, and also Wembley, the national stadium. Could I do it in one season? I knew at this stage of my career that my chances of playing at the highest level had probably gone and that playing in a League game at Old Trafford would never happen. I thought my only chance would be to draw United in one of the Cup competitions, never thinking of playing there in an FA Cup semi-final as it was a neutral venue.

We had another great night out after the Wrexham game, again everybody just wanting to talk about football and to buy you a drink. After a few days it was then announced that Old Trafford was to be the venue. I was ecstatic. I was not playing in any League games by this time but there was no way on earth I was going to miss this game. It could not come quick enough!

The build-up to the semi-final was manic and we were in great demand. Everybody wanted a photo and to wish you good luck, and for those few weeks we could see what it would be like to be a top player, always in the public eye. If we all went for a beer, the press would be waiting for us. This was not a problem for us as a group of players because even though we had more nights out as a squad than was probably normal, we always behaved ourselves. If somebody stepped out of line, they were soon put into place. On the week of the game (the game was to be played on the Sunday) we went to have a look around Old Trafford so that it would not be too much of a shock when we found ourselves there on the match day. We had a joke with Bomber (Mark Williams) when we were stood on the pitch saying that he would 'struggle to clear the stands here'. It was a standing joke that wherever we played Bomber would kick at least one ball over a stand and out of the ground. In fact, early in the season on a night out, we were taking the mickey out of him for it and he bragged, 'You haven't seen anything yet. I will do it in every game for the rest of the season'. The challenge was on and to be fair to Bomber he pretty much kept to his word. He had to do it in the game itself, it did not count if he did it in the warm up. I am sure that sometimes he did it accidentally when he was trying to keep the ball on the pitch! Passing was not Bomber's strong point but he and Dychey were a fantastic centre-half pairing and probably played the best football of their careers that season. Even without a crowd in Old Trafford, the place was intimidating. It was a fantastic arena and I was in my own little dreamland walking around. I was thinking of all the times when I had been a spectator there when I was younger, watching my heroes play on the exact pitch that I was standing on. We had a tour around the changing rooms, and in the museum the lads were giving me some stick because I was in a trance like a school kid. They virtually had to drag me out of the museum to get back on the bus at the end of the day.

When we went into Saltergate to report for training the next day, all the arrangements were being made for the weekend and the game. John Duncan sat us down and asked what we wanted to do about staying over at a hotel before the game. I am not sure why he asked what we wanted to do, as when we usually said what we wanted he would overrule us and do what he wanted anyway. Normally when we had a game that required an overnight stay we would travel down in the afternoon of the day before the game, have an evening meal and then an early night. We decided as a group that if that was good enough for a League game then we should do the same thing even if it was the FA Cup semi-final we were preparing for. We told John and Kevin that we wanted to do as usual, but they said we were either going and staying two nights or we would just travel on the day of the game. None of us wanted to do that so we argued again that we wanted to stay for just one night. John's argument was that it was a big game and that we would very likely struggle to sleep due to nerves the night before the game, and that coupled with sleeping in a strange bed would mean a bad night's sleep the night before the biggest game of our lives. He said if we went down two days before the game that first night we would be perfectly relaxed and away from all the hype that was happening in Chesterfield. Yet again John and Kev had thought of everything down to the last detail, and as usual their preparation was perfect.

We left Saltergate on the Friday with all the media and press there to see us off. This was for real now! The biggest game in our football lives was now less than 48 hours away. I shared a room with my usual roommate, Jamie Hewitt. From day one we really hit it off, we were always in each other's pockets and the lads did rip us about it. That first night at the hotel went exactly like John and Kevin planned. The evening meal was beautiful, we had a bit of a team meeting and then the night was pretty much ours to do as we pleased, as long as we stayed in the hotel and had a reasonably early night. All the lads could speak about was the game, we were like a bunch of Under-11s before their first ever Cup Final. Jamie and I retreated to our room fairly early, but spent a couple of hours talking about the upcoming game. We tried to switch off and forget it, the whole squad did, but it was impossible. Eventually we dropped off and I slept like a baby. I think the pressure of it all had made me shattered and it was the best night's sleep I had had for years. If I slept like that again the following night I would be happy I can remember thinking to myself (we all had a great night's sleep the night before the game but for a completely different reason). We all got up on the Saturday morning and met for a late breakfast. Feeling relaxed the team could not wait to actually get out on the training pitch to get some normality back into the system. We went out and had a bit of a jog and stretch and tried to go through a bit of shadow play and team shape, but it was a bit false really. We had a bit of a laugh and a joke when the gaffer was mentioning the likes of Juninho, Ravanelli and Emerson and we were waiting for Kev to say, 'Don't worry about Juninho lads. He is exactly like Chris Marsden, a Pontins League player.' We did just enough to get the legs going. The afternoon was pretty much ours, and a few of us went to watch a game at Macclesfield to make the afternoon go a little bit quicker. Anything to make the game come around sooner. I sensed that the atmosphere was a little bit different around our evening meal on the Saturday night. The game was less than 24 hours away and the lads were unusually quiet. I think the pressure was starting to tell a bit and the nerves starting to kick in. Obviously John and Kev had sensed this as well, and they did something like Cloughie would have done. They ordered a couple of bottles of wine for the tables and said if we wanted a glass then we were allowed and that it would not be frowned upon. I think John and Kev were starting to feel the nerves as well as the players and understandably so, as it was something that none of us were used to and nobody was sure how the game would go the following day. It was great that we had reached the semi-finals, that was a fantastic achievement in itself, but there was no way we wanted to make fools of ourselves. We were massive underdogs, nobody expected us to win, but there was still pride at stake. The bottles of wine soon went, and John and Kev ordered another couple and it did the trick. The lads were soon themselves again and the usual banter was flying around once more. The gaffer had sensed an anxiety in us and done something a bit unexpected, and it had worked perfectly. Fantastic management. We stayed at the tables after our evening meal for about half an hour and somebody joked about going to the bar for a pint. John amazed us when he said that if we wanted a pint then that would not be a problem. After all we were all adults and John knew that there was no way people would take advantage and go overboard because they would not want to spoil the build-up to the game. We all waited for each other to make the first move, not wanting to be the first one to go to the bar. Eventually Billy Mercer (our goalkeeper) got up and like sheep we all followed. When we got to the bar, there was Rushy (David Rushbury), our physio, having a glass of his favourite tipple, red wine, chatting away to a young lady. There were a few cries of 'Ay up' but we all fell quiet when the lady turned round. We immediately recognised her as Caroline Aherne, the actress who played Mrs Merton and Denise Royle, the daughter in *The Royle Family*. We all got ourselves a drink and sat down with them. A couple of producers from her show also came round and for a couple of hours we were in hysterics. We had a couple more pints and basically listened to her; her jokes were brilliant and she was great company. At around half past 10 we all made our way upstairs to go to bed, feeling a lot more relaxed than we did a couple of hours earlier. The few drinks had had the desired effect. For a couple of hours our minds were away from the football the following day and everybody was tired and ready for a good night's sleep. As soon as my head hit the pillow I was gone. I woke up the next day feeling refreshed and buzzing. It had finally arrived.

We had breakfast and then reported for our pre-match meal about three hours before kick-off. Again everybody was a bit quiet, but there was no way the wine would be out this time! We left the hotel and made the short journey to Old Trafford. On the way we saw a few cars with Chesterfield scarves hanging from the windows. They would pip their horns and give us a 'thumbs up'. I thought to myself that it was a bit quiet, but all that changed about a mile from the ground. Word had obviously got round the route we were using to get to Old Trafford as the streets were jam-packed with Chesterfield fans making their way to the ground and wanting to give their team a wave. They started singing their songs, it was awesome! It seemed to take forever to travel that last mile to the ground. At such a small club like Chesterfield you get to know a few of the fans, so it was nice to see them in the crowd also enjoying what was their big day. Supporting a lower League club can be hard so it is nice for the real fans to have days like that, to reward their loyalty and devotion to the club. On a usual match day at Chesterfield we would probably have got about 4,500 home supporters, but for this game we had 25,000 Spireites there. The club had sold out their quota of tickets as quickly as they could sell them, and could have probably sold them four times over. As we turned the corner into the car park at Old Trafford I saw my mum and dad waiting in the same spot I used to wait for Bryan Robson many years earlier. It brought a tear to my eyes. Here they were to support me at the home of Manchester United, a million miles away from the rec 15 or so years before. I gave them a quick wave and then I can remember saying to myself. 'Get a grip Dutch! You have a job to do.' We fought our way through the crowd and eventually got into the dressing room. As the kit was being put out we had a walk out onto the pitch. The ground was only starting to fill up and so you were unable to really get a feel for what it would be like in about 40 minutes when we went out to warm up. We all went through our usual routines, but I think we rushed through them as we were ready about five minutes earlier than we would have been for a normal League game. John knew we were on edge so just said 'Go and enjoy it.' We all went out of the door together and made our way down the corridor and into the tunnel. We stopped and shook each other's hands and said 'Good Luck', took a deep breath and jogged out onto the pitch. The noise that hit you nearly knocked you off your feet. As we were warming up the usual music was blaring out, when all of a sudden Tina Turner's classic hit *Simply the Best* started. All of a sudden the Chesterfield fans started singing it and waving flags and scarves. I have never seen or heard anything like it. It made the hairs on the back of your neck stand up, and, me being me, it brought tears to my eyes. Amazing!

When we got back into the dressing room John Duncan had his final word with us. He said how proud he and Kevin were of what we had all achieved so far, and that we should not worry too much about the result and just to go out there and enjoy the occasion and give it our best shot. It seemed strange lining up in the tunnel alongside Ravenelli and Juninho. They looked so relaxed, but they would have done. They were used to this every week of the season except they were playing lower League opposition. There was no chance of them taking us lightly as they had some good old-fashioned professionals in their line up with the likes of Robbie Mustoe and Steve Vickers and a manager with plenty of FA Cup experience in Bryan Robson, my hero. When we emerged onto the pitch the noise once again deafened us. I was determined to enjoy the occasion; this would probably never happen to me again.

The game started at a frenetic pace and to be fair we gave as good as we got in the opening stages. It was typically nervy stuff but we had not conceded that early goal that we were so desperate to avoid. The game was heading towards half-time goalless when Kevin Davies, who had started to cause Kinder, the Middlesbrough left-back, a few problems, received the ball. He went past Kinder and Kinder pulled him back. I saw David Elleray reach for his pocket, and I thought 'Good, a yellow card. He will have to be careful up against Kev now'. I looked away and then I heard a roar from the crowd. I quickly looked back and to my amazement and to everybody else's inside the ground, Elleray had shown Kinder a red card. Middlesbrough were down to 10 men. Half-time came and John and Kev had their work cut out trying to calm us all down. We now realised that we had a great chance of reaching the Final. I think that was the first time, I am sure all the players and staff would admit to this as well, that we had considered this. Middlesbrough were still going to be dangerous, and their little Brazilian (Juninho) had been immense in the first half even though Mark Jules had done a fantastic job in marking him. Our game plan was to remain the same even though they were down to 10 men, play a tight game that we had to keep our shape in. That was vitally important as if we 'opened up' their superstars could come to the fore and murder us. I was loving it! I had been up against Middlesbrough's other Brazilian Emerson, a midfielder with great power and finesse. He had the longest hair of anybody I had ever played against and every time you got anywhere near him his hair would swish in your face. God knows what he had on it, a mixture of sweat and a cocoa butter solution or something like that, but every time it hit me it would leave some kind of goo on my face. Lovely.

We came out for the second half and immediately took the game to Middlesbrough. Then the unthinkable happened. Kev Davies managed to get a shot away, Ben Roberts the Boro 'keeper could only parry it straight into the path of Bruno, big Andy Morris. He could not miss in front of the Chesterfield fans. Andy rolled the ball into an empty net and the Chesterfield fans went berserk. Big Andy casually raised his arms as if he had just scored in training. He hardly showed any emotion, a bit different to the rest of us as we piled on to Andy's back. We were 1–0 up against 10 men. I think deep down we still expected Boro to come back at us.

Our front three attacking players were now starting to cause Middlesbrough all sorts of problems and Andy Morris went through and was brought down by their 'keeper. He did catch Andy but Andy made the most of it. It was the most over-exaggerated dive you will ever see from a 16st, 6ft 4in footballer. However, it did the trick. Elleray pointed to the spot and then confusion set in. For all of our methodical preparation we were not sure, I definitely was not the designated penalty taker. All eyes went to Tom Curtis who had scored from the spot in the fifth round against Forest but this was different and Tom had missed from the penalty spot since then. John Duncan was shouting frantically from the sidelines, still to this day, I do not know what about, but Dychey, being captain, saw it as his responsibility if no one was volunteering and he stood up and placed the ball on the spot. If you watch the video of the game you can see somebody stood on the halfway line with their head in their hands. That person was me. I had my eyes shut. I couldn't bear to watch so what Dychey felt like god only knows. I listened for the noise to tell me the outcome. The roar told me he had scored.

If this sounds possible it was the worst thing for us. We had gone and scored a second goal. From being 1–0 up and still concentrating hard, we went 2–0 up and allowed our minds to wonder, thinking about Wembley and an FA Cup Final. If we had managed to keep it at 2–0 for 10 minutes we would have been cruising and our minds would have switched back to concentrating on our team shape and all the things that would normally have been second nature to us. We did not. Middlesbrough went virtually straight up the other end and Ravenelli slid the ball home to make it 2–1. We were now rocking. Middlesbrough threw everything at us for 10 minutes and somehow we survived. From having a man advantage and looking comfortable, it was as if Boro now had an extra man. I can remember Emerson getting the ball near the touchline with me and Tommy Curtis closing him down quickly. He had nowhere to go. We had it covered! Or did we? He sold us both the biggest dummy ever seen on a football pitch! With the smallest of moves of his hips he had sent me and Tommy one way while he went the other. He had got himself loads of space without moving. Tommy and I still laugh about it to this day.

With a little bit of luck we held on and then came the incident that is still talked about to this day and what the semi-final will be remembered for. The goal that never was! It must be in the top three of the worst decisions of all time. Jon Howard had managed to find himself a little space about eight yards out and let fly with a shot. It beat Roberts in the Boro goal, hit the underside of the bar and came down and bounced down and hit the floor. Had it crossed the line? I was not sure. The ball went back up in the air and Andy Morris was about to head the ball into an empty net when he was climbed over by a Boro defender. It was either a goal or a blatant penalty. I immediately looked at the linesman when the ball bounced down off the crossbar and he was pointing towards the halfway line. He had given a goal. We were leading 3–1. Hang on a minute, Elleray had blown for a penalty, or had he? 'What the bloody hell is happening?' I thought. Somehow Elleray had seen a foul on the Boro defender by Bruno. We pleaded for Elleray to go and speak to the linesman who had by now put his flag down as he obviously thought Elleray had seen something. Total mayhem! Middlesbrough took the free-kick and got on with the game before the two of them could consult. There was no way I could see from where I was whether the ball had crossed the line or not, but by looking at the linesman's reaction it had to have done. Our heads were spinning. If the goal had been given, it would have been game over. Boro would have been beaten and we would be on the way to Wembley. There would have been no way they would have got back at us again. Looking back it again was the worse thing that could have happened to us. Yet again our heads were all over the place. Middlesbrough, realising they had had a massive let-off, came pouring at us and when Juninho went on one of his runs at pace we were stretched. Just as Juninho was about to enter the box, Dychey hung a leg out and over Juninho went. This decision was never really discussed because of the other incident in the game but whether the foul was committed inside or outside the box was again debatable. Elleray yet again endeared himself to the Chesterfield public by pointing straight to the spot. No looking to the linesman to see whether he had a better view of the foul. Elleray wanted to be the star of the show. He was calling all the Middlesbrough players by their first names as if he knew them personally; it was as if he was star-struck. I know he had contact with Premier League players week in week out, but it really did not seem fair. Craig Hignett converted the penalty and for the rest of normal time it was real back to the wall stuff. We threw bodies in the way of shots and wasted time at every opportunity. Bomber even nearly cleared the main stand (it is the smallest) in the final few minutes as we hung on. The final whistle was welcome as it gave us a few minutes breather before extra-time. I had come off with about 20 minutes of normal time left, yet again resembling the tin man after half-time due to my double hernia.

John and Kevin told us we had to really dig in and keep our shape and try to frustrate them. Yet again it was real back to the wall stuff and it came as no surprise when Festa pounced on a loose ball and smashed it into the net to put Boro 3–2 ahead. To be honest, Boro could have easily extended their lead a couple of times and as the last minute of extra-time came we were dead on our feet. The mental pressure had finally taken its toll (nothing to do with the couple of pints the day before) and we probably had one more attack in us. Chris Beaumont picked the ball up right over on the far touchline from the dugouts. He threw an aimless ball into the Boro 18-yard box. Darren Carr went up for the challenge and forced the defender to miss it. The ball bounced towards Jamie Hewitt.

He somehow managed to get his head to the ball and get enough power to direct it towards goal. Ben Roberts was wrong-footed in the Boro goal and the ball seemed to take an age to leap past him and into the goal. We had got the equaliser. Cue probably the worst celebration by a goalscorer ever seen in the history of professional football. (Jamie did not score that many!) Pandemonium broke out in our dugout. Kev Randall knocked the gaffer's glasses off in celebration and that clip was to be shown many times over the next few months on television. We had held on for a memorable draw. What a game! We stayed out on the pitch for ages after, celebrating and clapping the fans. We swapped shirts with the Boro players (I managed to get Curtis Fleming's and later Juninho's in the replay) and eventually ended up back in the dressing room. We were exhausted but Manchester United had left a bottle of champagne in there for every player. On the table in the middle of the room were about four more bottles of champagne left by Roy Keane, who had been a youth-team player a few years earlier with Dychey at Forest. What a gesture! After many pictures and interviews we all made our way up to the players' lounge at Old Trafford. It was a free bar and we stayed there for an hour or so watching highlights of the game. It was only then when we saw the disallowed goal that we realised how far the ball had actually crossed the line. We had been robbed! However, we did not let it spoil the day – or the night. On the way back to Chesterfield there was a real party atmosphere. Every pub we passed was full of Chesterfield fans and once again the word got out about our route back. Fans were everywhere, applauding and dancing in the streets. It was great to see. When we arrived back in Chesterfield we went straight out to the club where we usually went. Obviously the rules had been relaxed and we went upstairs into the VIP lounge. When it was announced that we were in the club the place erupted. When we went to the balcony, it was a sea of scarves and flags. I spent the night at Jamie's house and after only a couple of hours' sleep we were woken up to banging on the door. It was the national press wanting photos of the hero of the day!

Things settled down over the next few days. A good job, as we were all mentally and physically exhausted. It would be hard for us to recreate that same level of performance again. Realistically we knew we had had our chance and what a chance it had been. We had been 2–0 up against 10 men and only 25 or so minutes away from an FA Cup Final at Wembley. Looking back we should have done it! We had been a bit naïve, understandably so, and that coupled with one of the worst refereeing decisions of all time had robbed us of making history and becoming the first team from the third tier of English football to reach an FA Cup Final. But nobody can ever take away that Sunday afternoon at Old Trafford from us and nobody will certainly ever forget it.

The replay at Hillsborough was a massive anticlimax. We were well beaten, 3–0, and it never came close to reaching the heights of the first game. Not many do!

What a game! What a season! Nothing could ever get close to that FA Cup run, it was that special. Thank you to everybody associated at Chesterfield FC, from staff and players to supporters, for making that 1996–97 season so memorable.

Chapter Twenty-Two
Back Down to Earth

There was no way the previous season's achievements could be surpassed or even got anywhere near so it was a strange pre-season. All the hype had died down and now it was a case of getting back to the bread and butter of League football. Chances were that we would never get that far in a Cup competition again in our whole careers, especially in the FA Cup, let alone emulate it the following season. The season was a massive anticlimax. It was always going to be, and our results mirrored this. Once we got on a bit of a run we were fine but they did not last long enough, and vice versa with some terrible runs of results. The League season could really have been split into five periods, three good little spells and two horrible spells. We started the season on fire: confidence was still high from our Cup run and after six League games we found ourselves second in the table with 14 points from the first six matches. A great start. We had also disposed of Wigan Athletic in the League Cup, winning both games, and we had drawn Barnsley in the next round, a club who were definitely on the up.

Our next game was a massive one, away at Watford who were the only team above us at that early stage. They had two very different strikers in Jason Lee and Ronnie Rosenthal, but they were two players who had competed at the top level and were now probably playing below their level. It was a great game but Watford eventually came out on top, deservedly winning 2–1. That result knocked us badly for some reason, none of us knew why, and we went nine games without a win, including being comfortably knocked out of the League Cup by Barnsley. In our seven League games we only picked up three points courtesy of three draws, and we were sliding rapidly down the table. The team spirit was still there even though some of the personnel had changed, and we rallied round. It is strange what outside influences can affect morale on the pitch and it was around this time that we set up a little golf League between ourselves. The idea was that you would play in pairs and play everybody in the League twice, once at a course of your choice and the other at a choice of the other pairing. I was paired with my midfield partner Tommy Curtis. At that time we were a similar standard on the golf course, both of us playing off a 16 handicap. Nowadays Tommy has obviously had too much time on his hands and plays off a handicap in single figures. He never lets on what it actually is, but I do know he has played below par a few times. So be careful if you ever get on a golf course with him, he is a bandit! Those games of golf brought the squad closer together again and it seemed to relax us again. In the next nine League games we went unbeaten, winning four games and drawing five. We were back on it.

We also beat non-League Northwich Victoria in the first round of the FA Cup 1–0 at home. Everybody's hopes were high for another good Cup run and what better way to start than getting the same scoreline as against Bury, 12 months earlier? Could we do it again?

The second round saw us play Grimsby, and the chances of a similar Cup run seemed a million miles away when we found ourselves trailing 2–0 at half-time. It looked like it was over but our resolve and determination saw us fight back and take the tie to a replay. However, it was to be a false dawn as we lost the replay at Saltergate 2–0. Our Cup dream was over! This knocked us once more. We knew realistically that we could not emulate the heroics of the 1997 FA Cup run, but deep down we all hoped for the same. One thing that did show our strengths as a squad was the amount of goals we conceded. John had got us so well organised defensively we only let in three goals in nine games, a fantastic achievement. After the Cup loss, that all went out of the window. We went on a terrible run in the next 16 games, winning only three and losing eight. We were not being thumped but we had lost our way a little and teams had worked us out somewhat. We were still sitting back and letting teams come at us, but had lost the individual brilliance that could win you a game out of nothing. In this run we played away at Grimsby who were a decent team, especially on their own patch. John and Kev were not bothered about their centre midfielders having the ball as much as they liked as long as they did not pass the ball into the feet of their strikers. That role for us was really the same as what we did every week but with the whole team playing abut 10 yards deeper. No problem with that. Unfortunately nobody had told Billy Mercer this. He had been doing some specialist work with the other 'keepers when we had been working on this game plan and had no idea that we were going to play that little bit deeper as a team. The idea behind this was that because Grimsby were a small, quick team we did not mind them putting balls into the box because with our sheer size and power we should deal with that quite comfortably. The problem would be if we opened up and they would then be able to isolate their attackers against our slower defenders.

The first 10 minutes or so of the game went perfectly. Grimsby did not get in behind us once because we were playing that deep, and even though they probably had 80 per cent of the possession they had not had one effort on goal. They were becoming frustrated with just playing in front of us and I think it was out of sheer frustration that Wayne Burnett, their midfielder, picked the ball and let fly at goal from all of 40 yards. That was the plan, frustrate them and make sure that if they were going to have a shot at goal it was from a distance. The problem was Burnett had one hell of a shot on him. The ball whistled past my ear and crashed against the bar. We all looked at each other. Where did that come from? That was not part of the plan. Surely a shot like that was a one-off? Burnett must have had six or seven shots at goal in the remainder of the first half, and only a mixture of the woodwork and some world-class saves from Billy meant we went into the interval at 0–0. Every time he had a shot we used to look over to the bench to see if the game plan was to change but John and Kev just stood there motionless. When we got into the changing room Billy went mad. He could not believe what was happening, and said so in no uncertain terms. Just as he was ranting, John and Kev came in and said 'Well done lads. It is working perfectly.' We could not believe it, but more importantly Billy could not believe it 'You what!?' We all burst out laughing and for about two minutes we were in hysterics. Billy eventually saw the funny side and it was decided that we would go back to our usual way of playing, still very defensive but a bit further up the field so that Burnett could not have another 45 minutes practising his long-range shooting. The plan had not worked perfectly in the first half, but rather than coming in ranting and raving John and Kev had defused the situation perfectly and that was what they were good at. We hung on for a 0–0 draw without too many alarms second half, certainly fewer than the first half.

Our next game was at home to Fulham and saw me come head-to-head (virtually) with Paul Peschisolido. He was a great player but a bit cocky and arrogant on the pitch. Apparently he is a great lad off the pitch, but we definitely did not see eye to eye, especially when we were having a few words and he said, 'How much do you earn?' He was obviously on decent money at Fulham, a lot more than I was at lowly Chesterfield. Fair play to him, but I have played with and against a lot better players than him, but they let their football do the talking and were not the type to brag abut how much they were earning. They beat us comfortably 2–0 and he was chirpy all the way through the game. I shook hands with him after the game and wished him all the best, and to be fair to him he shook my hand and said the same back. I would have my moment the next time we played against each other, I thought to myself. We lost our next game away at Gillingham but then finished the season off well with another decent run. We picked up 17 points in our last eight games with five wins, two draws and the one defeat away at Luton.

That season was a strange one. Not just because it followed the greatest season ever in the club's history, but because you could split the season into five distinct spells. There was not a spell in the season where we were on a so-so run, where we might win one, lose one, win one etc. We had three very good spells through the season· comprising a total of 23 games (exactly half the games) where we picked up 48 points and two spells where we were awful and only picked up 17 points. When we were good we were very good (if we had played like that and been consistent we would have won the League) but when we were poor we were awful (we could have been relegated, finishing bottom by a distance).

A strange season for the club and a worrying one for me. My right knee was now becoming a serious problem and I had two more operations on it over the summer to try and solve the injury. By this time I had had five operations on my right knee, not good news. Would the 1998–99 season be better?

Chapter Twenty-Three
Pads On

A s you can see from the last couple of chapters, the spirit in the squad was unbelievable. Whatever was thrown at us we would stand up, dust ourselves down and get on with it. No other club I played for had that same spirit. Mansfield came close a couple of times but under Andy King we were too young and too naïve to be really successful, the promotion team of 1991–92 under the management of George Foster while coming very close (because there was a good spirit) did not have that same closeness as at Chesterfield. The things we had to put up with were unbelievable and the squads at Sheffield United and Bristol City would not have been mentally strong enough to put up with such problems. For starters we never had a training ground. The amount of times we were thrown off a pitch by an irate groundsman was unbelievable. We would never know from one day to the next where we would be training. It used to make us laugh when Kev Randall would come back from his daily morning run, which he said was to keep his fitness up but we knew the real reason: he had been out trying to find somewhere to train. Most weeks we would end up at a grass area behind a pub about two miles from the ground. We would be getting changed at Saltergate into training kit and having tea and a chat and Kev's voice would bellow down the corridor telling us to get our 'bumpers' (trainers) on and then we would jog to wherever we were training. The grass area behind the pub was typical of the standard of our training facilities (if you could call them that). There were no goals and no markings, Kev would have to go round with a cone beforehand scooping any dog mess or any undesirable objects off the training area. Not many squads would have put up with it but we just got on with it. If anybody ever complained they would have been classed as a 'big time Charlie'. No way could you describe it as ideal, but that was life at the Spireites.

Another sport that many of the players were interested in was cricket. Every morning without fail, the three amigos (Tommy Curtis, Jamie Hewitt and myself) would be round the back of the stand with a ball and bat. We would be there for an hour or so before training and sometimes an hour or so after. We had our own set of rules and the rest of the lads used to give us some stick but one by one they would start getting involved and it was not long before all of the squad would come out before training. There were varying abilities, from Jamie, Tom and myself being the best cricketers, to Reevsie who looked like he had never picked a bat up in his life. He was that bad, but Reevsie being Reevsie was never out. At that time he was the joker in the pack, a likeable scouser who never shut up.

The cricket bug was catching on. Kev Randall, the assistant manager, was absolutely mad on his cricket. He said he was an opening batsman in the Geoffrey Boycott mould. Geoffrey Boycott was like Ian Botham compared to Kev, he was so boring. He never played an attacking shot and I certainly never saw him hit it off the square. He was very much a blocker. In fact, cricket had caught on that much we organised an annual friendly match against the likes of Glapwell CC or Sheepbridge CC. They were very much light-hearted affairs with us usually meeting beforehand in the pub and having a bite to eat and a couple of pints. There were always stories to tell about our escapades at cricket. I can remember the first year at Glapwell. We were fielding first and we were all out in the field waiting for their opening batsman to come out when we realised that our wicketkeeper was not out yet. Marcus Ebdon had volunteered to be the 'keeper and when he came out we all fell about laughing. The phrase 'All the gear no idea' comes to mind. He came running out of the changing rooms with his pads and gloves on but also with a traditional baggy white cricket hat on (very much like Jack Russell's). The look was completed with a pair of Oakley sunglasses and he lined up behind the stumps ready for the first ball. He looked like a professional wicketkeeper but that was where the resemblance stopped. Tommy bowled the first ball just outside the off stump: the perfect line. The batsman was in two minds whether to play at the ball or not. At the last minute he let the ball go and it missed the off stump by a couple of inches. Perfect cricket. A good ball by the bowler, a good decision by the batsman. All that was left now was the routine stop by the 'keeper. That was when the perfect cricket stopped. Taffy (Marcus) got himself in position perfectly, his gloves were ready and in position to catch the ball. He certainly looked like he knew what he was doing. However, I think the speed of the delivery had surprised him and he did not get his hands together in time. The ball thumped against his chest. You could hear the air knocked out of him as he fell backwards. He did not get a lot of sympathy, we were all too busy laughing.

It didn't get much better for us in the field. Billy Mercer, our goalkeeper, was not allowed to be wicketkeeper in case he broke a finger or something. John Duncan was not particularly happy about Billy playing but Billy was desperate for a game. Finally the gaffer relented but gave Kev Randall strict orders to keep him out of the way. This he did until Billy came on to bowl. With the strangest of actions he bowled his first delivery (I say first delivery – his first four efforts were wides) and the batsman absolutely smacked it straight back down the pitch, about a metre wide of Billy. Instinctively he put his hand out, and the ball hit his fingers. He let out the biggest scream and doubled up. I looked straight at Kev. He had gone white in an instant. How was he going to explain to the gaffer that our number one 'keeper had broken two fingers playing cricket? How would John explain that to the press? You could see all these questions rushing around in Kev's head. I was one of the first to get to Billy. He gave me a wink and I immediately knew what he was up to. The lads soon did as well. We all waited for Kev to get over, all of us looking concerned. Billy gave Kev a wink. 'You t★★t! You bloody idiot!' Kev screamed. Eventually he saw the funny side of it.

That was not the end of our inept field display; the best was still to come. The boundary rope was very close to the field and when one of their batsman cracked the ball towards the boundary, off went Jon Howard and Tommy to try and stop a four. Jon got to the ball just before it crossed the boundary and flicked it back. Tommy threw the ball in. Perfect. Not quite! After flicking the ball back, Jon's momentum carried him over the rope and head first into a hedge out of sight. You just could not make it up!

As you can tell, we used to do many things together as a squad away from the football club. This definitely helped us to become a very close-knit group of players. We used to do everything together. From cricket to golf to go-karting. The first time we went to the indoor track on the outskirts of Chesterfield there were quite a few of us there. You were only allowed six racing at any one time so the first six went out togged out in their red costumes and helmets. We were stood in the pit lane, which was surrounded either side by a wall of tyres, and the owner was giving us instructions, such as where you could overtake and what different colour flags meant if we saw any of the officials waving them. Harry (Roger Willis) was the first to get in his cart and off he sped on his first practice lap. We were still in the pit lane waiting for our carts to be switched on when Harry came flying down the final straight. At the bottom of the straight Harry was supposed to hang a left and fly round the corner in front of the pits. But he had forgotten and instead he came flying through the pit lane, which was only just wide enough for a cart to fit through, heading straight for us. There was no way he could stop. We dived for safety any way we could. If John Duncan could have seen us he would have had kittens!

Soon we were well into the race. I can remember looking behind me and seeing Ian Breckin and Mark Williams vying for position. They were about half a lap behind and had a few corners to face. Bomber (Mark Williams) went into a corner too quick and spun and Brecks with nowhere to go went straight into him and over his legs. For about a half a lap I was unsure as to whether he was really hurt or not. When they came into view Bomber was at least standing but his cart had seen better days. He was limping but being the tough (?) man he was he did not like to admit he was hurting. Again, it was a good job the gaffer and Kev had not seen it. They never knew the half! (Until now!)

Chapter Twenty-Four
Injury Concerns

This season was to be very similar to the previous one. We were still very sound defensively (we had to be the amount of time we spent working on it!) but we still had a major problem, even more so this season, of scoring goals.

We started the season with a defeat away at Colchester, but then won our next three games without conceding a goal. Two of the three games were against our local rivals Rotherham United, a team that we always seemed to do well against. In the second leg at Saltergate I used my experience to get the better of one of their younger players. I sound like a right old pro when I say that, I was only 25 but quite experienced! Rotherham had a young lad playing for them called Danny Hudson. Jamie Hewitt and I had got a corner routine going where we left a big vacant area about 10 yards out in line with the near post. Jamie had a great dead-ball strike on him and managed to hit that area nine times out of 10, not with a high-floated ball but with a hard-drive ball coming into that area about head height. It was a well worked set play with the rest of our players making decoy runs towards the back post. This left me to try and get a half yard on my marker and time my run with Jamie's delivery. It had worked well but never as good as that night. I knew where the ball was going but young Danny Hudson was marking me tightly. I thought I would try a little trick. 'You've had a good start to the season, Danny. Keep it going mate. You've got a great future ahead of you,' I said just as I started to walk behind him. He lost concentration a little and went to turn round and as I heard him say, 'Thanks Paul', I was already on the move. It was too late for Danny. He was facing the wrong way and he was wrong-footed. The ball was on its way and it was perfect. When I headed it Danny must have been 10 yards away from me. He had been well and truly kippered. The ball flew in the net and all their players looked at young Danny. He had not got a clue what to say. I shook hands with him after the game, and apologised. He actually said, 'Thanks. Nobody will ever do that to me again'. It was a harsh lesson, but he would learn from it as we all do.

Yet again our early season form was indifferent. We managed to pick up 14 points from our first 10 games. The highlight of those games was playing against Manchester City at Maine Road. I found myself playing at centre-half, and this was becoming a more regular thing. I can remember Barry Statham, my old physio at Mansfield, saying that he thought centre-half was my best position. Towards the end of my career I would have to agree. Injuries were beginning to take a toll on my knees and they would take a lot longer to recover if I played in midfield because of the extra running it entailed. I still say to this day that centre-half is the easiest position on the pitch. We drew 1–1 against City with our second-choice 'keeper Andy Leaning making a penalty save and having an excellent game. The atmosphere that day was brilliant, and City fans must be some of the best in the land seeing how well they were supported that one season in our League, the third tier of the Football League.

We were doing alright, but we had only scored six goals in our opening 10 games. Simply not good enough! We played Stoke City in early October at their new ground, the Britannia Stadium. It was a great stadium and the facilities inside were superb. The changing rooms were very modern and spacious, quite unlike their old ground. The Sky television cameras were there to see what should have been (it certainly was on paper), a good competitive game and a good advert for lower League football. Anyone who watched that game to see what lower League football was all about would never have watched again. It was a terrible game. It was boring to play in, so god knows what it was like to watch. The game ended 0–0 and it has to go down as one of the worst ever televised games, if not the worst. It was that bad.

We went on to win our next four games, all at home. The highlight of these was the 3–0 demolition of Notts County. I managed to score twice in this game, made all the sweeter as they were scored past my old Mansfield teammate Darren Ward. I think one of the goals was from the infamous corner routine. Our inconsistency was to strike again though as we went out of the FA Cup in the first game at Wycombe. The FA Cup had become special to the Chesterfield public since the 1997 run so it was disappointing to go out at the first hurdle. That was to be my last FA Cup game for Chesterfield.

Our next game saw us go to high-flying Fulham. They had spent big under the chairmanship of Mohammed Al Fayed, and with the players they had bought they were firm favourites for automatic promotion. I was to see an old mate again, in the form of Paul Peschisolido. Fulham absolutely battered us in the first half, playing us off the park, and we thoroughly deserved to go in at half-time two goals to the good.

We had a bit of a reshuffle at half-time and decided to come out and try and take the game to Fulham (very much unlike us!). We might as well lose 6–0 as 2–0. It was definitely, to use the old cliché, a game of two halves. We played them off the park. We pulled a goal back to make it 2–1. It was only a matter of time before we equalised surely. But the goal would not come. I knew now what it must have felt like playing us. The board indicating there would be three minutes of added time was put up. We still had a chance. The ball went out towards the touchline where Geoff Horsfield, the bully centre-forward, picked the ball up in oceans of space. Instead of looking for a pass he decided to do a bit of showboating. He flicked the ball up and started doing 'keepie ups'. The crowd was loving it. The score was 2–1 not 5 or 6–0, and we saw it as a p★ss take. I would not have even dreamt of doing that, even if we were 10–0 up. It is disrespectful. Tommy and I were fuming and went flying towards him. The steam must have been visible coming out of our ears. Tommy got there first about five yards ahead of me (he was always quicker than me!). Tommy tried to smash Horsfield but the

Fulham player nonchalantly flicked the ball over Tommy's head and he ended up on the track at the side of the pitch. There was no way he was going to do the same to me. If I could not get the ball then Horsfield was going to end up on the track with me. Just as I was preparing for the contact (it would have been some contact as well, we were two big lads) my favourite man, Peschisolido, nipped in and took the ball off Horsfield without the ball touching the floor. It would have looked great in an exhibition match. I was fully committed now and there was no going back; Peschisolido, not Horsfield, took the brunt of it. He went down as if he had been polaxed. It looked a bad challenge to be fair. Phil Dowd was the referee, somebody who I had always got on with and still do to this day. 'I'm sorry Holly. You are going to have to go', he said. I am not sure what I was more upset about: being sent off or being called Holly. I had never been called Holly before and thankfully have never been since. Over the next few months I gave Tommy some stick saying he had cost me half a week's wages by missing his tackle and leaving it to me to get sent off, 'You may be quicker than me Tom, but Horsfield did make you look a tad silly that day!'

I was to be suspended for three games so it was the perfect time for another operation on my knee. Three operations in less than six months on the same knee, it was not good but it needed doing. We did not win a game throughout December and by the turn of the year we found ourselves in 11th place. In the 23 games so far we had played that season you could see quite clearly where our strengths and weaknesses were. We had scored a paltry 23 goals (one a game on average) and let in a mere 19 goals in the same amount of games. We must have been so good to watch! In 23 games there had been a total of 42 goals scored. Hardly stuff to bring the fans back.

The new year came and we got ourselves back on track, even scoring a few goals in the process. We won four games out of five in January and this took us up to seventh in the table, one place off the Play-off spots but level on points with Gillingham in sixth. We were one place above the mighty Manchester City so we can not have been doing too badly. We were to play City in one of only three games in February and that ended in a 1–1 draw. Yet again they travelled in their numbers to support them. In the end they got their reward (just) when they beat Gillingham in the Play-off Final to achieve promotion. Without a win in those three games we slipped three places to 10th, but we were ready for one last push in the remaining 15 games to try and put some pressure on those clubs in the Play-off places. The push did not materialise. In the remaining games we only won four out of 15. We drew five and lost six to finish in ninth place. Not a bad position seeing as there were some big clubs in the division, but we had missed the Play-offs by 12 points. I think we were becoming easier to play against now, and as a squad we were beginning to become a bit stale (so it proved the following season). In our heyday we could beat anybody, but those days were becoming less frequent! One such example is when League leaders Fulham came to Saltergate. Fulham were riding high on the crest of a wave and looked like breaking the 100 point barrier in a season – a mean achievement! What did we do? Beat them 1–0, but a comfortable

1–0. It was good to beat them after Horsfield's antics at Craven Cottage earlier in the season and I got a little bit of revenge on Peschisolido as well so it was a good day. The ball was played along the touchline for him but was played too far in front of him. I was playing at the back and I could have dealt with it comfortably and knocked it out of play easily before he got to the ball. I saw my chance, not to injure him but to give him a good whack so he would know I was there. I slowed right down to give him a chance of getting the ball (it was not too hard for me to slow down as I was not that quick!). As I went for the ball Peschisolido was just getting there at exactly the same time. Bang! I won the ball and my momentum took him up into the air flying backwards. It seemed like slow motion as he flew through the air, over the hoardings and straight against the window of the police box. I don't know whose expression would have been better, Peschisolido's face as he went towards the window or that of the safety officer's in the police box as a player hurtled towards them. Horsfield came over and I was ready for a row, but he winked and said 'Great tackle. He had that coming.' I went over and ruffled Peschisolido's hair and was tempted to say, 'It doesn't matter how much money you are on. It still bloody hurts, doesn't it?' I refrained and eventually shook his hand after the game. We had closure!

A disappointing season, but little did I know at the time that this would be my last full season at Saltergate. I should have seen it coming really and to be fair it was the right decision for Chesterfield. My knee was now a major concern and I required another operation during the summer of 1999, the eighth on my right knee.

Chapter Twenty-Five
Pastures New

T he operation on my knee had gone well. I had had a really good pre-season and felt as fit as I had done for a long time. The friendlies had not particularly gone well, so we were not sure what realistic aims were to be for the season. For the last three seasons we had finished just outside the Play-offs after being around them all season. However, I felt, as I have said previously, that we were not as strong as previous seasons so perhaps a mid-table position would be classed as a successful year.

We lost our opening two games, and John Duncan was starting to get a bit of stick from the crowd. We managed to beat Rochdale 4–2 on aggregate in the first round of the League Cup so that appeased the fans a little, especially when they found out who our opponents in the next round were going to be – a re-run of our 1997 FA Cup semi-final – Middlesbrough over two legs home and away. Something to certainly look forward to.

Remember my story about me becoming an 'old pro' when I managed to trick young Danny Hudson when I scored against Rotherham? Well when we played against Cambridge United at home I found myself playing at centre-half again alongside Ian Breckin. Cambridge had an up-and-coming striker called Trevor Benjamin. He had already built himself a reputation as a powerful young forward with tremendous strength. I thought that I would have to let him know who was boss early on in the game. I would always back myself in a physical battle on a football field so I was looking forward to the challenge. After about two minutes I had my chance to show him that I was just as strong as he was. The ball got played into his feet as I tried to get round the side and pinch it in front of him. This was a strength of mine, as usually I could battle through the centre-forward and come away with the ball. Not this time. I bounced off Trevor, he turned me and I tried to trip him before he was through on goal. Somehow I managed to find myself on his back. He carried me for about 10 yards on his back (he must have been strong) before unleashing a shot into the bottom corner. Plan B. I failed to battle through him so I would have to out-think him instead. He did not cause me much trouble for the remainder of the game which we went on to win 4–2. A lesson learnt for the 'old pro' in that there is always someone bigger and stronger than you!

Our next game was away at Millwall, a game that saw my last 90 minutes in a Chesterfield shirt. About halfway through the first half I went up with their centre-forward for a header. I won the header and as soon as I came down I landed on my knees with the bottom of my legs behind me. Their lad came down from a height and landed straight across my left calf. It hurt at the time but I could carry on. I put some ice on it at half-time but it was sore at the end of 90 minutes. I iced it on the way back but it was starting to swell quite badly. Rushy (the physio) told me to keep an eye on it over the weekend and ice it regularly which I did, but come Monday it was nearly twice the size. My calf was that big I could not get my jeans on. When I got to the ground Rushy nearly fainted. My calf was red-hot even after I had iced it for 20 minutes, and he was getting concerned. After a few days, it still had yet to reduce in size, and it was decided that something had to be done. They made a little incision in my calf and drained the blood out. It was scary how my calf reduced in size, literally in front of my eyes. The doctor said I was not to play for a couple of weeks because of all the muscle trauma and damage to the calf.

I missed the away victory at Preston and the home defeat against Stoke City. Our next game was Middlesbrough at home. I was still sidelined but I was looking forward to the game to see the likes of Paul Ince and Paul Gascoigne in action. Gazza got injured just before half-time and went straight to the dressing room. One of the youth team at Chesterfield went into the Boro dressing room after half-time to collect the teapot. When he knocked he heard a shout to come in and found Gazza sat in there icing his calf. He asked the young player if he would go and make him a cup of coffee. The lad did as he was asked, who would turn Gazza down!? When he went back in Gazza thanked him and asked him to sit with him while he iced his leg. The lad did it, even though he was a little star-struck – who would not be at 16? When he had finished icing the lad was about to leave him to get showered when Gazza asked what his name was. He picked up his boots and signed them to the lad, 'Best Wishes, Gazza'. Brilliant!

The return leg was to be my last appearance for Chesterfield. I came on as substitute for about the last 20 minutes when we were 1–0 down on aggregate. I enjoyed pitting myself against Paul Ince and we soon levelled the scores with a minute to go. The tie looked like it was heading to extra-time, when they scored again to make it 2–1. We had lost with the last kick of the game. Little did I know that when I clapped the Chesterfield fans at the end of the game that was my goodbye. It was a shame as they had been brilliant with me and I would have liked to say goodbye and thank them properly.

The following morning my phone went early. It was an agent saying that a club was interested in me and would I like him to represent me in the deal. I put the phone down. Agents should not ring you directly behind the clubs' backs. He kept on ringing and I kept on ignoring him. I had signed a contract with Colin Gibson (the ex-Manchester United player) to act on my behalf as part of the PFA. I had had no contact with anybody from Chesterfield or Colin, so as far as I was concerned there was nothing in it. I was happy at Chesterfield and did not want to leave.

My phone rang again and I looked at it half expecting it to be the agent. It was the club! It was Kevin Randall saying something had come up and that I had to come to the ground. When I got there Kev and John Duncan quickly shepherded me into their office. They said the club had accepted a bid from Bristol City of £200,000, and although they did not want me to leave it had been accepted by the club so it was down to me. I asked them why the chairman had agreed to the deal, and they said it was down to my injuries and also they did not know how long I would be able to command a fee. Fair enough. By this time I had had eight operations on my knee, and with my contract about to expire the following summer I might not get offered a new one judging by the chairman accepting this bid. While I was with them, my phone rang. It was Tony Pulis, the Bristol City manager. He had obviously been given permission by Norton Lea, the Chesterfield chairman, to ring me directly. I asked if he could ring me back in about half an hour. This was real. Kev Randall was really upset. We had always been close, ever since my days as a youth-team player at Mansfield when he was the youth-team manager. I was honest with them and said I would speak to Bristol City out of courtesy but Norton had made it very difficult for me. I shook hands with John and Kev but we all knew it was probably a thank you and goodbye. I spoke to Pulis again and he invited me to go to their Cup game against Forest that night in Nottingham. He left me a ticket, I thought it perhaps would be in the directors' box but intead it was right behind the goal in the middle of the City fans. It was a weird feeling. The night before I had been playing on the pitch at the Riverside Stadium against Middlesbrough, and 24 hours later I was sat with the Bristol City fans at Forest. Surreal. I travelled down to Bristol the following day to talk over a proposed move. It was a good deal they had on offer, and I rang John and told him I was going to sign. I thanked him for all of his help over the four years I had been there, and wished him all the best for the future. It really did happen that quickly. I was genuinely gutted to be leaving Chesterfield but the chairman had pushed things through (I do not blame him) and left me with little option but to leave. I had had some fantastic times and made some great friends at Saltergate with the highlight obviously being the 1997 FA Cup run. Thanks for the memories!

Chapter Twenty-Six
The Wembley Spoiler

I travelled down to Bristol on the Thursday morning and met with Tony Pulis, while Colin Gibson from the PFA went in with the chairman to thrash out a deal. I was still struggling a bit with my calf injury but I had to try and hide that when I was going through a bit of a running session with the reserves on the Thursday afternoon. It was not too strenuous so after I had showered it was a case of having a meeting with Colin to see what City had offered. There was more money being offered and understandably so, seeing as I would have to move down to Bristol where the house prices were significantly higher. A lot of it was incentive based so that you had to be in the team and the team doing well for you to see the difference in wage. I had no problem with that because from what I had seen, and from the players that they had got in their new squad, Bristol City was a sleeping giant seriously underachieving. Tony Pulis had it spot on when he said the squad was full of southern softies and it needed somebody to come in and have a fallout with a few, upset a few people who were just coasting and going along with the flow. He saw that person as me along with another target he was after, strangely enough from the same club as I had just come from. Billy Mercer and I were soon to become teammates again for the third time at different clubs. It would be nice to have a familiar face in the Ashton Gate dressing room.

It was arranged for me to stay in a hotel in Bristol until I found myself a house down there. That was okay but it is not ideal when you are living out of a suitcase. There was another player in the hotel as well called Steve Jones, who was probably one of the ones Tony Pulis talked about. A nice lad but you could never really say he had his heart and soul into football. However, there was no way I could travel everyday. It was a two and a half hour drive from Chesterfield so the hotel was definitely needed.

The contract was signed and I reported for my first day's training on the Friday morning. Again I could not believe the size of the squad. From walking in on my first day to the day I left, the club, the players and everything about the place reminded me of Sheffield United. There were over 40 professionals, and you could see from day one that there were little cliques formed all over the dressing room. The facilities were brilliant, but they were spoilt. Their kits were washed and laid out for them every day just like it was as Sheffield. All they were asked to do after training each day was fold their dirty kit into their dirty towel and take them down to the laundry for either the wash lady or the kit man to sort out. Not hard! The majority of the players could not even be bothered to do that, instead just throwing it on the floor in the middle of the dressing room floor for Buster (the kit man) to sort out. That drove me insane and after a few weeks at the club, and after my settling in period, I would have to say something.

My first game for Bristol City would be on the Saturday after joining on the Thursday. With only one training session under my belt, I expected to be on the bench for the home game against Burnley. When the team got announced at the training ground on the Friday morning, I was to line up in central midfield. I was starting! No problem I thought, it was a good opportunity to show my new teammates and fans what I am all about. All you want to do when you first join a club is get through that first game, a goal or a win is a bonus. Did I manage that? You should know by now that my career was never that simple and never went according to plan. I did not even get through the 90 minutes. The first half went well on a personal level. I had been told to get forward as much as I wanted which is what I enjoyed doing, I had always felt frustrated at being held back in a more defensive role at Chesterfield. I had got on the end of a couple of crosses, gone close to scoring a couple of times and put in a few crunching tackles, something that fans always like to see. I was enjoying it. Then my unlucky injury jinx hit again. I went into an innocuous challenge on the halfway line, and as I came out of it I went over really awkwardly on my ankle. It was agony. I immediately thought I had broken it. Gill O'Shea, the physio, came on and straight away called for the stretcher. What a start!

When I got into the physio room the doctor carefully took off my boot and cut my sock off with a pair of scissors. I had never had any problems with my ankles all throughout my career, from a seven-year-old right up to my last game at Chesterfield and yet here I was in my first game for my new club, laying in the physio room with an ankle the size of a melon.

This injury was a nightmare to shake off and it was five weeks before I played again. To tell you the truth it was not quite right when I came back, but a mixture of things made me say it was okay. Firstly and most importantly was the fact that I had just joined the club and there is nothing worse than when you are trying to settle in a new club and being laid up on treatment from day one. You know what people are saying – that you are there for the money and that you are just happy to be 'picking up the dough'. That could not have been further away from the truth. I was desperate to get started and that is why I was determined to play, even if my ankle injury had yet to heal properly. The second reason was that the next game was the first round of the FA Cup and we had been drawn against my first club Mansfield Town at Ashton Gate. I had never played against the Stags since I left Mansfield more than four years earlier and I was eager to play even though I was only about 50 per cent fit. People would say that you should never play in a game unless you are a 100 per cent fit as you are letting your teammates and fans down. If that was the case I would never have played a game since 1994! I loved my football and if I did think I was letting people down by not being a 100 per cent, I would not have played. Besides, I passed a medical at Bristol City, despite having eight operations on my right knee!

When I ran out for the game against Mansfield, I was not sure what reception I would get from the Stags faithful. Would I get warm applause for what I had done for the club in my four years where I had always been a fans' favourite or would I get called a Judas for being a so-called traitor and playing for the enemy, Chesterfield? I soon found out. Ninety five per cent of the fans were brilliant and gave me a great ovation, realising that I had gone to Chesterfield because they were playing at a higher level than Mansfield and purely for football reasons. My decision, in my eyes, had been vindicated by the success the club had in the four years I was there and the majority of the Stags faithful knew that and acted accordingly. The other five per cent went mad, with cries of 'Judas', 'Traitor' and 'Spireite' being the more polite of the insults levelled at me, but you get idiots at every club and if they fail to see what is right in front of their eyes then they are not worth bothering with. Any true Mansfield fan would know that I would have run through a brick wall for them, and even when I went back there as a coach you would get those same morons directing abuse at you.

The game against Mansfield, as I said, was my first game for five weeks and in fact I had not played a full 90 minutes since the Millwall game for Chesterfield on the last Saturday in August more than two months previously. I wanted a nice easy game to get myself back in the swing of things. After one minute Mansfield had a shot at goal and it was handled on the line by our captain Shaun Taylor. A blatant penalty and to make matters worse for us the referee sent him off. The spot-kick was converted by a great friend of mine, Tony Lormor. Mansfield had the initiative now and were in the box seat playing against 10 men. For some strange reason they sat back and allowed us back into the game. I had been pushed back to play at centre-half in Shaun's absence and I expected a tough time with Mansfield bombarding us but it never materialised until about the 80th minute. We cruised into a 3–1 lead, and I can remember looking over at the dugouts when Mansfield were bringing on a substitute. They were bringing on a young lad who did not look old enough to be playing, a guy called Michael Boulding who I was to coach in that last couple of seasons at the Stags. A true gentlemen and an absolute credit to his family. Not that I thought that when he knocked the ball past me and went after it. 'Young upstart. Who the hell does he think he is, knocking it past me and thinking he can get it the other side when he has given me a 10-yard start?' Ten-yard start! I needed 20. He was lightning. He would easily have beaten me to the ball, but I was not about to have this young whippersnapper taking liberties with me. I blatantly body-checked him, even though I tried to make it look as accidental as possible. I deservedly got booked but I now knew to be a bit careful about this young Boulding's pace. Mansfield pulled a goal back to make it 3–2 but we held on for a deserved victory. I gave the Mansfield fans a clap, they had always been good to me and they still were when I went back to the club on the coaching side of things, and I wanted to show them that it was appreciated.

We were 16th in the League, clearly not good enough for a club the size of City. There was something very wrong at the club, there must have been. You can not have the players of the ability City had and be in 16th position in the third tier. It was not the manager's fault. It was the players. Everything had to come easy to them; they did not want to work for anything. They were simply not bothered and that p★ssed me off no end. I had been used to the tight spirit at Chesterfield and the things that went on at Ashton Gate would not have been tolerated at the Spireites. It would have been sorted out, not by the manager but by the players themselves. They had a pride in each other and a pride in themselves, a pride which was sadly missing at City. The dressing room was full of 'big time Charlies'.

We continued to flatter ourselves winning some, drawing some and losing some but the urgency to put things right was lacking. On a cold night in December we went to Chesterfield and played at Saltergate. Chesterfield had had a terrible start to the season and were near the foot of the table (they were eventually to finish bottom) but I knew exactly what the lads in their dressing room would have been saying. 'Let's beat these big time Charlies. Let's kick them and see what they are made of.' Billy and I went round the City players that night and told them exactly what to expect, and to be fair they stood up and were counted as we won comfortably 2–0. The Chesterfield fans gave me a fantastic reception, they knew I had not wanted to leave the club and had had my hand forced if you like. It was nice to go back there.

We lost in the third round of the FA Cup away at Sheffield Wednesday and people were now starting to call for Pulis's head. We went into the Christmas period in 13th place. Yet again I was to spend Christmas night away from home preparing for our away fixture at Brentford. I hated it. At the end of the day, we were professionals and you should be able to refrain from the luxuries at that time of year, instead of having to be treated like kids (I felt this way a lot during my time at Bristol City). I probably played my best game for City on that Boxing Day. The team were awful so I think my effort and passion to try and salvage something out of the game went noticed by the manager and fans alike. After the game Pulis singled me out as the only player who should have been proud of the way they played that day. It was nice to hear but what happened next came as a shock.

Two days later we were to play Luton at home. I had done alright on Boxing Day so imagine my shock when the team got read out and I found myself among the substitutes. I was fuming but kept my cool. The only thing I could think of was that Pulis had already got his team worked out for the Luton game prior to the Boxing Day fixture. I did come on in the second half in a dull 0–0 draw and found myself back in the starting line up for the next game away at Wrexham in the first game of the new year. We won 1–0, a good result, and the lads were saying 'New year, new start'. That summed them up, they would say all the right things, the things that people wanted to hear, but actually going out and doing it was a different kettle of fish. I had played my part in a good victory. Everybody expected the side to stay the same (never change a winning side they say!) for the home game against our local rivals from across the border, Cardiff City. The game was to be played on the Sunday and when the team was read out, there was only one change to the team that had beaten Wrexham. I had been left out again. I could not believe it and neither could the lads. Being left out once when you do not deserve it you can handle, but for it to happen again made my blood boil. I am ashamed to say I did not try a leg in that training session, the only time I can honestly say that I could not be bothered. Not a good attitude to have but that is how I had come to feel in my early days (well, most of my time) at City.

I came on in the second half again, but we again drew 0–0. The fans let their feelings known, and during the following week Tony Pulis and Bristol City went their separate ways. I liked Tony Pulis as a man but did not enjoy playing for him. He has gone on to prove himself as a great manager, so perhaps he was right on those occasions and I was wrong, but I would definitely argue my case. I shook hands with Tony before he left and wished him all the best. I have spoken to him since but I have never once asked why he would play me away from home and leave me out for that spell when we played at home. Very strange. Who would take over? Three caretaker managers were announced. Tony Fawthrop (the chief scout), Leroy Rosenior (reserve team coach) and Dave Burnside (I am not sure what his role was apart from 'bigging up' the youth players) were the men in question and were to be known as the 'Three Amigos'. I got on fine with Tony and Leroy but not well with Dave. Dave was a purist. His ideas were full of football, silky skills and a good technique. Nothing wrong there but on a cold winter's night when you are playing away at the likes of Saltergate you need a little bit more than that – basically a pair of b★llocks. I was not his type of player. End of story!

Tony was the head man when it came to dealing with the press, Leroy took on most of the training, while Dave – I am not sure what Dave did. I can award him the prize for putting on the strangest training session I have ever been involved in, in all my time in football. It was an XI v XI game on a full-size pitch, nothing strange there, but with two balls on the go! There must have been some logic, but the 22 players on the training pitch that day failed to find it.

Things were improving though. We beat Cheltenham 3–1 in a game which saw my first goal for Bristol City. It had been a long time coming but I enjoyed it. We won our first away game at Bournemouth 3–2, a game where I played at the back in a three-man defence. It was a tough game but a great result. However, the Pulis problem was to occur again. I was called into the office on the Friday before our home fixture against Wigan Athletic to be faced by the Three Amigos. They said that they had a problem as one of them wanted me to start the Wigan game while one of them was adamant that I would start on the bench (thanks Mr Burnside!), and because they could not agree I was to start on the bench.

Changing rooms are a cruel place and rather than be sympathetic with my problems, I was to be nicknamed 'spoiler'. Every team needs a 'spoiler' – somebody who does all the horrible stuff and can be left out at home while the rest of the team play nice attacking football. That was to be my name throughout the rest of my stay at Bristol. We drew against Wigan Athletic, yet again 0–0. Perhaps they needed a spoiler! We won our next game on penalties in the Auto Windscreens Shield game at home to Bournemouth. Our League form continued to improve and we went unbeaten for 15 games in all competitions. It was too late to make a push for the Play-offs; we were too many points behind. I had now become a regular in the side again. We beat Chesterfield 3–0 at home before winning away at Blackpool, and we were on a roll now that the weather was picking up. We beat Reading 4–0 at home to book our place in the area Finals of the Autoglass Trophy, where we were to face lower League opposition in Exeter City. However, just as I was hitting a decent run of form the old knee troubles came back to haunt me. I had to come off in the Reading game and missed another nine games through injury. I was pig sick and starting to really worry about whether my right knee would be the end of my football career.

We beat Exeter City 4–0 in the first leg of our semi-final. We had one foot in Wembley. However, our League form was to take a little dip – I would like to say it coincided with the injury to City's spoiler, but who knows? I also missed the second leg against Exeter which we drew 1–1 to book our place in the final against Stoke City at Wembley. It had not been as exciting as the 1997 FA Cup run but it was a chance, all the same, to play at the Twin Towers, a great dream of mine (along with playing at Old Trafford). The day after our semi-final victory we went on a celebratory day out to Cheltenham races. It was a great day and towards the end of it I witnessed one of the funniest things I have ever seen. The Chelsea player, Jody Morris, was also present and he had obviously had plenty to drink, we all had by the end of the last race. He was giving it the 'big one', and all you could hear was his voice. It was driving me mad. A young lad who was at City at the time was Kevin Langley, a quiet chap who would not say boo to a goose. He had had a fair bit to drink and was tucking into his battered sausage and chips. He too had obviously heard enough of Morris, and promptly picked his battered sausage up and threw it about five metres where it bounced off Jody's head. Kevin went back to eating his chips as if nothing had happened. Morris was fuming but everyone was killing themselves laughing at him. He did not have a clue where the sausage had come from which made it all the more funnier. (You really had to be there!)

I came back into the side for the Brentford game which we won and in a rehearsal for the Autoglass Final, I also featured in a 2–2 draw against Stoke City.

I now had two games to convince the Three Amigos that I was fully fit and worthy of my place in the starting XI for Wembley. I played and did well in the two games, both of which we won. My return to the side had improved results (just coincidental I think) but a few people said that I was now becoming an integral part of the team. I was not bothered what they said as long as I played at Wembley.

The build-up to the game at Wembley was similar to that run at Chesterfield. The press were milling about everywhere, and whereas at Chesterfield we travelled to the semi-finals in normal club tracksuits, Bristol City being Bristol City decided that we would be measured for suits. We went away for a couple of days before the Final and stayed at Bisham Abbey. It was a lovely venue and we had a perfect run up to the game. The bus journey to Wembley was memorable and when the Twin Towers came into sight, the nerves really started to kick in. All you could see everywhere was red and white, those being the colours of both teams. We eventually got into the changing rooms and went out on the pitch. We wore navy blue suits, lime green shirts, red Bristol City ties and, to complete the look, red carnations on the lapel of our jackets. It sounds shocking but we did look the business.

When we came out to warm up, the ground was nearly full. The atmosphere was building by the minute and when the famous Stoke City song *Delilah* came on it made the hairs on the back of your neck stand up as 35,000 Stoke City fans sang along. Bristol City's song that day was *Hi Ho Silver Lining* with the words replaced by 'Hi Ho Bristol City'. Bristol also had 35,000 fans there and it was a great occasion. When we walked out into the stadium from the tunnel, the two teams side by side, it made me think of all the FA Cup Finals I used to watch as a kid with mum, dad and Jamie and now here they were, watching me walk out at the home of English football under the famous Twin Towers.

The first half of the game was not particularly memorable, especially for us, and Stoke City thoroughly deserved to go into the interval leading 1–0. Apparently the television commentators had been saying before the game that the key area on the pitch where the game would be won or lost was the central-midfield battle. Stoke were very strong in that area with James O' Connor and Graham Kavanagh, but people also saw City's strong area as the midfield with Brian Tinnion and myself (they probably feared Tinnion's left foot more than anything because he had great ability). It promised to be a great battle, but the Stoke pairing definitely had the better of the first half.

Things changed in the second half and we started to dominate. We won a succession of corners and on the last of these I managed to lose Peter Thorne who was marking me. The ball dipped and I threw myself at it. I got a good connection and I saw it deflect off somebody but it was going in anyway. The ball hit the net and that end of the ground erupted. I had scored at Wembley! I wheeled away in celebration and went towards the City fans. What a feeling! My best in football for pure emotion. The joy did not last long as Stoke regained the lead and eventually hung on for a deserved victory. I think they were the better team and were definitely physically and mentally stronger than us. When the final whistle went I slumped down on to my haunches. We had lost. This might be my only chance of ever playing on the 'hallowed turf' but at least I had scored! They could never take that away from me, could they? Yes they could. On the way back to Bristol Damian Spencer, a young centre-forward who had come on midway through the second half, said my header had in fact deflected in off of him. I must admit I thought it had at the time but because he had not claimed the goal immediately I thought it must have gone in off a defender. Never mind. I had had the goal announced at the time as my goal, and deep down it really did not matter. I asked Damo why then had he not celebrated it straight away but he just shrugged his shoulders and smiled. Apparently Andy Gray, the Sky television pundit, had analysed the goal numerous times on the slow motion replays and eventually credited the goal to Damian. Thank you Andy Gray.

A party had been arranged back in Bristol win or lose. We drowned our sorrows and I actually sang a duet with Leroy Rosenior on the microphone. What did we sing? *Ebony and Ivory.* What else could it be? I can remember being dumbstruck when a lad called Ivan Testitamanu, a Moldovan international, started putting a shot of vodka (his national drink) into the top of his pint of Stella because he found Stella too weak!

The rest of the season was a bit of an anticlimax. We had five games left in which we won two, drew one and lost two. We finished ninth. Things had definitely improved under the Three Amigos and I felt more relaxed at the club. It was not Mansfield or Chesterfield, but I was still playing the game I love — well, at least for another seven and a half games!

Chapter Twenty-Seven
Back to Form

It was a strange summer at Ashton Gate. For some reason the Three Amigos could not agree a deal and so the club was on the lookout for a new manager. All sorts of names were mentioned but the man given the task of getting the club promoted was Danny Wilson, the old Sheffield Wednesday and Barnsley manager. I was pleased with this as I had met Danny a few times in Chesterfield when I had played there as Danny lived in a village just outside the town. I had had a drink with him and talked about football and he seemed like a reasonable guy. Danny bought in Frank Barlow, another guy linked with Chesterfield, and they worked together as a team brilliantly. From day one it was clear that we were going to try and get promoted by playing football. They had done it at Barnsley and gained promotion to the Premier League, so why not do the same at Bristol City, which, to be fair, was probably a bigger club than Barnsley.

Pre-season was okay, a lot of football but not enough physical work. I never thought I would hear myself saying that, but as at Sheffield United I did not think we worked hard enough pre-season. You are fine until Christmas after doing that kind of work, but once the games start coming thick and fast and the pitches start getting muddier and heavier that is when you really feel the benefit of a hard pre-season. But hopefully we could be up there near the top of the table come the festive period. Things started well away at Wrexham, always a difficult place to go. I had been given specific instructions to man mark Darren Ferguson (son of Alex), who was the Wrexham playmaker and a very good footballer. My remit was to make sure he did not get on the ball. It did not matter whether I had an impact on the game or not, just as long as he did not get them playing. I felt sorry for Darren, a lad who I had always and still get on with very well, he will definitely go on and be a successful top-flight manager. Back then he just could not get rid of me. Everywhere he went, I followed. I bet first half we did not touch the ball 10 times between us. I hated it but that was the job I was given. During the second half the game was a bit more open and I scored the second goal in a 2–0 win. A great start for the club and on a personal level.

Also on a personal level things went from strength to strength, though results were terrible. We lost our next three home League games all by the odd goal and the team were struggling. I managed to get Man of the Match in all of those games, perhaps I stood out more when a team I was playing for were struggling because of the way I played. I was not a flair player by any means, just an honest, hard-working grafter. I felt as if I was getting somewhere back to my best, my right knee had not given me any stick for a few months and I had started scoring again. I scored my second goal of the season in the second leg of our League Cup time at Brentford in a game that saw us lose 2–1 and go out of the competition 4–3 on aggregate. That was to be my last ever goal. We lost 1–0 at home to Swindon the following Saturday, but again as the team struggled I did well again. I loved it. I was enjoying my football again but there was to be a shock around the corner.

It all happened on Saturday 16 September in an away game at Oldham Athletic. The day my career ended.

Chapter Twenty-Eight
They Think It's All Over – It Is Now

Saturday 16 September 1999. A day I will never forget for all the wrong reasons. It still seems like yesterday. It was a day that started off as a normal away fixture but ended with my career in tatters. When we arrived in the changing rooms I went out onto the pitch as I always did to see what the pitch looked like. It looked perfect. There was not a blade of grass out of place and the sunshine was making Boundary Park look heavenly; it looked that good.

My nightmare started as I got changed and prepared myself for the game. I had my warm up t-shirt, shorts and socks on and crossed the dressing room to where all the boots had been laid out ready. Usually players would take two or three pairs of boots to each game with them so as you can imagine there are loads of pairs of boots there, sometimes up to fifty pairs. I looked down for my boots but could not see them. I looked again, thinking I had simply missed them. No sign of them. I asked Buster (the kit man) whether he had seen them but he said he had not. The youth team players all had two professionals' boots to clean throughout the season, both training boots and match boots. They did not mind doing them as they were usually well tipped at Christmas and again at the end of the season, and if a pair of boots was not quite right with one of the pros then they would normally give them to their boot boy. I would probably give my boot boy £100 at Christmas, £100 at the end of the season and up to three or four pairs of boots every season. It made a difference to the kids because they were not on massive wages. Most of the pros would be fine and look after the kids, but there would always be the odd ones who did not give their boot boys a penny which I thought was scandalous. To be fair, I would not have minded doing my own boots but in football there is that boot boy tradition.

Anyway, my boots had obviously not been packed. My boot boy must have forgotten to put them in the boot skip. What could I do? Mistakes happen. The lads wanted to know what I was going to say to him when I saw him, but I knew it must be a genuine mistake and that he would not have done it on purpose. *C'est la vie.* I borrowed a pair of boots, something I had never done before in my life, but I was not unduly concerned about it. To me a pair of boots is a pair of boots, but some footballers are very particular about their own boots and they wouldn't have known what to do. Whether it was through wearing somebody else's boots or just pure coincidence, but after 44 minutes my football career was all but over.

When we went out to warm up we went through our normal running warm up, and then through our usual passing drills. It was strange though. When we passed a simple ball along the floor, it seemed to be running along its path peculiarly. It seemed to wobble about when it was travelling in a straight line, nothing major but definitely a little bit odd. Somebody came up with the reason that though Oldham's actual playing surface was made up mostly of natural grass fibres, a small percentage was made up of artificial fibres. Whether that was the reason I suffered a career-ending injury that afternoon I will never know, but it does make you wonder. The grass, wearing somebody else's boots or just plain coincidence, I always ask myself the same questions whenever I think of that game. The answer never comes and it still goes around my head every so often.

The first half was a forgettable affair. A minute before half-time Danny Boshell, Oldham's midfielder, picked the ball up around the halfway line and went towards his own goal. I tracked him when he suddenly changed direction. I was at least five to 10 yards away from him and went to follow him. My foot stayed in the same place as my body turned 180 degrees. You could hear the noise of my knee 'going' from the sidelines, it was like a really loud popping noise. The pain was excruciating and it threw me up in the air. After watching a replay of the incident I am actually waving for a stretcher before I hit the floor. I was squealing like a pig and when Gill, the physio, reached me I pleaded with her not to touch my leg at all, just get a stretcher on as quickly as possible and get me off the pitch. I knew then how serious it was. I had been injured before, many, many times, but I had never felt pain like this. The stretcher came on and I can remember being carried off. I had my eyes closed because of the pain and because of the tears in my eyes. It hurt that much. The crowd, realising that it must be a very serious injury, gave me a warm round of applause as I was stretchered off. When I eventually opened my eyes I was in a street lined with terraced houses. Where the hell was I? Was I dreaming? At Oldham there are steep steps from the playing surface to the changing area, too steep to carry a stretcher. So I had been stretchered out of a corner of the ground and found myself in a street just outside Boundary Park. Bizarre.

I was taken straight to the physio room which was joined onto the home dressing room. It seemed strange being able to hear the oppositions team talk but to tell you the truth that was the last thing on my mind. The Oldham club doctor came in and examined my knee. It was obvious to everyone there that this was a bad one and then he started doing tests on it. I knew what he was testing for because I had practised the same test when I had passed my physio exams, which I had taken when I was playing at Chesterfield. He was testing for cruciate ligament damage, and I could tell by the looks on every face that it was not good news. The thing that I could not believe was that it was not my right knee, the knee I had all the operations on, but my left one which I had never really had a problem with.

Andy Ritchie, the Oldham manager, came in as did most of the Oldham players to show their concern, which was nice. The second half got under way and I hobbled down the corridor, already on crutches, to the away dressing room where I showered and changed. The pain had gone and I can remember thinking to myself that it might not be as bad as I first feared. It stiffened up a little on the journey back to Bristol, but was not anywhere near as painful as I had first thought it would be.

I had to report for treatment the following day and when I got up in the morning I was in bits. My knee had swollen up but the swelling was not actually around the kneecap itself, but in a band just above my knee. I knew that meant bad news. It was the classic sign of a cruciate ligament injury. I got a lift to the ground that morning to let Gill have a look at it and she looked worried. She was about to say something when I interrupted 'Cruciate?', 'I'm afraid so. It certainly looks that way,' she replied tentatively. We had a chat about the possible damage, and Gill was trying to look on the bright side but I feared the worst. My knee was not at all painful, but it was really unstable and kept giving way over the next few days. Everybody was showing concern but to be honest I just wanted to be on my own. Later that week I went to see Dai Rees, the top knee specialist in the country, at the Orthopaedic Hospital in Oswestry. He examined the knee but it was still very swollen. He confirmed that I had injured my cruciate ligament but until I had a scan he could not tell to what extent and what other damage there might be. However, he did say because of the laxity of the ligaments in my left knee that he expected there to be quite a lot of damage. A scan was arranged for a couple of weeks later and I was pencilled in for the operation on 17 October 2000. It may seem a long time to wait for the surgical procedure but it took that long for the swelling to go down.

When I had the scan, the bad news was confirmed. I had completely ruptured my anterior cruciate ligament, snapped my medial ligament, snapped my lateral ligament, torn my medial cartilage and to finish off torn my lateral cartilage. There was other significant damage that was not picked up on at this point but would be discovered a few months later. I was finished. The reconstruction of my left knee was performed by Dai Rees and Von de Klerk, both knee specialists. They were pleased with how it had gone and I stayed in hospital for four or five days to see how I progressed. They gave me a programme to adhere to and said what I should be doing over the coming months and what stage I should be at, at different times.

The next few weeks went really well. Even though the progress was very slow it was going okay. The only trouble with being injured long term is that you are on your own a lot. You are no use to anybody to be brutally honest and you feel very isolated. The other injured lads suffered short-term injuries so were into the later stages of their rehab and were therefore doing different things to me. I spent hours and hours either at the gym or at the pool, all by myself. I felt like I was the forgotten man. Results had picked up and the club was buzzing again, and even though I was pleased I did become a bit bitter.

As I said, I was progressing, but I kept complaining of a pain across my kneecap, particularly in one point, but I was told it was perfectly normal and the surgeons confirmed this. When I started doing a little bit more the pain was a lot more intense and I was in agony. I had started doing light weights on my left leg, a good sign, and apart from the pain things were going well and I was ahead of schedule. The weeks passed and I was doing more and more but the pain was not going. I was getting really concerned by this, but again the specialists did not think it was anything to be unduly worried about and told me to keep going. I can remember one day in the gym I was doing my weights on my bad leg, I was lifting them just with my left leg and tears were running down my face I was in that much pain. Everybody has a different pain threshold and I would say that I have a high one, but the pain was becoming unbearable. Gill could see the agony I was going through and she arranged for me to have an injection in my knee to see if that would help; it did not. I was becoming desperate, something was seriously wrong.

I can remember reaching my lowest point clearly. Everybody had gone training and I was once again sitting on my own in the dressing room when I broke down in tears. I sobbed and sobbed. I had to find out what was wrong and whether I could run. I went out on to the track around the main pitch and set off. I picked up the pace but I was limping badly. I knew I should not have been doing it but I was at my wit's end. Gill had come out to see where I was and could not believe what she was seeing. She went mad and I broke down again. She realised how low I was, and we had a real heart-to-heart. I said how worried I was that I would never play again.

It was decided that I would go to Lilleshall for a change of scenery. Lilleshall was a place you could go and carry out your rehab with their physios who had the most modern equipment at their fingertips. I can remember on the first morning they asked me to do some squats without even a weight. After I had done five squats, they stopped me and said I was doing it wrong. They said I was leaning slightly so all my weight was going through my good leg and that I was not even working my injured left leg. To the naked eye you could not tell I was even doing it, but when they straightened me up, only by a couple of inches, and asked me to do five more squats, the pain hit me. They told me to stop immediately. That afternoon I went on a machine that was to measure the strength in both my legs. I was sat down and strapped into a chair. I had to kick out as hard as I could against the resistance offered by the machine, and it would then be measured by a graph that came up on the screen. They didn't tell me what results they were expecting until I had finished the exercise. I had to do it on my right leg, and then on my left leg. While they were waiting for the results I asked them what they were looking for. They said that if they did the test on a fit player, they would expect about an 11 per cent difference between their stronger leg (the foot which they kick with) and their weaker leg. With somebody who had the type of injury I had, and with the stage I should be at, they expected there to be about a 20 per cent difference, certainly no more than 25 per cent, between my good leg and my injured leg. When the results came through I could see the puzzlement on their faces. They came back and said there had been a mistake with the exercise and that I had to do it again. This I did, and they again waited for the results. They seemed to be taking an age looking at the printout and pointing at the first set of results and then the second set. When they came over I could tell there was a problem. The difference in strength between the two legs was a massive 66 per cent. They said they had not ever seen that before, not anywhere near, and that there must be a deeper underlying problem which was causing the loss of power in my left leg. For the rest of the week I did hardly anything. My head was in bits.

When I got back to Bristol it was decided that I would have to have a really deep bone scan. When the results came back it was a shock to say the least. My kneecap was in two. I had fractured it all the way across the patella and there was a big hole in it between the two parts. What now? I think this was the point when we all knew that this was the end. I went to see a new knee specialist, Mr Bickerstaff, with all my scans and x-rays. Could he do anything? He said that how I had managed to lift a single weight at all with my left leg he would never know, 'you must have been in agony'. I was not lifting one weight, I was doing the bloody full stack! He told me that he was prepared to try something but the likelihood was that it would fail. I was booked in for the next day. He was going to take a bone graft from my hip and position it in the void in my kneecap and then give it time to see whether it would fuse the two parts together again. He was not hopeful and I appreciated him being so frank.

It did not work. After about a month's rest I was still experiencing the same pain. Bristol City and its hierarchy were obviously hearing alarm bells ringing and they started to put a bit of pressure on me. I had 18 or so months left on my contract and they were not particularly keen on paying somebody who, to put it bluntly, was probably no longer any use to them. It seemed very harsh, after all I had been playing for them when I got injured, but I could see where they were coming from. I had a meeting with Danny Wilson and the chairman and it was decided that I would go and see Mr Bickerstaff one last time. I poured my heart out to him that afternoon. I pleaded with him to 'go into my knee' one last time to see if he had missed anything. He said he would, but told me that I should not build up my hopes. He said that after the operation he would be brutally honest and give me his opinion on whether I would ever play again. I appreciated that.

When I came round after the operation, it was late and the nurses told me that Mr Bickerstaff would be round in the morning. That night seemed to go on forever. He came round at about 9.30am and as soon as I saw his face, I knew what the news was. 'I'm sorry Paul. It's over. If you want to be able to walk about for the rest of your life then you have to pack it in. I'm sorry to say this, but you will always run the risk of your knee exploding again and it could happen as easy as when you are walking down the stairs. It is like a time bomb.'

Yet again I sobbed. I knew it was coming but it did not make it any easier. It was all over. He had said that I should never kick another football again, not even go for a light jog. I thanked him for trying. He said my knee would always be very painful, not just when I had been doing a lot but all the time. He did not exaggerate. I am in constant pain in both knees, and for all those people who have said to me that I have piled the pounds on you now know that even though I would have loved to train regularly it is not possible. I always laugh it off, and people do not really mean anything by it, but it hurts. I had always been fit and it hurts like hell when you are unable do any exercise without running the risk of ending up in a wheelchair.

All that was left to do now was to tie up the loose ends with Bristol City. They had been okay, I think I could have been treated a lot better but that's life. I was not sad to see the back of Bristol. There were some good lads there in Billy Mercer, Mark Lever, Keith Millen and Peter Beadle but it was a strange club at that time.

My career was over. I would never kick a ball properly again. At the age of 28 it was time for a new chapter in my life. I was to go full circle and end up back at Mansfield Town, my first club. It had changed a lot from what I had remembered.

Chapter Twenty-Nine
Full Circle

I had been a bit cute. I had known for about six months, probably longer, that I was struggling to play again, and so I had to think about life after playing football. Whenever I was back up North I would always pop into Chesterfield or Mansfield to see people who I had been at the clubs with. I would catch up with Jamie Hewitt, who was now the physio at Chesterfield, and Dave Rushbury, who had gone from being physio to first-team manager. When it looked like I was going to have to retire, Rushy was kind enough to try and find me a role at Chesterfield. He said if the worse came to the worse then I could go there as the 'odd jobs man'. That sounds a bit of a comedown from being a professional footballer but it would involve doing the kit, preparing the food on away trips and a bit of coaching. I was really grateful to Rushy for at least trying to find me something. However, I lived in Mansfield and if there was a job there it would be a lot more convenient – I was prepared to do anything, literally anything. Towards the end of my rehab I had spent a lot of time back down at Field Mill working with Barry Statham (Mansfield's physio) and a young player called Michael Sissons, who was also coming back from a cruciate ligament injury. I watched a lot of Mansfield's games pre Christmas of the 2001–02 season and they were playing wonderful football. They were such a young side and were playing with absolutely no fear. It was a pleasure to watch. Billy Dearden, who had come back to the club a few years earlier, was the manager, Stuart Watkiss the assistant and Neil Richardson the youth team coach. After the games I would go for a pint with Barry, and Stuart and Neil would join us. They were really serious about their football but also liked to enjoy themselves and I hit it off with Stuart straight away. I had known Neil for many years and had always got on with him and I thought it must have been a great place to work. Towards Christmas 2001 I had a beer with Barry. I explained to him that it was no good and I was going to have to retire. I could tell he was genuinely gutted and he said he would keep his eyes and ears open to see whether something came up at the ground that I might be interested in.

I had only just signed my settlement deal with City, the ink was literally still drying on the paper when my phone rang: it was Barry. He had heard something that might interest me. It was rumoured that Billy Dearden might be leaving in the near future and both Stuart and Richo were being promoted, so Stuart would be the manager, Richo would be his assistant and the youth team manager position would be…well, up for grabs. The Stags were due to play Leicester in the third round of the FA Cup and I got a phone call on the Thursday before the game on the Saturday. Did I want the job? I accepted immediately. Billy was leaving after the Leicester game to become manager of Notts County and Stuart and Richo were taking over the reins. It was all to be kept quiet. The first-team squad were going to Portugal for a few days after the game so it would be a perfect week for me to come in and get acquainted with the youth team players and my new surroundings (it had changed a little!).

I can remember not sleeping the night before my first day because I was slightly nervous. I had never coached before, and it does not matter how experienced you might be as a player, nothing prepares you for that first team meeting and that first team talk as a coach. I managed to get through my first meeting with the young players relatively unscathed and prepared for my first training session. It was going really well and I decided to join in towards the end as I missed the football, and also to try and show the youngsters that this coach could still play a bit. I had yet to touch the ball and after a few minutes it came towards me as one of the lads came to close their new coach down. Trying to impress, I sold the lad a bit of a dummy and let the ball run across me. I looked the part but then as I went to push off my left leg collapsed on me and I ended up in a heap on the floor. I could hear the lads trying to keep their giggles in. My pride was wounded. I dusted myself down and carried on but I had a big hole in the knees of my tracksuit bottoms. What a start!

One thing I was pleased about was that I would be learning the ropes of the youth team football with Ivan Hollett, who, a few years earlier, had helped me progress through the ranks of professional football as a teenager. Who better to learn from? I have always had the utmost respect for Ivan and without a doubt he is the unsung hero at Mansfield Town. The man is a legend and it is only the people who have the fortune to meet and work with him who realise what he is all about. He should definitely have been the first team manager at the Stags at some point. I can honestly say that I have never heard anybody say a bad word about him. From that first day of working with him we have become the best of friends and he is without any question my best friend in all my time in football. I would like at this point to thank Ivan and his lovely wife Ann for their friendship and put on record how highly my wife Clare and I regard their friendship. Thank you.

I had got the football bug back. I loved working with the kids at Mansfield and looking back I should never have moved from that role as youth team manager. The enjoyment I got from seeing one of them making their debut was every bit as good as scoring a goal myself. I loved Saturday mornings and seeing the kids compete against other League clubs. Working with all the staff at the club was definitely my happiest time on the coaching side of things. Stuart and Neil were great to work for, their football philosophies were exactly the same as mine. Every day after training all the playing staff would get together and have a bite to eat and a couple of cups of tea. Barry (physio), Seamus McDonagh (goalkeeper coach), Stuart, Neil, Paul Molesworth (chief scout), Ivan and I would sit for hours talking about football and having a laugh and a joke. There were some fantastic players at the club as well, with the likes of Bobby Hassell,

Liam Lawrence and Lee Williamson. The things Liam and Lee were capable of doing in training and games were frightening. Out of the two I thought, and still do think, that Lee was the better and I still think he will do well in the Premier League. One thing I did wish was that I could have played in that team in the 2001–02 season. They were a great team, the best I have seen at Mansfield Town as a player and a coach, but I felt these young players could have achieved even more as a squad with a bit of experience and guidance in the team. They were a joy to work with, on the odd occasions I worked with them, and I am sure, in fact I am certain, if that team had stayed together, Mansfield Town would have been playing in the Championship. That they were allowed to leave Mansfield Town in the way they did was a disgrace, but I will come onto that later.

The young team were learning together. Stuart and Neil were certainly learning game by game too. Again I have no doubt that Stuart will one day manage at a higher level as he is one of the best young coaches in the game. I feel that at lower League level, the most important attribute that a manager or coach can have is man management skills. Stuart had this in abundance and all of the squad, not just the starting XI, liked and respected him. The players are at this level for a reason but if you can get them working for you and get that good team spirit in the camp then you are halfway there. It is also important that the manager gets on well with his staff and that the staff have respect for their manager. Stuart had this.

While the first team were doing well and always moving around the top three in the closing stages of the 2001–02 season, I was enjoying working with the youngsters at the club. The likes of Jake Buxton, Chris Beardsley, Jason White and Alex John Baptiste were starting to come to the fore and they were a joy to work with. The facilities were not great but, as I have said many times before in this book, that is what lower League football is all about.

One familiar face at the club who, along with Barry and Ivan, had been there when I was there as a player, was the chairman, Keith Haslam. Keith was still a young man when I was a player, and he loved nothing more than having a few beers and cracking a few jokes with the players. I think Keith was a frustrated footballer deep down, so the nearest thing to that for him was to be chairman at a football club. At that time he spent a lot of time with the squad, so much time that really he was 'one of the lads' rather than the man who made all the important decisions at Mansfield Town. When I came back to the club in January 2002 there was a similar atmosphere in the club as there was back in my days as a player. It was, as my mum always used to say, a 'family' club, a nice place to work. It was a pleasure every day to go in and work (how things changed in the course of a year). Towards the end of that season the club was on a high. In the final two home games of that season there were attendances of 8,663 for the Cheltenham game and 8,638 for the must-win final game of the season against Carlisle. How the figures of 8,000 were accounted for I do not know, because there were over 10,000 people at both games although one of the turnstiles had been kicked down!

The Carlisle game was a nail-biting affair. We won 2–0 and with results going well for us elsewhere, we had been promoted. This young team had surpassed all expectations and had been successful playing some great attacking football. It could not have gone any better for Stuart: in his first job in management and since Christmas he had steered his club to promotion. The future looked bright and with all these youngsters maturing at the same time the sky really was the limit. Could we go on and compete at the next level? I believed that having played in that division for most of my career there were no doubts we could, and I felt we had a chance of challenging again. The only thing Stuart did not need was injuries. He had strengthened the squad towards the end of his first season with senior players like David Kelly and Scott Sellars coming to the club. They were great professionals and great to have around the place and the younger pros loved them. I particularly grew close to Scottie; again he is one who conducts himself in the right way and shows everybody respect no matter who they are or what they have achieved. He was one of many people who I was to meet over the next few years who had played at the top level, but he was by far the least affected and the most approachable and that is why one day he will also become a fantastic manager.

My first few months in coaching had gone really well, the club was a pleasure to work at and I was really excited about the future. Everybody seemed to be enjoying themselves, enjoying coming to work and that is half the battle at a lower League football club. From players to management, from administration staff to ground staff, you all need to pull together in the same direction.

Chapter Thirty
Watkiss Out

The thing that Stuart feared most happened. Injuries, and lots of them. Things had started well with a great 4–3 victory against Plymouth in the opening game of the season but that was to the only real highlight at the start of the season. Things went from bad to worse, both on the pitch and the news coming from the treatment room. We only had a small squad and that, along with injuries of key players, particularly defenders, was the kiss of death for Stuart.

The team were struggling at the foot of the table, but with the injury situation improving I was still hopeful of the first team climbing away. They had too much quality. There is the old saying in football that you are too good to go down but I genuinely believe that we would have been okay if Stuart had been allowed to keep his job. There were rumours going round that Stuart was living on borrowed time and that Keith Curle, who had been seen at a few games, would soon be in the hot seat at Field Mill. I thought it was just idle gossip. I knew that the two Keiths used to drink in the same pub in Sheffield.

While the first team had been struggling the youth team had gone from strength to strength and were currently top of our respective League. I had managed to get a real closeness in the youth squad and they were really enjoying their football. That is my philosophy, if you are enjoying your football you will play better. It sounds simple but I feel managers often complicate things and forget this simplest of facts. Mansfield played away at Port Vale, their last game in November. They lost 4–2 but I certainly did not expect what happened on the Monday morning. I knew Keith had been in Stuart's office first thing, but that was nothing unusual. He did it a lot. When I went in about 10 minutes after Keith had left it was like walking into a morgue, Stuart and Neil were just sat there. They had been told by Keith that enough was enough. I thought at the time, and I am pretty sure he still does, that Keith would regret sacking them so early in the season when the injury situation was improving and with the key players back soon. I hated the situation. My job was still there but the people who had given me it had been relieved of their duties. I shook hands with Stuart and Neil and thanked them for all their help and wished them all the best for the future. It was horrible. I then had to go and take the professionals training. You feel as if you are being disloyal to those who are leaving the club, but you have to carry on. I was really sorry to see them both go but the decision had been made and a new manager was coming in. Would it be Keith Curle? Would he bring an assistant in or would he promote somebody from within the football club? I would soon find out.

I first met Keith Curle on Monday 2 December. I can remember this date because it is the start of the period when, for the first time in my life, I failed to enjoy football. My love affair with the sport and with Mansfield Town was put on hold for nearly two years. I had heard differing stories about Keith Curle but I was determined to put all things to the back of my head and take him as I found him. News got round before I had ever met Keith that John Gannon, my ex-teammate at Sheffield United, was going to be the new assistant manager. Ganns was the Under-16 manager at the club and knew Curley from their time together at Wimbledon as part of the infamous 'crazy gang'. The next two years were certainly crazy. I could also think of a few more adjectives to describe them, not many of them printable.

My first impressions of Curle were all good. He was immaculate and definitely talked a good game. He wanted to bring a professional approach to the club, right from the training facilities to the state of the ground. All great ideas, but Rome could not be built in a day. I went with Curle and Gannon in the car late on the Monday afternoon and showed them where we trained. They were nowhere near up to standard according to Curle and rightly so, but we had encountered many problems about trying to find decent pitches on which to train. Ivan had been at the club for 15 or so years and was still trying. That night a fans forum had been arranged where the fans could hear what the manager had to say and where they could also ask questions. It had been arranged for Stuart and Neil to be there, but obviously with what had gone on earlier in the day Keith Haslam saw it as the ideal time to introduce the new managerial pairing to the fans. Curle was a natural in front of the fans and they quickly warmed to him. He answered every question brilliantly and to be fair I thought I could learn a lot from him. He had told the fans exactly what they wanted to hear and I could not believe how confident he came across. He exuded class and had that little bit of arrogance in him that every successful sportsman needs. My first few hours with Curle had been fine. We seemed to get on and after the meeting I went for a drink with Barry Statham. Barry was not keen and said he would hold his judgement back until a later date. After a couple of drinks Keith Haslam came into the bar and asked me what my first impressions were. 'Very impressed', I said. 'Well be careful. He wants shut of you. The first thing you do wrong, he will have an excuse. Don't give him that chance', the chairman said. The alarm bells started ringing. Looking back Keith should never have said it. From then on I was always watching my back.

Curle was a perfectionist and wanted everywhere immaculate. Nothing wrong with that. The youth team players were doing brilliantly on the pitch but you could never say that their cleaning of the ground was up to the same standard. They tried their best but with the lack of decent cleaning essentials to hand, it was difficult. So why not buy the cleaning essentials? It was not as easy as that. Why? Because Mansfield Town is Mansfield Town where nothing is simple and straightforward, however easy it should be. I lost count of the hours I spent cleaning up the ground after the youth team players had 'finished' their cleaning duties. For the next two years I was a coach and also a professional cleaner. I could not run the risk of leaving the jobs to them because it would not have been done down to the last detail. So I used to scrub the toilets, scrub everywhere just so I knew that when Curle went round and checked everywhere he could not say that the kids were failing to do their jobs right and that therefore I was not doing mine right; the place was immaculate. I was determined he was not going to have that opportunity to get rid of me. I had a checklist (only Ivan knows this) that I used to tick off every day before training, after training and before I left the ground. The balls were washed and pumped up every day, bibs washed and cones washed. You think of it, it was done.

Results picked up and Curle was doing a great job. The thing I was most impressed with was his organisation. The training pitch would be set up before the players even got there and it was something that I thought Curle had got spot on. After a couple of weeks at the club he said that the whole of the dressing room area needed decorating. No decorating firms were brought in; it was all hands to the pump. Fair enough. By Christmas Eve all that was left to do was the home dressing room and that was when my first problem with Curle surfaced. The professionals left the club after training at about 1 o'clock and Curle and Gannon got showered and changed, ready to go for a few Christmas drinks in Sheffield. We had a game at home on Boxing Day, so I asked them before they left what to do with the home changing room. He said 'It will only take an hour or two if you and the kids start now!' Five hours later we were still there. It was Christmas Eve and at 6 o' clock we finished. Another test passed!

As I have said before, I think Curle was a good coach and his professionalism was to be admired. However, results did not improve enough and we were relegated when we lost away at Tranmere Rovers. Curle had played quite a few games since he came to the club and was in great shape considering he was nearly 40. I had got on okay with Curle, not brilliantly but okay. For some reason he felt threatened by me. The only reason I can think of was that I knew Mansfield and knew a lot of people around town. I am a people person and enjoy being sociable and can talk to anybody. Never once did I speak to people around town about personnel or tactics. I am not like that. I think if we had stayed up that season Curle and I would have been fine. From that day we did not get on. Keith Curle was not a man I liked and I am sure that he would say the same about me. However, we were both professionals, and when we had a heart-to-heart it was decided that I would just concentrate on the kids and make sure my own house was in order. I had no problem with that. Perhaps the summer break would see us both coming back feeling refreshed and a bit more relaxed towards each other. Not a chance. I am not saying that Keith Curle was totally to blame for us not getting on through the rest of his time at the club; I was probably to blame just as much through my stubbornness. The harder he tried to get to me, the bigger my false smile got. The next 15 months were to be the most miserable of my life.

Chapter Thirty-One

Keith Curle

The summer break did not help our relationship. In fact it made it a hundred times worse. Before we went on our summer break we had been asked when we were taking our summer holidays and when we were due back. No problem there then, as I was due back in England on the Monday night before the arranged start back date for pre-season training on the Wednesday. I was in the middle of my holiday lying next to the pool when my mobile rang. It was Keith Curle. He was ranting and raving about me going to Chesterfield as assistant manager. News to me! 'Why have you gone behind my back?' he shouted. 'Look Keith. I am not going to Chesterfield. I haven't spoken to anybody from Chesterfield, I am on my holiday,' I said trying to calm him down. I put the phone down, bewildered about the phone call. Where had he got this from?

I later found out the reason when I spoke to Scott Sellars. Scott had applied for the vacant managerial post at Saltergate and had put in his application that if he got the job he would try and get me to go back to the club as his assistant. We had spoken about this when Scott was a player at Mansfield and we had both said that if we ever got a managerial job that we would bring the other in in some capacity to their club. We both had the same principals on football and we got on, so why not? I did not even know Scott had applied for the job so I knew nothing about the Chesterfield thing. Scott did not get the job anyway!

Later on in the holiday, I got another phone call from Mr Curle asking when I was due back. He had already got this information when I handed the holiday request form into him and he had accepted it. He did not know but I had photocopied it just to cover my own back with his signature clearly on the bottom of it. I was beginning to learn very quickly! I told him that nothing had changed and that I was still due back on the Monday evening, in plenty of time for when the youth team players reported for their first day on the Wednesday. He told me that he had changed his mind and that he now wanted the kids in on the Monday morning. 'But Keith I am not back in the country until 5pm that day', I sighed. 'That's your problem. Sort it out!' Curle said before slamming the phone down.

There was no way on earth that I was coming back early from a pre-booked holiday that had been agreed to. No chance! I arranged for Kevin Philliskirk, another Sheffield chap who helped with the kids, to take them on that first day. Kevin had been brought in to report back to Curle on everything I did. He was Curle's eyes and ears when he was not about. Me and Ivan knew this from day one. When I got back to England on the Monday evening I switched my phone back on at the airport. I had a message from Curle telling me not to bother coming in on the Tuesday and that I should not go to the club until I had heard from him. Basically he had suspended me. I went in on the Tuesday morning to see what the hell was going on. Curle went mad and tried to send me home. I went in and saw the chairman, not to tell tales but as I said I wanted to know what the hell was happening. It still makes me mad now while I am writing this.

Eventually Curle and I sat face to face, and he said he had tried to get rid of me from day one but that Haslam would not allow it. He said I had some kind of hold on Keith but that could not be further from the truth. I liked Keith as a person, but we had had some real humdingers of arguments about the club. I do not agree with a lot of the things he has done at Mansfield Town and I am sure he would say the same about some of my decisions on the playing side of things, but there is a mutual respect there. We are not and have never been close friends as such, but I can assure you that if I had stepped out of line I would have been out of the door like anybody else. I admire Keith for being loyal to me when Curle was trying to get me out of the club, and one thing that you can say about Haslam is that he will do what he thinks is right and stick to his guns no matter who he upsets.

Back to the season 2003–04. Curle and Ganns had got the club playing some fantastic football, very entertaining with lots of goals. The youth team were having an okay season, and Curle's lad Tom had come in during the summer as a youth team player. I really liked Tom, he was a lovely lad who had got some ability like all the other boys but still had plenty to learn. He was never a problem, and he never once used his dad as a weapon to anybody at the club. However, I had a dilemma. Did I play Tom just because he was Curle's son or did I treat him like a normal youth team player? I had no choice. Tom would be treated like everybody else and there was absolutely no way I would not pick him just because I did not get on with his dad. Tom knew all this and I did not have a problem with him. One Saturday morning the youth team were playing at Port Vale. Tom was substitute and after about half an hour, Curle rang to see how the kids were getting on. When I told him that Tom was actually a sub waiting to come on in the second half, he asked me to organise Tom to get straight back to Mansfield as they were a man short due to injury and he wanted him to be sub for the first team that afternoon. I shouted Tom over and told him, and then Callum Lloyd's dad, Steve, took Tom back to Mansfield and Tom later went on and made his debut that afternoon. I was pleased for the lad but I had a mutiny on my hands when the rest of the kids found out.

As I said, that season Curley and Gannon did a great job getting the club into the Play-offs where they eventually lost to Huddersfield at the Millennium Stadium. Keith Curle eventually lost his job in November 2004. I am sure everybody will know the story and the subsequent court case where Curle was found not guilty. Contrary to what a lot of people say, I was not the one who made the formal complaint to Keith Haslam – I was not even at the club at the time. I was on the golf course with Ivan, having a regular weekly game with two of Ivan's friends, Ron and Vic. I loved this weekly time away from the club – that was how bad I felt. I had become totally disillusioned with football and if there had been another job offer at that time, I would have jumped at the chance. I do not think the club has ever been the same. If it had not been for my wife Clare and my family, I am not sure what I would have been like. I dreaded coming into Mansfield, let alone the club, and at that time I really found out who my true friends were. For legal reasons I am unable to go into the story about Keith Curle's dismissal, but as you can imagine it was not a nice time to be at the club. As I have said numerous times, there is no doubting Curle's ability to coach on the training pitch. I would go as far to say he is one of the best I have seen, but we are completely different people with completely different characters. What happened has happened but I do not think it will ever come to me and Keith Curle being on speaking terms.

Pictured winning the ball off future Mansfield manager Carlton Palmer – Ian Baraclough in the background.

Holland nails colours to Blues mast

The day I signed for Chesterfield January 1996.

Chesterfield.

Heading for goal against Blackpool 1996.

The semi-final team 1997, pictured with the FA Cup in Chesterfield's first-ever kit and fake moustache.

The worst celebration ever. Left to right – Jon Howard, Jamie Hewitt (goalscorer), Andy Morris (Bruno), Darren Carr.

My last League game for Chesterfield.

Scoring at Wembley 2000.

Me and Clare – May 2005.

Me and my son Christopher.

Me and my daughter Megan.

Family support at the Shrewbury game April 2008. Left to right: Jak Holland, Zak Yadgar, Sargon Isaac, Banny Isaac, Clare Holland, Chelsea Holland.

Clare's favourite photograph.

Me and my great mate Phil Shields in his dream place – St James' Park January 2006.

My son Jak with Alan Shearer when he was mascot for Newcastle.

Chelsea and Amy.

Clare and I with our barge friends Clare and 'Captian' Dave at the end of season dinner at the Civic Centre.

More family support – Notts County away. Left to right – Chelsea Holland, Amy Leivers, Clare Holland and Jak Holland – doing their winner's dance. Spot Alan Wilson, the legendary tannoy man, in the background and Kevin having a bit of lunch!

Great kids – Chelsea and Jak.

My son Jak with Stags ex-captain Jake Buxton.

Clare and I with heavyweight boxing champion 'The Tongan Terror' (Melekiseteki Naufahu – 'George').

My son Jak with Stags centre-forward Lewis Trimmer.

My daughter Chelsea and I at Vicky and Neil's wedding – August 2007.

Chapter Thirty-Two
Carlton Palmer

o Keith Curle had gone under a cloud but as is often the case, you have to move on. It was a horrible time to work at the club and you would do well to find anybody there with a smile on their face. The club had gone backwards off the field with numerous staff leaving and not being replaced, and there was negativity around the club. We were 12th in the League table, just two points outside the Play-offs, but the team was unrecognisable from the one that had lost only five months previously in the Play-off Final. Four of the club's most promising youngsters had been allowed to leave the club. It was a similar situation to when we lost in the Play-off semi-final in 1995 when the nucleus of the team had been sold. I had gone to Sheffield United for £250,000, Darren Ward and Ian Barroclough had gone to Notts County both for £150,000 and Steve Wilkinson had gone to Preston North End for £90,000. The fans were not happy at this time but Keith Haslam had at least made the club £640,000. This time round only Liam Lawrence commanded a fee. Lee Williamson (a travesty) and Craig Disley were both allowed to leave on a free transfer, and Bobby Hassell passed his 24th birthday at the club without anybody realising and was therefore allowed to leave on a free. Somebody had dropped a major trick there but as usual it was covered up. This time round, with four much better players leaving, the club had only received £175,000, all of that being for Liam. This is the reason that Mansfield Town are where they are now, no other. All four should have gone for money, proven by the fact that one of them is starring in the Premiership, two in the Championship and one in League One.

Who did Keith Haslam bring in to replace Curle? Carlton Palmer was the man and he was on a hiding to nothing from day one. People saw him as Keith Haslam's buddy and that was the only reason they thought he was brought in. Again Carlton was a very confident person but I found him totally different from Curle. He was a lot more approachable and I enjoyed his company. I would not say that I agreed with a lot of his footballing decisions but at least he listened to your opinion. However, the fans never gave him a chance which made Carlton even more stubborn than he was. I can remember having a drink with him once and he told me that as a young lad he realised that the only way he was going to play at the top level was not by being a brilliant footballer but by making himself the fittest player in the top League, which he did. He was in great shape, just like Curle, and I never once saw Carlton not looking a million dollars. He was, or tried to be, a winner at everything he did, and I am sure if he came into the club under different circumstances the fans would have had a different outlook.

Carlton is a fiercely loyal person. He was a friend of Keith Haslam and has stuck by Keith through thick and thin, often to his own detriment. He has made a living out of football and really only came to Mansfield to help out his mate, but as I have said from day one it never worked out. My wife Clare would never hear a bad thing said about Carlton or Keith. She always says you should judge somebody by how you find them personally and both Carlton and Keith always treated her and my family with the utmost respect.

The atmosphere on the terraces at Field Mill had now changed. Instead of the usual rumblings of discontent that you get at every club, things were starting to get nasty and there was a lot of bad feeling towards both Haslam and Carlton. On some things I can see where the fans were coming from, on others I felt they were totally wrong, but there is a right way and a wrong way of showing your feelings. If you are a brave man, you would go and see the people you are not happy with and have a discussion face to face. If you are a coward, you go on message boards and voice your opinion under a pseudonym. If you feel that strongly about something why not speak to people in the right way, unlike a couple of idiots who confronted Carlton at the end of season dinner in 2005 knowing full well that he was unable to do anything in front of main sponsors and supporters. Would they have done it outside, one on one, with Carlton away from the safety in numbers inside the Civic Centre? Exactly. Cowards to the end.

Carlton would be the first to admit that he made mistakes at Mansfield Town and that really he should never have come to the club. I would agree with him on that point, but I can honestly say that Carlton always treated me perfectly well. He was a nice person who deserved a lot better. I think this was the beginning of the end for Mansfield Town as a Football League club. The fans were not happy and Keith Haslam was not happy. Who was in the right and who was in the wrong? Both parties to a certain extent. A small minority of fans stopped supporting the players when they needed it most, instead turning their attentions to getting the 'Calver One' out while Keith Haslam refused to budge, believing he deserved better as in his eyes he was the one who saved the club. I could see where both parties were coming from.

By this time I had become really close friends with a friend of Clare's, a man called Banipal Isaac, better known as Banny. I have never met anybody so full of life and he would put a smile on anybody's face whatever the circumstances. I have met some funny people in football but none funnier than Banny. He is only small but when he enters a room he is like a whirlwind. I have never met anybody who would willingly drop everything to help somebody like he does, whether he knows them or not. He has always been there for me and my family and I can not thank him enough. He was a great help in getting me through the period when I left football. I can remember the first time I left him a ticket for a game at Field Mill. It was around this period and as I was youth team manager I used to watch the game with Ivan behind the dugouts in the Bishop Street Stand. It was about 15 minutes before kick-off but I could not see Banny in the West Stand. I gave him a quick ring – he was just turning into the ground and I could hear a steward say to him that the car park was full and that he would have to park somewhere else. 'You what? Get out of the way! Quick! I am the referee and the game can't start without me! They said you would know about this! What is your name?' The steward stepped aside and apologised. That was not the end of it. I told Banny where to pick his ticket up and told him to get to Gate Eight and somebody would tell him where to go. I saw Banny appear at the top of the staircase near the directors' box but instead of turning left he had a quick look around and turned right and went in and took his seat or rather the chairman's seat! I could not believe it. I rang Clare and said, 'You will never believe where Banny is!' He got some strange looks but nobody said anything to him and he watched the whole game in comfort. (Luckily Keith was away in Portugal). It did not end there…after the game I had arranged to meet him for a drink in the Sponsors' Lounge. When I got there I saw Clare and asked her where Banny was, she pointed to a corner where there was a long row of kids queuing up waiting for an autograph from Banny. I walked over and Banny gave me a wink. He was signing bits of paper to the kids, 'Best Wishes, Eusebio'. He turned to me to check he was spelling it right?! Banny you are the best!

We finished 13th in Carlton's first season and when we started poorly in the 2005–06, the writing was on the wall. Not many people know this, but Carlton did not get a penny when he left the club. He could have done, he was certainly entitled to a pay-off but he felt that it was the right time to go. He would leave the club on mutual terms rather than another lengthy court case involving court fees and compensation. Fair play to Carlton, but yet again a small minority of fans did not see this. Carlton Palmer had his heart in the right place: he was loyal to his mate Keith Haslam, prepared to fight his and the chairman's corner, but ultimately he failed at the Stags. Who would be next in the hot seat? We would soon find out.

Chapter Thirty-Three
Peter Shirtliff

Carlton started playing again at the start of the 2005–06 season and, to be fair, he thought that they needed somebody more experienced than me on the touchline making decisions while he was playing. I thought I was capable enough of this but Carlton spoke to me face to face about it and said he was going to bring Peter Shirtliff in as his assistant and that I would go back with the youth team. I was not particularly happy with this but at least it was said to my face. Peter came in and had a really calming influence on the first team squad. He was an excellent coach and to be fair he did have a lot more experience than me.

I had gone back with Ivan to coach the kids and I had no qualms about this as I loved working with him. The set up was typical of Mansfield, little equipment and poor facilities but some of my best mornings in football were spent with Ivan and a new physio at the club called Paul Madin, or Mad-Dog as we had christened him. He had started work at the club just as Keith Curle was on his way out. Mad-Dog was a joy to work with and had plenty of experience, not in football but in life itself. Football changing rooms are a strange place to be around and the banter is often cruel. You either sink or swim. I have never known an outsider (somebody who has not been in the game) to come into the football circle and be accepted as quickly as Paul was. His sense of humour was brilliant and he definitely gave as good as he got. He really was a joy to be around. He had come from a hard-working background, and at the end of the day he was a football fan who had snatched a chance to work in the game he loved. We talked for hours on end, we still do, and along with Ivan and Muggy he made my last few months at Field Mill the more memorable. If it had not been for those three on the playing staff it would have been a sad place to work.

Carlton left the club after the Rochdale game where they had been beaten 2–0. The club were due to play in the League Cup the following Tuesday at home against Southampton. Shirty was put in charge and he asked if I could help. No problem. We won the game 1–0 courtesy of a Giles Coke goal. He was a strange lad. Ability wise he was better than Liam and Leroy. He was as good as I have seen at that level in training and on his day, but for somebody who was so laid-back and confident in the dressing room he was like a little boy out on the pitch. I would have loved to have played alongside Giles, to make him believe in himself and to be able to talk him through games. Jon Hjelde always used to say to me that he was as good a young player as he had ever seen and he has played at the top level. Cokey was a typical member of the Mansfield squad when I came back to the club as a coach, to the day

I left. All the potential and ability in the world, but mentally very weak. We always offered a lot and we did deliver for the occasional game but when the going got tough, we sank!

Shirty was the total opposite to Carlton and Curle. He was calmness personified; well at least he was in the early days. He was great to work with on the training pitch and from when he got the job to the turn of 2005 he did brilliantly. I was his assistant on a permanent basis from the end of October when we won away at Cheltenham and Shirty was confirmed as the full-time manager. I was delighted. I never got a pay rise but to be perfectly honest I was not bothered. I was enjoying myself again. I learnt a lot from Peter on the training pitch and he was always looking to try new drills and work on different things. He wanted his team to play football on the floor, how it should be played, and we worked on that every day in training.

However, a problem, as was so often the case in my playing career and my coaching career, was just around the corner. I was due to get married that Christmas to Clare. When we booked the date of Saturday 2 December 2005 I was the youth team manager and therefore nothing to do with the first team. It was the day of the second round of the FA Cup so I thought I had got things covered. If we won in the first round and got through to the second round it was not a problem. If it was away I would not have to go, if it was at home I still would not have to go as Ivan would cover the youth team match for me in the morning and then supervise the youth team players at the match at home in the afternoon. However, when Carlton went and I got made the assistant it became a problem. I had spoken to Shirty about this and we decided to wait until after our first round game to see what we would do. We had drawn Rotherham away, a team who were a League higher than us. All the signs were that we should struggle but in a great display we won 4–3. Now the wedding became a problem. I spoke to Peter about it and he said he wanted me at the game (we had been drawn against Grays at home on Saturday 2 December), if we could get round the wedding problem. Clare and I went to see the manager of where we were getting married to see whether we could change the date (all the money had been paid at this point). The only way we could get round it was to move it to Friday 1 December but it would still cost us about another £500 on top. It was not ideal but we changed the date. I told Shirty this and everything seemed okay. Then the unthinkable happened. The game was to be shown live on Sky TV. At first I was delighted because kicking off on Sunday gave me another day to recover from the wedding. Wrong! It was to be a 7.45pm kick-off on the Friday night. I could not believe it. I went to see Shirty and I told him there was no way I could afford to change it again and that I was going to have to miss the game. Getting married to Clare and my family were more important to me than a game of football. The fortunes had conspired against me and I missed the game. Shirty was not too impressed. Many people may disagree with my decision and say I was wrong, but you will never alter my train of thought. Football is only a game and there are a lot more important things out there.

Shirty had got us through the third round of the FA Cup and we drew Newcastle United away at St James' Park. What a day! Not only for the club but for a great mate of mine, Phil Shields. Phil is a massive Newcastle fan and a big supporter of the Stags and he and his family are wonderful people. He sponsored the game and everything else he could sponsor. I have never seen anybody as proud as when he was stood on the pitch with his hero, Alan Shearer. We eventually lost the game 1–0 to Shearer's record-achieving goal but that was a real highlight of my coaching career. Phil had organised for my son Jak to be mascot for Newcastle for the game and I am sure Jak will never forget that. Thanks mate!

Our season drifted along after that and we eventually finished in 16th place. Not a brilliant season but we had got through it. I had enjoyed working with Shirty and it worked well. Although we are completely different characters, we complimented each other well. Shirty was the quieter, studious type while I was the joker in the pack who kept spirits up. He was definitely a better coach than I will ever be, but I was closer to the players and could sort things out before they escalated into a problem. That is what a management team should be. I was enjoying it again and I loved the away trips, being able to talk to Mad-Dog on the way down to games. I hated overnight stays as a player and I hated them as a coach, but you do get to know people better, especially fellow staff members. I became really good friends with Paul Madin. We were always trying to outdo each other, he would be forever cutting the toes out of my socks, but I would always manage to outdo him. I noticed that before games he used to leave his medical bag on the side unattended so I sneaked some jacket potatoes wrapped in tinfoil out of the hotel prior to one game and at the last minute put four big jackets in his run-on bag. I waited. Eventually somebody went down injured and Paul had to run on. I was laughing so hard inside. When Paul got to the player, he unzipped his bag and he immediately looked over at me. I was killing myself. He mouthed something that is unprintable but I had got him. Another time we were having a drink at a hotel in Torquay. The restaurant manager had put some lovely chocolate squares on a silver platter, very similar to After Eight mints. The only problem was that they had started to melt. I went down to sniff the chocolate and said, 'Those are off. No wonder he is giving them away. Smell these Mad-Dog', and as he leant forward I pushed his face right into the melting pile of chocolate. I quickly ran off laughing and Paul could have died when the restaurant manager came out and saw his face absolutely caked (pardon the pun) in chocolate and dripping off his chins (sorry chin). That is what we were like. When it was time to be serious, we would get our work heads on but we did have a laugh at other times.

I think my philosophy changed a little. I was determined to enjoy my life again and not worry too much about things. I was as happy as I had ever been in my personal life but something happened on Saturday 17 November that totally changed my outlook on football. Peter Wilson had just started at the club as goalkeeping coach and he seemed like a really nice man. I had only just met him but already he was one of us. What happened at Shrewsbury was horrible. I will not go into the gory details but to see someone like him die at the pitch side from a heart attack changed my thinking on football, and the importance of its place in the bigger picture.

The season yet again fell away in the last 10 games and we ended up finishing in 16th position – nowhere near good enough.

Chapter Thirty-Four
Billy Dearden

The start of the 2006–07 season mirrored that of the 2005–06 season. We were capable of beating anybody on our day but those days were few and far between. A young chap called Danny Reet was at the club at this time, a centre-forward with bags of potential. However, he had a problem, a lot like me in many ways. He was susceptible to putting on weight. There was a big difference between us though. I may be a lot heavier now than when I was playing, but I never once got fined for putting weight on as a player. I was disciplined. I knew when I could relax and when I needed to have my professional head on. Danny did not. We tried everything with him. I say we, I mean Peter Shirtliff, Paul Madin, myself and Billy Dearden all tried and failed miserably to get into his head and make him appreciate being a footballer. I tried everything from giving him an absolute rollicking, to putting a sympathetic arm around his shoulder. It just would not sink in. I beasted him physically for a month and he started knocking the goals in, most notably two goals against our rivals Notts County, but I was fighting a losing battle with him. He would get weighed on the Friday, play on the Saturday and then get weighed again on the Monday morning. He would sometimes be five or six pounds heavier. What could you do? We fined him and that did not work. We tried everything and in the end I gave up on him. He was a likeable lad but in the end I could not stand to see how easily he was letting his dream job go, when I had had my dream smashed by an injury. I could have swung for him.

Shirty was getting more and more fed up with things at Mansfield, and rightly so. We all seemed to be doing far more than what was in our job descriptions, and Peter's cool head was getting hotter and hotter every day. Something had to give soon. I do not think he and the chairman were particularly seeing eye to eye on a lot of things and you could see Shirty was no longer enjoying it. The fans started giving him a bit of stick as well and after the Barnet game, in which we were awful, Shirty was at breaking point. He went berserk at the lads, totally out of character. I felt it needed doing a long time before, but he felt as if the squad could not have handled it as they were naïve and weak mentally. That is the one thing where Shirty and I were of totally different opinions. By this time I was ready to tell a few home truths, the losses we were getting did not seem to bother the players. When I played a defeat would spoil my weekend but a defeat this season did not upset the players enough and it would be forgotten before they even boarded the bus back to Mansfield. I was ready for walking out. Yet again it was a horrible place to work, everyone talking about each other behind their backs. Mansfield Town was no longer the club I had joined many years earlier. It had changed.

I went up to see Shirty on the Monday morning after the Barnet game to find him sitting at his desk. 'He has only gone and sacked me!' he said. Again people said I must have known that Shirty was getting the sack and that I was in on it with Keith Haslam. Not a chance. I thanked Peter for all his help and I am sure now that he believes getting the sack from Mansfield Town was one of the best things ever to happen to him. He has gone on and become assistant manager at Tranmere Rovers and I am sure he is a thousand times happier there than he was in those last few months at Field Mill. It is surprising when you lose a job how your perception on what is important changes and I am now realising that, the same way I am sure Peter did two years earlier.

Christmas Day 2006 was a strange one. I had been put in temporary charge of team affairs on 18 December and was looking forward to taking the reins for the first time properly in a Football League match. We were due to play Chester at home the Friday night before Christmas in what was a winnable game, before going into a difficult Christmas period. The game was called off and I was gutted. I was so looking forward to the game and hopefully my first win as a manager. I gave the lads Christmas Day off and after dinner I was working the team out on numerous pieces of paper when I had two phone calls within the space of five minutes. First Jon Hjelde rang in, his calf was not feeling any better, followed by Danny Reet, he had a sickness bug! My mind on him was made up from that point.

I have never felt as nervous before a match in my life as I did before that first game in charge against Darlington. I was determined to try and enjoy the occasion and boy did the lads do me proud! They were brilliant. We won comfortably 2–0, and had a massive 21 efforts on goal. I have never felt, and I honestly mean this, as proud to be involved in a football match as when the final whistle went that Boxing Day. I felt a million dollars. We had a great journey home and I had got the buzz back. When I got home Clare and the kids had decorated the front of the house with all the yellow and blue kits and memorabilia they could find. It looked a picture.

However, that was to be my last game in charge for the time being. I knew before Christmas that Billy Dearden was coming back to the club as manager. Keith Haslam rang me, by this time he did not even really come to the ground, to tell me the news and I met Billy over a drink. It was all kept hush-hush, but Billy had been at the Darlington game in the stands even though I picked the team. Deep down I was gutted, I had really wanted a crack at it, but what better man to learn the ropes from at Mansfield Town than Billy Dearden. Billy was coming back to the club for his third spell – he must either have been mad or a glutton for punishment.

The rest of that 2006–07 season went the same way as the previous three. We climbed away from the foot of the table and with 11 games to go people were talking about pushing for a Play-off place. Things had certainly improved performance-wise on the pitch, but it was still a first-class comedy off it. Before we played at home to Chester

City at the start of March James Derry, the potential chairman, came in and said that he would take the whole squad to Barbados if we got in the Play-offs. When the press found out about this they slaughtered the players as they did not think they deserved a weekend in Skegness never mind anywhere exotic.

By this point Keith Haslam had put the club up for sale. The supporters were desperate to get him out and people were doing all sorts of strange things to make it known they wanted him out. People forgot about what was important. The important thing is that your football team wins on a Saturday afternoon or Tuesday night. That is all that should matter. Clare told me one night that she had spoken to one of the wives of one of the high-profile supporters of the club who had said that she had lost count of the number of times she had woken up in the middle of the night to find her husband not there. She would go downstairs and there he would be in the dead of night typing a letter to Haslam saying what he thought about him. I am not sure if these letters ever got posted and we all love Mansfield Town but you have to get things into perspective.

The season petered out but optimism was high going into the 2007–08 season. Billy had done a great job in steadying the ship and I was learning from the master. On the managers' side the club had people who genuinely cared for it. Billy Dearden, Ivan Hollett and myself were all Mansfield Town people who cared passionately about the club. Things were definitely on the up.

Chapter Thirty-Five
The Final Season

The season no Mansfield Town fan will ever forget. Not one person could foresee what was coming and it will go down as the worst season in the history of the football club, a season that saw them lose their proud Football League status.

It all started fairly quietly. The club was still up for sale but the takeover was about to happen at any time. How many times did we hear this! We had had a half decent pre-season and we got a great point away at Brentford on the opening day of the season courtesy of a brilliant goal by Mickey Boulding. Mickey had had a disappointing first season back at the club, but was now playing in his favoured position and he did not look back from that game. If it was not for his goals we would have been dead and buried a long time before the end of the season. Single handedly he kept us in with a shout but it should never have got to that stage. On paper we were a good young squad, but on paper ability does not win anything. This is not meant to sound big-headed, but if I had played central midfield in the team, even the size I am now, we would not have gone down. People will say that all the off-field stuff was the reason we went down. Bullshit! We were simply not good enough.

We did not record a single win in August, and in our three games we only picked up one point. It was still early days and confidence was still high. We showed what a good team we could be when we demolished Stockport County, who went on to be promoted. We raced into a 4–0 lead after about 25 minutes and also missed a penalty in the process. In our next game we lost against Peterborough, nothing to be ashamed about, but in two games we had shown we were a match for the better sides in our division. That is where the problem was. In our next three games we were embarrassingly awful. We lost against our local rivals Chesterfield at home, never a result to please the fans, but then lost our next two against Accrington Stanley and Dagenham and Redbridge both 1–0. No disrespect to both of those teams, but Mansfield Town should have been wiping the floor with teams of that standard. The players can not say they that were not well prepared. Billy and I always had the opposition watched, we had the best training facilities we had ever had at the John Fretwell Centre and the morale and spirit were fairly good. Looking back I think that is where the problem lay. We were too nice. The players were all good mates and did not like to say anything that might upset one another, but that fails to breed the habit of winning football matches. In numerous meetings I lost count of the number of times I said we had to be nastier. If somebody had a go at you, do not take it personally as it was meant for the good of the team. Trouble is we never took it on board. If somebody had a 'pop' at someone, that person would sulk. As a football club the whole place, not just the players, was full of sulkers.

Yet again we played very well at home against good opposition in MK Dons, but once again, as we did 17 times that season (a record in itself), we lost by the odd goal. I was completely p*ssed off and ended up squaring up to one of the players, Jude Stirling, in the tunnel at the end of the match. I should not have done but I was becoming so frustrated – why did it not hurt the players, or seem not to, as much as it hurt me and Billy?

By the time we played Barnet away on 13 October we had fallen to the bottom of the table. However, we performed well there and looked as if we had grown some b*llocks from somewhere. We drew 1–1 but it was the spirit that pleased us more than anything. We were getting blocks in, defending for our lives. It was more than that though. We played some good stuff and the confidence seemed to be returning. We battered Notts County at home in the next game, and even though the scoreline was only 2–0 it could have been a lot more. We were looking good, the takeover was happening any day, the whole atmosphere of the fans had changed with that news and everybody was looking ahead again. It is amazing that when the fans are happy and relaxed, the team look the same. I am by no means blaming the supporters for having a moan at the players, they are entitled to their opinions, but it just emphasised how weak mentally we were as a squad. Whenever we scored first in a game confidence would grow and we would steamroll teams like we did against Macclesfield at home. We were 4–0 up at half-time with a first half hat-trick to Simon Brown, a player who was typical of how we were as a squad. When the team were doing well Brownie could be a world-beater, but when the chips were down something would be stiff or sore. The total opposite to me as a player really. I would shine when the chips were down, but you would hardly notice me in a 5–0 victory even though I was probably doing the same things as I was doing when we were losing. Strange.

In our next match away at Hereford we were the victims of probably one of the worst decisions I have ever seen from a linesman. Billy went mad cursing the linesman, but he did not flinch. Billy carried on, 'Fourth official. He is bloody well ignoring me. Why won't he acknowledge me? He knows he has dropped a clanger! Is he deaf?' 'Yes Billy. He is,' the fourth official piped up. Looking back it was hilarious but not at the time. I have never seen Billy so mad.

A nice distraction from our League troubles was the FA Cup. We comfortably beat Lewes 3–0 at Field Mill to put us through to the second round. We were drawn away against Harrogate Railway, the lowest-ranked club left in the competition. With the possibility of a massive upset the game was scheduled for television. We were on a hiding to nothing. Paul Madin and I went on a scouting trip to see what they were like but mainly to see what the facilities were like and if the infamous slope was as bad as people said. I did not think it was that bad, I had seen a lot worse. If I had been going there as a player with Chesterfield I would not have been worried at all, but with the current crop of players at Mansfield Town I feared the worst. If we did not show them the respect they deserved there was a good chance we would come unstuck.

What happened next annoys me to this day. I have mentioned it before on the radio and got slaughtered for it, and rightly so. The timing of my outburst was wrong, what with it coming straight after a defeat and I should have waited but I felt, and still do, so strongly that somebody who calls themselves a Mansfield Town supporter could do such a thing. We were due to play Harrogate Railway on the Sunday, and there was a knock on my door on the Thursday morning before training. One of the senior players at the club was at the door looking worried. He said he had had a phone call from a so-called supporter who wanted the team to let Harrogate run through unopposed from the kick-off and score in some kind of protest against Keith Haslam. What would have happened if we had not then equalised in the game? Billy and I would have got the sack and the whole team would have made themselves a laughing stock on national television. What was this person thinking about? If we had not won this game there might not have been a Mansfield Town because the money we generated from the Cup run kept the club afloat. It was that important to the club, but this one fan, and it was only one fan, thought it would be the perfect way to publicise his own personal vendetta against the chairman. As I have said previously, there are ways of doing things. This man apologised to me about the incident saying that he should not have done it, and that he did not know what came over him. I accepted his apology but when I kept seeing him at games and events organised for the club it riled me. I am sure he was having a laugh when I later got sacked, but I can sleep at night knowing that I did my best to keep Mansfield Town in the Football League. I failed but I did my best. Can he say the same? I think not! For the record we beat Harrogate 3–2 in a game that typified what the FA Cup is all about, and we were drawn against Brighton, again away, in the third round. A horrible draw.

As Christmas approached we were again beaten by Chesterfield. This game means so much to both sets of fans and is the massive game of the season for them. If you win those two games a lot of other things can be forgiven. To lose both games to them in this season was unforgivable. We had gone into the festive period bottom of the table. We performed heroically to beat Peterborough at home, but then when we had the perfect chance to back that result by beating what has to be said was a poor Accrington team we failed miserably. We got beaten 1–0. Unbelievably, by the turn of the year we were yet to win away from home. We had picked up a paltry three points from 11 games away from Field Mill. Pathetic.

How things changed in the new year. In our next seven away League games we won five and drew one. Sounds good? It would have been but we went nine games without a win at Field Mill. No wonder we got relegated!

We had done brilliantly in the FA Cup beating Brighton away, and then we all got the draw we wanted: a premiership club at home. It was a good reward for our fans, with the majority sticking with the club they loved in very bad times. We played really well and were unlucky to lose 2–0 to Middlesbrough. It was a great day, with the highlight being a drink with Gareth Southgate and his staff after the game. They were so down to earth and it was nice for somebody who had achieved so much in the game to show us some respect. He and his staff were a credit, as were all their players, to their club.

It was back to the bread and butter stuff of League football. That performance should have kick-started our quest for safety, but it had the opposite effect. We picked up great away victories at Wycombe, Darlington and Lincoln but they were wasted by home defeats by Brentford, Morecambe and Chester City. Our form against teams in the bottom half of the table was the reason we got relegated. Nothing to do with the ongoing takeover saga at the club, which by this stage had become embarrassing. Keith Haslam had, by this time, employed a businessman by the name of Stephen Booth to oversee the sale of the club. More of that later.

Billy's final game in charge came in the 4–0 defeat at home to Rochdale. How Billy got the news was embarrassing, and it did not show him the respect he deserved for all he had done for the club in the past. Billy was having a pop at the players and rightly so, they had performed awfully and badly let him down. Somebody, one of Derry's men, was trying to barge his way into the dressing room to say that Stephen (Booth) and James (Derry) wanted to see Billy upstairs. It was laughable but again typified exactly what it was like at the club at the time. It was like a soap opera. Looking back the club was a total embarrassment.

Billy had gone. I have got so much respect for Billy and all that he stood for. His contacts in the game were second to none and I had thoroughly enjoyed my time working with him. He had helped me so much as a player and as a coach, and I thank him for that. I only wish the end could have been in different circumstances.

Stephen Booth told me that I would be in charge for the next two games: the following Tuesday at home to Hereford who were in the top three and our away game the next Saturday at Valley Parade, the home of Bradford City. Did I want the job? I could have probably turned the job of saving the club from relegation down. And probably have still been at the club in some capacity now. Not a chance. I wanted to be the man who saved the club and preserved their League status. Ultimately I failed, but I can assure everybody I gave it my all, and I was as disappointed as any Mansfield Town supporter when we got relegated. I really thought I could achieve what was dubbed 'The Great Escape'. I failed, which meant I lost my job; I took the chance when many others would have hid and played safe. But as I have said many time before, 'That's football!'

Chapter Thirty-Six
The Great Escape?

There was not a lot of time before the Hereford game to pick the lads up. We had been awful against Rochdale the previous Saturday and here we were with only one morning on the training pitch behind us before our next game was upon us. We had the worst possible start when we conceded a very early goal to go 1–0 down. Exactly what I did not want to happen. I half expected us to fold like a pack of cards but to the lads' credit they kept their heads up and played some terrific football. We did everything but score in the 90 minutes of football. We went into extra-time, where we were awarded a penalty and the chance to equalise. Mickey Boulding stepped up but their 'keeper made yet another great save. The final whistle went and we had somehow lost a game that we definitely deserved something from (how many times did we say that that season?).

The fans had seen the effort the players had put in and we were given a standing ovation when we left the pitch. I felt proud of how the players had performed that night, especially young Nathan Arnold who I had played in a central attacking role with Mickey. He was brilliant and showed what he is capable of. Nathan is an outstanding prospect potentially as good as Liam and Leroy, and with the right manager guiding him will have a great career ahead of him. Get the wrong manager who does not know how to treat Nathan and he could fall by the wayside. It really is that fine a line. My biggest concern after the game was to try and pick Mickey Boulding back up. He was nearly in tears, believing his penalty might have cost me my chance of getting the job. I told him not to worry as without his goals we would have already been relegated. In all the interviews after the game the media praised me for the way in which I had got the lads to play. They wanted to know what I had done differently, if anything. The answer is nothing really. All I had said was for them to go out, enjoy themselves and not be frightened of expressing themselves or making mistakes. To get the ball down and pass it, the tempo high, to get on their front foot and play their part in getting us out of the sh*t! I still think that some thought they had a god-given right to stay up and the sooner they realised we were in the proverbial the better. However, despite all this praise, the simple fact remained: we had lost another match.

We went to Bradford for what could have realistically been my last game in charge. Muggy (Carl Muggleton) and Ivan were helping me out and I trusted them both with my life. They, along with Paul Madin, are such loyal people and I wanted the three of them around me for one final push. We beat Bradford 2–1 in a nail-biting game and again after the final whistle the lads got a standing ovation from the hundreds (1,000+) of Stags fans behind the goal. I felt so proud of the lads when we walked off and told them so in the dressing room after the game. I had identified already by this time who would play a part in trying to stave off relegation and who would not. I knew the players who were up for a fight and those who were not. We now had 10 games to save our season. I was buzzing on the bus all the way back from Bradford, the atmosphere was electric. I did not get a phone call from anybody at the club on the Saturday saying well done, which set the alarm bells ringing. I thought I had, or at least the lads had, done enough to get me the job until the end of the season at the very least. We had played some great football in the Hereford and Bradford games and the lads really were on a high.

Eventually, as I was walking round the supermarket on the Sunday morning my phone rang. It was Stephen Booth asking if could I pop round for a drink at his house that afternoon. No problem. I clenched my fist. I must have got the job. Well, not exactly. When I arrived at Stephen's house we had a glass of wine and he said how pleased he was with the previous day's result and the much improved performances in the last two games. I can remember thinking 'For God's sake. Just offer me the job'. He eventually said that he would like me to have a chat with somebody who was coming to the house in 15 minutes. Who was it? Mr McEwan.

Stephen left us, two strangers, for half an hour to talk about football. It was embarrassing for both of us. We couldn't believe we had been left alone, in strange surroundings, to talk about football, not Mansfield Town, but football in general. After about 30 minutes Mr Booth came back in and said 'How did you get on?' I asked him what the club's plans were and he said they would like Billy and I to work together to get the club out of the drop zone. I wanted to know who would make the final decision on things. I was sure Billy would not be willing to take orders from an inexperienced coach like me and I wanted to be the one in ultimate charge, and I said so. Stephen asked if we would be able to sort things out for ourselves, but neither of us would budge really. We did not fall out, far from it, but why should we have been put in that situation. It was obvious that Billy wanted the manager's job and so did I, and neither of us were prepared to accept anything less. I was getting fed up. I thanked Stephen for inviting me over, and said seeing as I had spoken to him many times about my thoughts of the run in and my ideas it was only fair that Billy had his say without me being there. I shook hands with Billy McEwan and wished him all the best. I was fuming. When I got home Clare and the kids were waiting at the door to see whether I had got the job. The champagne was on ice as they knew how much managing Mansfield Town meant to me. They could see from my face that things had not gone well. I can remember my mum telling me I should just get out of football as it was not worth it. She had been seriously ill in hospital and the extra stress on Saturdays was not helping her to get better.

My phone rang later that night. It was Stephen Booth again. He had had a chat with Billy and Billy had agreed he would come in as director of football and I would remain as manager with the final say on things. Was I okay with that? I said to Stephen I wanted a couple of hours to talk it over with Clare, if I was to take the job I wanted people around me I knew and trusted. I did not know Billy McEwan and if I agreed to him coming into the club what would happen to Muggy and Ivan who were both working with me? I was still confident in my own ability and I wanted the job permanently, not just until the end of the season, and I wanted Muggy and Ivan as my assistants. I was happy with that! So I rang Stephen and said I was not happy with his plan and that they now had to make a decision. I felt that I was still the right man to save the club from relegation.

I had a meeting with the players the next morning. I had said to them before the Hereford game that I would keep them informed of what was happening behind the scenes. They were gutted. They wanted me to have the job, along with Ivan and Muggy. It was announced later that afternoon after training that I would keep the job, but only for another couple of games. What good did that do? Stephen Booth was just the messenger, I am sure of that! It made everybody nervy again, and from the massive high we had after the Bradford game the uncertainty was back again. It was my job to relax them. I told them not to worry about me but to still just go out and enjoy their football. They might not have been too worried, but I certainly was. It was now basically sh★t or bust. I had made the decision to take the job on, be it for only two games; if we managed to stay up I would be a hero, get relegated I would be sacked. It was that simple.

We played okay in our next game at home to Grimsby and probably deserved at least a draw, but we were beaten by a wonder goal. We now travelled to Bury on Easter Monday in what was now a must-win game. We were awful and that is being kind. We had lost 2–0 and for the first time in four games they had let me down. In the changing room after the game a few home truths were told. When I talked to the press after the game I said all the right things about staying positive and that we could still stay up, but deep down I thought we had blown it. My chance of becoming manager had probably gone too.

This time I was dreading the phone ringing. Before the Bury game I had talked to a chap in the hotel before the game who was with James Derry. He seemed okay but I did not know him and it looked at this point as if he was going on board with James's consortium. Over the next few days I was sick of hearing this man's name: John Batchelor. What he had planned for the club and what he was going to do! I had heard it so many times over the last six months that I just switched off. This took a bit of pressure off us ahead of the weekend's game at Notts County. I had been offered the job of trying to keep Mansfield Town in the Football League. All of the senior professionals had been in to see Stephen Booth. They wanted me there; they said I had made a massive difference to them and that the Bury game was only a blip. I appreciated that. At this level, my philosophy is that you are never going to coach players to become much better players, they are at this level for a reason, but if you can get them on your side and playing for you it means much more. I certainly had them on my side.

We now had eight games to save our season, and to save my job. We had a team meeting and I said if we could get 12 points we would have been safe. The next three games were our 'biggies': Notts County away, and Wrexham and Barnet at home. I wanted at least seven points. We ended up with five but should have had nine. We were seven points from safety before the County game and we went on to draw the game 0–0. We deserved to win. We were the better of two poor teams on the day.

The Wrexham game was now a must-win game, they were the only team below us in the League. Win this and we would just about send Wrexham down. We won 2–1 on a very nervy night at Field Mill. We had given ourselves a chance, the team now just had to beat Barnet. That bloody game still comes into my head regularly. We were 2–0 up and coasting. Should I play safe and shut up shop? I would get slaughtered if we did that and invited Barnet back into the game. Go for the kill, be positive was my attitude. Jefferson Louis, our big 6ft 4in centre-forward, missed an absolute sitter to make it 3–0 and I mean a sitter. When there was a break in the play he came over for a drink of water. 'Don't worry about that mate. You will get another chance. Keep your head up' I said, still not believing the miss that would have made the game safe. 'Sorry Dutch, I thought their lad was going to kick me in the face and I shut my eyes', Jeff replied jogging back onto the pitch. I looked at Ivan and Muggy and shook my head with a smile on my face. Here was our big strong target man, armed with the chance to make himself a hero, frightened of getting kicked in the face!

Barnet made three substitutions all at once and for some reason we panicked. Perhaps I should have brought Kevin Horlock on at this point just to go on and kill the game off with his experience but before I could even think they had pulled one back. I was trying desperately to get orders out to the players but we were shell-shocked. Barnet equalised and could have gone on to win the game. In the end we drew 2–2 but it felt like a loss. Had I just blown our chance of staying up?

We now had five games to get a minimum of seven points. At this point I would have taken four points from our next four games to leave us having to play Dagenham on the last day of the season and needing a win to stay up. We had to get something from our next two away games. Anything. Three points would be a bonus, two points would be acceptable. We lost 2–1 away at high-flying Stockport in a game that we again definitely deserved to get something out of. To make matters worse we had Bucko (Jake Buxton) sent off in the game and that meant we lost our skipper for the next two games.

Our next game was at Macclesfield, probably the worst game I have witnessed for many a year. We drew 0–0. Mickey Boulding and Gareth Jelleyman both played, despite being only 60 per cent fit they were massive players for us and difficult times called for difficult measures. It was a credit to them that they both played.

Had I made Mickey's injury worse by playing him? We would soon find out. Next up was Shrewsbury at home. We simply had to win. We were outstanding and won 3–1 courtesy of a Mickey Boulding hat-trick. 'The Great Escape' was truly on. The fans believed in us and for the first time I was absolutely certain we would stay up. The changing room was buzzing and the club was alive again.

How one week can change things! The build-up to the game had been good and at half-time in our penultimate game we were drawing 0–0. Our two main rivals for that dreaded relegation slot were Notts County, who were drawing 0–0 at half-time at home to Wycombe, and Dagenham, who were losing 1–0 away at Darlington. So as things stood we were out of the relegation zone. We had done okay in that first half, but we looked really nervous and edgy and at half-time I told them to go out and make themselves heroes.

I had asked Dave Jackson to text me the scores on my phone, and I waited for the vibration in my pocket to tell me somebody had scored. The players did not know I knew the other scores but it was vitally important I knew in case I had to change things quickly.

After about seven minutes of the second half my phone went. I crossed my fingers (honestly) and saw Darlington had gone 2–0 up against Dagenham. Our game was getting tight. It was not a good game because of what was riding on it, it was edge-of-the-seat stuff. Over the next 15 minutes or so everything had turned on its head. My phone was going mad, but I had to wait until a break in play to have a look. With 20 minutes to go in all their games, Notts County had scored in the 66th minute to lead 1–0 (3 points would make them safe) and somehow Dagenham had got themselves back to 2–2 against Darlington. Rotherham scored the goal in the 71st minute, the goal that would ultimately send us down. It would not have been so bad if it was a wonder strike but it was a freak goal from about 50 yards out that sailed over Jason White's head. It was unbelievable. At this point we still had a chance. If results stayed the same as they were, we would go to Dagenham knowing a win would keep us up. As I said earlier, four weeks previously I would have taken that.

However, my phone was to go one more time. Surely Darlington had restored some normality to the day and were now leading? Dagenham had scored yet again to lead 3–2. We were as good as down. We had a couple of half chances but we had lost 1–0. The other results stayed the same. Things then turned nasty. I know people were upset, but there are right and wrong ways of doing things. The majority of the fans were dumbstruck, as was I, and I just went to the manager's room and sobbed. I would be remembered as the man who took Mansfield Town out of the Football League. I had managed only 12 games, I wish it had been a few more because I would have kept us up. We had got ourselves in the position so many times where it was in our own hands – a good result and we would be out of it – but time and time again we choked. At the end of the day, we got what we deserved. Relegation. We were simply not good enough, and I include myself in that. I really felt for the true Stags fans, they have always been brilliant with me and they know I gave it my all, but for those idiots who caused the trouble after the Rotherham game, you do not deserve Mansfield Town.

Our relegation was confirmed on the Tuesday night when Chester drew at home to Stockport. I have never been so down.

The final game away at Dagenham was the worst of my life. It was a horrible game. Nobody wanted to be there. For the record we lost 2–0. I stated after the game on the radio that a quick decision was needed on the managerial position for the sake of the club. I said I needed an answer by the middle of the week. I needed to know, the players needed to know. The next two months were embarrassing but again typical of the club in the last four years.

Week after week passed. I had to do something. By the end of May no decisions had been made either on my future or the players' futures. Pre-season fixtures had to be arranged, a new squad drawn together, players targeted, budgets made etc. The only man who was more frustrated than me was Stephen Booth. We would spend hours together working through stuff. Over the next few weeks I put a budget together, had spoken to players and got a squad together. I had put my retained list in, and told the club which players I wanted releasing. Unbelievably, the list that I gave to the people in power, by the time it was told to the press had changed. Carl Muggleton and Jonathan D'Laryea had been put on to the released list. I went mad. I stormed into the office demanding to know what was happening. Stephen could not tell me. He did not know. All he could tell me was that a deal that he had sorted out was nearing finalisation. I knew then that Stephen was as much in the dark as me.

The things I sacrificed for Mansfield Town were unbelievable. The club had a Spanish trialist come over, Adrian, from Benidorm, for two weeks and they could not find anywhere to put him up, so Clare and I had him stay with us, gave up our room so he could have privacy and we slept on the settees. The club never paid us any money for him and in the end his parents had to sort it out. He was with us for eight months! He was a great lad and now a great family friend but this is just one example of us having to do things beyond the call of duty.

I had got my squad, my brand new squad, waiting by the phone. I had worked on a budget that would save the club about £200,000 a year. I had agreed contracts with some good players and I was confident, once we were given the green light to go ahead, of regaining our League status at the first attempt. Many people had told me not to bother preparing pre-season games, budgets and squads until I knew for definite what was happening but I had to be professional.

I got the phone call on Monday 30 June. The players were due to report on the Wednesday, so you can imagine what it was like. A nightmare. Stephen Booth was on the other end, 'It's done. The deal is done. Come into Mansfield and meet the new owners.' So I came in with Clare and met Colin Hancock in Il Rosso, a pub near the ground. The deal had been all but signed; he was 99.9 per cent confident it would happen. His plans for the ground and stadium were brilliant but all that interested me was did they think I was the man for the job and if so could I bring in my players? Yes and yes were the replies from both Colin and Stephen.

That night we cracked open a bottle of champagne. I had the chance to redeem myself, and with the squad of players I had ready next to the phone we could do it. The squad I had ready, and they had all agreed, was:

Goalkeepers	A. Marriott
	J. White
Defenders	J. Buxton
	A. Moses
	G. Jelleyman
	A. O'Hare
	R. Goward
	K. Briggs
	A.N. Other
	Chris Wood
Midfielders	J. D'Laryea
	P. Evans (ex-Forest)
	N. Arnold
	W. Corden
	W. Burrell
	J. McGee
	A.N. Other
Strikers	M. Boulding
	M. Stallard
	A. Campbell (ex-Middlesbrough)
	A. O'Connor
	R. Boulding
	L. Trimmer
Assistants	C. Muggleton
	I. Hollett

I shook hands with Colin Hancock on a deal that was 99.9 per cent done. None of what happened next was his or Stephen Booth's fault. I got a phone call on the Thursday night saying that it had been officially announced that the takeover had happened. I could not believe it when I was told that it was not Mr Hancock. I could have cried. When I found out who it was, I knew the writing was on the wall.

I spoke to Mr Perry on the phone that night and was told to come in next morning. Contrary to what people said, I was not unshaven and wearing shorts and flip flops, I was appropriately dressed. I knew what was coming. I had been relieved of my duties, no longer at the club I loved, but decisions had to be made and fair play they made them. How did I feel? Words are not enough!

Chapter Thirty-Seven
The Final Chapter

W hat now? Do you know what? I have not missed football a bit! I have spent time with my family and friends and loved it. I had not had a weekend without football or some kind of sport since I was seven years old. I am now enjoying spending my weekends with Clare and Chelsea and Jak. They are growing up really fast and it is frightening. Chelsea is looking more like her mum everyday while Jak is like me in every way. They are a credit to Clare for the way they have turned out and if they turn out half as happy as Clare and I, they will not have gone far wrong. While the football was going on at the start of the season Clare and I would be with friends of ours Clare and Dave, on their barge having a glass of wine, relaxing and watching the world go by. A far cry from the pressures of football. I am afraid my love affair with football is over at the present time. Will I be back? Who knows. But I can tell you this, what has happened to me in my football career, especially over the last six years, has made me appreciate what is important to me. Clare, my children, my family and my great friends, and I would like to dedicate this final chapter to my sister-in-law Lisa with many thanks. She knows what for!

Tributes

I was delighted when Dutch asked me to contribute a few notes towards his book as he is a person I admire as one of life's real achievers. Before I actually met Dutch I'd played against him in the FA Cup for Mansfield at Bristol City and know from first-hand experience what a great player he was.

After working with him he has become a firm friend who I always look forward to meeting because he always has a smile and joke for everyone irrespective of his own personal situations, he's always cracking jokes with his sharp wit which is a key feature of his personality.

He possesses a good football brain and is a great coach and manager, always keeping things simple, spotting and analysing what was needed tactually on the field. Dutch was great at motivating players and had a good eye for young talent; his man management skills are second to none.

I was very disappointed he wasn't given time as Mansfield manager because I'm sure he would have produced a side capable of climbing the League and I would have stayed there with him.

Mickey Boulding

Ever since I can remember every Saturday I have been rushed off to football matches all over the country from Newcastle United to the Millennium Stadium. We have always been there to cheer the team and dad on. Win, lose or draw I know I'm going to get some stick from the lads in my form as they are all Nottingham Forrest and Derby fans. For all of you who don't know my dad personally he is a great man and we always have a laugh, whether it's teasing my little brother at home or cheering me up when I am upset. I am very proud to call him my dad!

Chelsea Holland

Paul Holland is one of the most interesting football coaches and managers I've ever met. The endearing thing about Paul was that he always managed to laugh at himself rather than get massively uptight when, if required, we asked him a hard question. That is not to say that he couldn't give a hard answer. But in the main, certainly from a media point of view, he was a prince, which in our industry is someone who you could deal with while providing fans with the answers they would like.

Football is a tough game, Paul knows that, but we as journalists just feed on the edges. For us there are the goals, the euphoria, the sadness and the passion in both victory and defeat. Whether it goes right or wrong we have our jobs.

At Mansfield Town Paul served the club well and at a time when frankly, and it's only an opinion, the club must have been a nightmare place to work, he did his best.

We wish Paul every success with his future and his book and I personally hope that one day I'll be sticking a microphone in his face again and saying either 'Great win Paul' or 'What went wrong this time?'

The great thing with Paul is either way you get an honest answer.

Tony Delahunty – Mansfield 103.2

Behind the main stand at Chesterfield FC was really where all the serious sport took place. Spectators may not have even noticed the potential, but Dutch, Jamie Hewitt, Jonathan Howard and me converted a tarmac walkway into a multi-use games area. There was a head tennis court and also a place to scoff down a 'BESI' bacon, sausage and egg sandwich before training, but the cricket square got the most usage.

I bought an old bat in and we would use a tennis ball, rolled up bit of tape or even a wind ball to bowl with. You could be out in any number of ways, including slip catches, hitting the ball into the stand or over into the road! Hewitt could turn a piece of tape off a pane of glass so was pretty unplayable from 10 yards away. John Howard needed a little more assistance and would place a few stones just short of a length to cause the batman problems. Dutch was pretty much an up and downer but always went on about playing for Lincolnshire U11s so thought he could play a bit. To this day I don't think he ever got me out. Randall would come down and do a bit of coaching every now and then. He saw himself as an opening batsman and a conservative Geoff Boycott, playing absolutely no shots and even going to the lengths of getting the same haircut.

It got to the point where we'd get in early, around 8 and clear the snow, frost or rubbish from the Saturday so we could have a full morning's play. Good times we will always remember. Dutch was definitely a better midfield player than cricketer, but not by much! I played both with him for a number of years and will always have great memories of my time around him!

Tom Curtis

Me and my dad always have fun, from him teasing me to me beating him at football! He will always put somebody before himself and will do anything for you. I have been to hundreds of football games with him and can't go to one without meeting someone new. One of my favourite memories with him is when I was mascot for the Mansfield/Newcastle game. I ran out with Newcastle (not Mansfield) so running out with Shearer on one side and my dad on the other was a dream come true. I really have got the best dad EVER!

Jak Holland

After a bit of a dodgy start which included going out of the League Cup by Blackpool we managed to put a run together and soon went to the top of the League. One of the games that started us off was against Chesterfield away, a local Derby, nobody fancied us to get a result especially after our bad start, but in this game suddenly everything clicked for the team; cheered on by a few thousand Mansfield fans we took the lead when Paul Holland scored with an absolute cracker from 30 yards. It set us up for a 2–0 win with Gary Ford getting the other. After that game we just went on and on. Rochdale had also been going well and we were due to play them away. Once again the away Stags support was in full voice and from a corner 'Jools', as he was known in the dressing room, rose like a salmon to put us 1–0 up. We won the game 2-0 with me converting Gary Ford's right-wing cross. The side had a great mixture of youth and experience and Jools benefited immensely with experience we had in the midfield line, with Steve Sooner, Steve Charles and Gary Ford amongst others. I am sure Jools would be the first to admit that he learned a lot from these players.

Phil Stant

For my friend of five years of friendship. I think I'll start with fond memories of baked potatoes and chicken and mushroom pies in my run-on bag!

I first met Dutch at Teversal Football Club where I was acting as physio in my first game ever for Mansfield Town. This was a preseason friendly and of course Mr Hollett was there too. This trio was a great time and I couldn't have wished for a better pair to guide me through induction at Mansfield. Paul mentored me through my early days at Mansfield and I am truly grateful for that. Anyway, that's enough bullsh★t! This all came at a great cost to me of course, with mickey taking and all the pranks we used to get up to on each other.

Paul and his family helped me through a difficult period in my life and there are too many good things to write about. If I get started it will turn into my book. Finally I would like to say a special thank you to my friend, workmate and mentor, 'Dutch'.

Paul Madin – Physio

When I began work at Mansfield Town as the physiotherapist it was October 1993. Billy Deardon was the caretaker manager at the time, and I met all the players at a hotel on the Friday evening prior to our match against Carlisle United.

After the formal meeting, Paul, who was one of the younger players, came over to me and welcomed me to the football club. He was very easy to talk to and I could already tell he had a keen sense of humour. This was highlighted in future years as he was always pulling pranks on other players. He never admitted it but I am sure to this day that Paul put some sort of heat rub in Kevin Gray's underpants. Mind you, knowing Kevin I don't think I would have owned up to it either!

On the training pitch and during matches Paul always gave a 100 per cent. He loved the people of Mansfield and the football club. I never saw Paul not sign an autograph that was requested or refuse to do an event that was outside normal working hours, be it attending a school or presenting trophies at a local football club.

When he was injured, and he did have a few because of the way he played, he was a delight to be with. Always worked hard and showed a keen interest in the physiological issues relating to the injury.

It was a shrewd appointment by Stuart Watkiss at the time to employ Paul as the youth team coach. He immediately settled in to the job and got on extremely well with everyone he came into contact with.

Paul was not only a very good footballer but he is also a very intelligent and extremely nice guy. I think the way he was treated by the football club when they sacked him as the manager was an absolute disgrace. I wish him every good fortune for the future.

Barry Statham

When I suggested to Paul that he wrote a book about his experiences as a professional footballer, he wasn't too keen. But I think he has really enjoyed doing it. There have been parts that really made him laugh as he remembered them and other parts that actually brought him to tears. He has made some good and loyal friends and I am very proud of all he has achieved.

I am sorry he didn't get the chance at the end, that he so deserved, but typical of Paul there are no hard feelings. Tony Delahunty (*Mansfield 103.2*) once asked me if he was the 'nice guy' all the time, as he appeared to be, and unbelievably he is. What you see is definitely what you get with Paul and that in itself is an achievement (particularly in the football industry.) He is a very special person.

Clare Holland

I have known Paul for five years and went to lots of matches when he was manager. He is really good fun and always managed to make us smile, win, lose or draw. Paul is always there for me and a really good friend, and I can't wait to see my name in his book!

Amy Leivers

I initially got to know Paul by playing in a staff v sponsors game at Field Mill. Sprinting (very slowly it has to be said) to get to the ball, myself and Paul were giggling at who was the fattest, sorry I mean fastest, when bang my hamstring went and that was that. We have been giggling about it ever since.

Since that eventful day we have become best of mates and have shared numerous special occasions. One in particular stands out. 7 January 2006. Venue: St James' Park, Newcastle; the occasion: the FA Cup third round, Newcastle United v Mansfield Town. I am a massive Newcastle United fan and have been since the day I was born (being a Geordie I had little choice) but I am also a massive Mansfield Town fan as I have lived and worked in Mansfield since the age of seven. I also had a box at St James', but sponsored various things at Field Mill. I had my football hero, Mr Alan Shearer. I had my mate and Mansfield Town legend and assistant manager, Paul Holland. What was I to do? I decided in my wisdom to sponsor the match, the match ball and the programme. This virtually gave me the freedom of St James' Park for the day. The day was over in a blur and I was fortunate to meet Alan Shearer, be presented with the match ball by Mr Shearer and I got numerous items of memorabilia all of which I am very proud of. However, the thing that made me more proud than any of that was standing arm in arm when the players ran out of the tunnel with my mate and genuine all-round good guy, Mr Paul Holland. A day I will never forget, a mate who deserves nothing but the best. I love you like a brother mate.

Phil Shields

If I had a pound for every mile I have travelled with Paul, taking him to matches, training sessions, bringing him home, going back to fetch things he had forgotten – his watch, his ring, his chain, his suit, his football boots – I would be a very rich man indeed. But money isn't everything. The enjoyment I got out of it meant much, much more. Not many dads get to see their son fulfil all of his childhood ambitions: playing for his school, his county, his country and playing on the hallowed turf of Old Trafford and Wembley.

Paul played competitive football from being seven years old until his career was cut short at 27 with a bad knee injury, and I didn't miss many matches! I enjoyed them all but none more than when he played for his country. How proud was I?

Paul, I wouldn't have missed it for the world.

Jim Holland – Dad

When I first went onto the coaching staff at Mansfield FC there was always a problem to be solved whether it was where to train, what equipment was needed or what players were training. Dutch always seemed to manage to solve it with a smile on his face, a joke to tell or a recollection of a similar experience, making light of most situations saying 'that's another chapter' in his ever growing book.

During season 2007-08 away trips four of us would play cards: Dutch, Mad-Dog (Paul Madin), John Mullins and I, keeping scores over the season. As expected the scoring was even, everyone winning the odd game. After a couple of weeks Mad-Dog didn't win a game and it became a joke each week. Dutch kept counting how far behind he was, taking the p*ss and Mad-Dog kept saying he wasn't going to play this week and always ending up playing after Dutch somehow sucked him into playing again. By the end of the season Mad-Dog had the lowest score ever recorded with Dutch still reminding him of it today.

Dutch is one of the best characters in the game. And it is characters like him that are sadly missing in football today.

Carl Muggleton

My best memory of Dutch would be his first-ever game in charge of Mansfield Town when we were struggling and played Darlington away on Boxing Day. Usually before games Dutch was the main joker, laughing, joking and looking for the opportunity to play a prank or get up to some sort of mischief. However, on this occasion he was as white as a sheet and speaking to him on the journey home, he had been dreading the team talk. Yet the team talk was great; he had the lads fired up, we went on to win comfortably and the feeling in that dressing room after the game was brilliant – knowing that the team had gone out there and won for Dutch was great. That was something I found with Dutch, he made you feel like you could do anything and gave you the confidence to express yourself, and in the changing room after the game you could see how proud he was of every single one of the players.

Dutch also has a great ability to turn on his workman's head almost at the switch of a button and he would go from causing havoc in the dressing room to screaming and shouting on the training pitch. On many occasions I would wind Dutch up but he would always have a better reply and put me in my place. He was great to work with and I can honestly say I enjoyed every minute and felt as if I learnt a lot.

I hope that Dutch can also get back into the game because as a young player he was great to work with and gave young players the belief and confidence to achieve. I also hope he can get back into the game as he has a hell of a lot to offer and showed that when we very nearly managed to pull off 'The Great Escape', and if we had had a bit more time, who knows?

Johnny Mullins

I first came across Paul as a young player playing for my youth team. It didn't take a genius to see that this boy was going to be a player. In season 1990–91 we were relegated to the then Fourth Division. I decided early in that year that I had to change things, so just before the transfer deadline I signed six players, a transfer deadline record at the time, and although relegated we were confident for the following season.

What I didn't know was a young player called Paul Holland, who I signed as a young pro at 17 years of age, was going to be such a big player in that promotion year even at only 17. He played all but a few games, in a side that broke all records. He was magnificent. He had the whole package – strong, great engine, good in the air, scored goals, saved them off the line – a real all-action, box-to-box player who in today's market would have cost millions of pounds. He went onto England Under-21 caps, had a big move to Sheffield United but unfortunately his career was cut short by a cruel injury.

He loved playing for Mansfield Town, this was his club. It didn't surprise me that he went on to manage the club he loved. Things didn't work out for him but I would say to Paul, 'Don't give up. Keep trying to get back into the game in some capacity, you have too much to offer the game to be out of it for long.'

George Foster

'The little blond curly-haired boy with a ball stuck to his foot', was how the neighbours described him. This was, of course, very apt as Paul lived and breathed football from a very early age. He always said he wanted to be a footballer and play for England, as I'm sure many young boys did, but for Paul it was to come true. His dedication and enthusiasm always shone through and he got his wish, but whether it was playing for his school, his county or his country, he always made us proud. We have spent many, many happy hours watching him play – winning and losing, but always giving 110 per cent. He worked hard at school, albeit with a little prompting sometimes, and apart from the usual boyish pranks he never brought trouble to our door.

Paul is a wonderful son, with a very warm heart and caring nature. If Paul is your friend he is your friend for life and you are indeed very blessed, as we are.

Sue Holland – Mum

It has been a privilege to work with Paul as both a player and manager at Field Mill. I remember he first turned up at Mansfield as a fresh-faced youngster who quickly forced his way into the first team at 17. Paul was intelligent and well spoken and it was obvious he was a cut above the rest in the centre of midfield and a real emerging talent, and on odd occasions when he played sweeper he could have done the job while balancing a cup of tea and smoking a cigar.

Sadly that rich promise never reached full fruition as injuries dogged him at Sheffield United and, after a spell at Chesterfield, he found a knee injury ending his career at Bristol City aged just 27.

The next time I saw Paul was on an away trip down south when he met up with the team in a bar and had a whispered conversation with then manager Stuart Watkiss. Paul had piled a few pounds on since I had last seen him and gleefully sank a few lagers as he and Stuart shook hands. Nothing was said about the conversation though he winked and smiled. Then all of a sudden he was back at the Mill as youth team coach and went on to do almost every job going there until his summer sacking.

Given the manager's job for the last 12 games of 2007–08 to try to save the club he loved from relegation from the Football League, everyone was willing him on to do it. Certainly the players responded well as they produced some of their best football of the season. But they fell short and it is to be hoped Paul won't only be remembered as the man in charge at the Mill when they lost their League status.

The way he conducted himself all summer, despite the threat of a new boss coming in, was typically professional and we will never know what he might have achieved over a full season. It was sad to see him axed. But my abiding memory of Paul is playing against him in a recent sponsors' game. Trying to tackle him in midfield I literally bounced off him as he kept control and sprayed another inch-perfect pass. Soon after, with hardly any effort, he crashed a net-buster home from 25 yards. You never completely lose class!

Paul is intelligent enough to make a living without of football and may well do so now. But it will be football's loss.

John Lomas – Chad

I could probably write a book myself all about Paul Holland's school boy days but let the following suffice.

My very first memory of Paul was when he was a primary school pupil playing in goal, wearing a large green goalkeeper's jumper, on the recreation ground at Sleaford. He was really quite small then but threw himself about in an attempt to save everything and his enthusiasm was infectious. Years later he joined Carre's Grammar School and I watched him go from school player to county player and then to England Schoolboys. Every game he played was like his last, totally committed and fiercely competitive yet unscrupulously fair and he took all these qualities into the professional game. We had several trips to the hospital together as a result of him going in for that tackle which most would avoid and we arrived at several matches when he had forgotten his boots.

If it hadn't been football it may have been cricket but professional sport needs more Paul Hollands. Paul provided me with so many memories, though not all could be put in print especially those from Carre's Grammar School soccer tours across Europe, and I hope we will always remain friends.

Colin White – teacher

It was clear from a very early age that Paul had that 'special something extra' that would turn him into a professional sportsman. Initially small for his age (hard to believe now!) he showed no fear on the football field, playing in the same school football team as me despite being two years younger. Despite this, his bravery (some might call it stupidity) frequently made me wince, most notably on a school soccer tour to Holland when he 'tackled' their star player off the pitch over the advertising hoarding and out of the game…swiftly to be followed by Paul who took some pride in being awarded the only red card in a game where several people ended up in the sin-bin!

This determination/foolhardiness very much became his trademark on the pitch and probably cost him in terms of the number of games missed through injury. The bitter irony is that his professional career ended on a cold day in Oldham when the clumsy git (only joking!) got his studs caught in the turf!

Paul was not just talented at football. His excellent hand-eye co-ordination also saw him excel on both the cricket and rugby field at school, and I am sure that he could now successfully turn his hand to darts or snooker if he put his mind to it!

To be fair (a favourite phrase of Paul's), growing up with him was a good laugh. Paul always was and remains very outgoing, friendly and has always made friends easily – a trait picked up from our dad. He is kind beyond words and as soft as they come! Indeed I would say that it was a great pleasure growing up as 'Paul's brother', as I was, and still am, widely known in Sleaford. All the best, mate!

Jamie Holland – Brother

If Paul could pick out the most special year of all, that would surely be 2003. Why you ask? Well it's simple, that's when I came into his life.

Every now and then there comes along a person in one's life and you know that someone is a special person who will be there at any given moment for what ever reason without asking anything in return, and that person is certainly not Paul Holland!

But joking aside I have never met a more genuine, thoughtful individual. 110 per cent throughout. He could have been 120 per cent but have you seen his ankles?!?

Banny Isaac